OPERATION FRESHMAN
The hunt for Hitlers heavy water

Contents

Forward 7
Preface 11
Heavy Water 13
A risk-filled mission 19
The Planning 27
Preparations for the mission 35
The Glider crash on Benkja Mountain in Helleland 41
The Tragedy by the Burma Road 49
The Tow-Plane's Fate 59
The Glider Crash in Fylgjesdalen 63
The Tragedy in Fylgjesdalen 69
The Red Cross is drawn into the drama 73
The Brutality of the Security Police 81
Gunnerside arrives 89
The Sabotage is successful 97
The Withdrawal 103
Mission Accomplished 107
The Germans' way of doing things 113
The Wehrmacht is brought to account 119
The chief commander is brought to account 125
The security police are brought to account 131
Persuing Freshman 135
The Funerals 139
Memorial markers 145
    The first memorial plaque (outside of Slettebø) 145
    Memorial stone (Helleland's churchyard) 146
    The second memorial plaque (outside Slettebø) 147
    Ceremonies 148
    Memorial markers (Benkja Mountain) 149
    Memorial marker (Eigersund's burial park) 151
    Memorial marker (Lysebotn) 151
    Memorial marker (Skitten airfield) 153
    Remembrance Day 155
Hunting for the past 157
What the British knew 163
Operation Freshman – an evaluation 171
Annotated sources and a literary overview 179

Operation Freshman – – The hunt for Hitlers heavy water

Foreword

Many readers are familiar with the adventure film *The Heroes of Telemark* with **Kirk Douglas.** Fewer are familiar with the full story of the allies' attempt to sabotage the German production of heavy water at Rjukan in southern Norway. **Jostein Berglyd's** book about *Operation Freshman* describes a vital but forgotten chapter about the British-Norwegian commando-force's dramatic sabotage efforts against German atom bomb production on Norwegian soil.

The object-target of the British sabotage planers was Norsk Hydro's vital industrial complex for the production of heavy water in Vemork, near Rjukan. This facility had already been constructed in 1934, as the first plant of its kind in the world, and was, at the time of the world war's brake-out, Norway's largest industrial complex. The Rjukanfoss River runs through Vemork with a water drop of over 100 meters, and thereby made enormous energy resources available for Norsk Hydro's use: Namely, the facility in Vemork produced hydrogen for artificial fertilizer products, a process that required a massive amount of energy. Heavy water results as a bi-product in the extraction of hydrogen and contains atoms of the special hydrogen isotope, deuterium ("heavy water"). Heavy water, moreover, has the property of being able to slow down neutrons, thereby preventing them from reacting with uranium inside a reactor which, in turn, makes it possible to fuel a reactor with natural uranium, instead of the very expensive, and very hard to access, enriched uranium.

In order to develop an atom bomb it's necessary to have, in addition to heavy water, yet another vital substance; uranium-oxide, which **Hilter's** army had seized through its invasion of Belgium in 1940, where the world's largest store of uranium-oxide was located. The supply of heavy water the Germans came upon in Vemork in 1940, however, was entirely too little for their atom bomb research requirements. Therefore, in May of 1941, **Hilter** demanded that the production of heavy water in Vemork be doubled.

In the beginning of 1942, the British received alarming reports from Norwegian intelligence sources within Norsk Hydro that the Germans had tripled production of heavy water at Vemork. These reports went all the way up the line to **Winston Churchill** who gave *Special Operations Executive* (SOE), the British organization responsible for sabotage and partisan activity in German-occupied nations, the order to knock out production of heavy water in Vemork. With this information in hand, **Churchill's** scientific adviser, **Lord Cherwell,** was very concerned over the possibility that the German's would win the race to produce the first atom bomb. The chief of *Combined Operations,* **Lord Mountbatten,** therefore suggested that small, air borne commando units be employed to carry out the destruction of heavy water production in Vemork. In October 1942, the British decided to sabotage Norsk Hydro's facility by means of transporting saboteurs to the area in gilders, called *Operation Freshman.*

But *Operation Freshman* ended in tragedy when British aircraft carrying the commando unit crashed in the Norwegian high mountain area in November 1942, and the German army thereafter murdered 14 surviving captured British soldiers. Five other surviving British commando soldiers from the same operation were later murdered by the German *Sicherheitspolizi* (security police) in Stavanger and Oslo. In all, 34 commando soldiers and three air crew died in this raid.

After the failure of *Operation Freshman,* the facility in Vemork at last became the target of one of the war's most successful sabotage operations. A young Norwegian radio operator, **Einer Skinnarland,** was already installed in the rugged Hardanger wilderness area near Rjukan at the beginning of 1942. For over a year, **Skinnaland** maintained radio contact with London providing information about what he observed around the Norsk Hydro facility and its security. On the night of February 17, 1943, six Norwegians parachuted over the terrain around Vemork, climbed up a steep, ice-cold mountain to the power station, overpowered the watchmen and blew up eighteen heavy-water producing cells. The enraged Germans set in three thousand men to fine-comb the area but all the saboteurs, including **Skinnarland,** succeeded in evading capture. When the plant was started up again after several months had gone by, it was partially destroyed as the result of an American bombing raid. In February 1944, skilful Norwegian saboteurs finally managed to sink the train-ferry that was meant to transport the remaining stock of heavy water from Norway to Germany.

Jostein Berglyd describes these, in part, unknown operations with the support of comprehensive source material and personal interviews. The book also relates the interesting judicial aftermath played out in 1945-46, when the suspect German soldiers and higher officials in the *Wehrmacht* (regular German army) and *Sicherheitspolizei* (security police) were tried and judged in allied courts for their part in the murder of the British commando soldiers in *Operation Freshman*. The central backdrop to these proceedings was the so-called "Fuhrer order" that **Hitler** decreed in October 1942, which clearly contravened international law. According to this "commando order," allied commando soldiers who were captured during an act of sabotage were to be immediately executed. **Jostein Berglyd's** excellent account of the judicial follow-up to the German army's execution of the 14 British commando soldiers in 1942 reveals, in an intriguing way, the German army's direct responsibility for these murders. After the war, the German commander of occupied Norway, **General Nicolaus von Falkenhorst,** was sentenced to death for his participation in the murders, but later had this sentence changed to 20 years imprisonment.

In this work, **Jostein Berglyd** shows how the British planning of *Operation Freshman* had several defects and to a certain extent followed in the spore of desperation and lack of time. The aircraft was less than totally suitable, the personnel were not sufficiently trained, the time of year was hardly ideal, the Norwegian mountain terrain was unsuited to glider missions, and the extremely risk-filled operation indicated little, if any chance of survival for the commando soldiers involved (regardless of the German army's brutal murder of the crash survivors). The allied military authorities and the SOE, however, drew several conclusions from the operation that would prove valuable for the second commando raid and also, in the final analysis, for the invasion of Normandy in 1944.

Ironically enough, there was never any risk that the Nazis would develop a German atom bomb. **Albert Speer** and the German atomic physicist **Werner Heisenberg** confirmed after the war that **Adolph Hitler,** beginning in 1942, choked-off resources to the German's atom bomb research that, for all practical purposes, was shelved right through to the war's end. The British fears about a soon-finished, German produced atom bomb were exaggerated but highly understandable and in turn resulted in the USA strongly pushing its own atom bomb program, the so-called Manhattan Project, which led to the bombings over Hiroshima and Nagasaki in 1945.

The allied sabotage against Vemork, and the accompanying loss of human life, therefore made no critical difference to the outcome of the war. **Berglyd's** book, however, is a well written memorial to the exceptionally courageous British and Norwegian soldiers and resistance participants' self-sacrificing contributions under the grim circumstances of war and occupation.

Lennart Westberg
Member of the Swedish Military History Commission
Co-author (with Lars Gyllenhaal) of *Svenskar I krig (Swedes in War)*

Operation Freshman – The hunt for Hitlers heavy water

Preface

There are five main reasons for my having written this book, *Operation Freshman – The hunt for Hitlers heavy water*. Firstly, I've chosen to recount a story that I have worked a great deal with over a long period of time. Secondly, I've chosen to make use of the comprehensive source material I've assembled over these many years. Thirdly, the theme is a vital one, and fourthly, I've long wished to honor those who took part in *Freshman*, attempting to carry out a life-threatening mission, despite miserable odds that forecast the chances of success as all but hopeless. And lastly, I've chosen to depict a comprehensive picture of the Norwegian sabotage efforts against the heavy-water production plant at Vemork. Much has been written about this sabotage over the years, but I have chosen to give a more comprehensive picture by incorporating the first – and unsuccessful mission.

The first time I got to hear about this subject was at the end of November 1942 – I was six-years-old at the time. Two British planes with saboteurs on board had crashed in the Eigersund area. According to rumor, something horrendous had happened to the British saboteurs in the German facility, Slettebø, near Egersund. It was said that the Germans had shot the saboteurs to death, even though they had been dressed in uniform. The youngest was only 18. This made a strong impression on me. What had this young man thought about, just as he stood before the execution platoon?

After the war a number of articles were published that told of what had happened in more depth. The goal of the sabotage, which the newspapers called Operation Freshman, was to destroy the facility for producing heavy water at Vemork. If this plant had not been destroyed, the Germans could conceivably have been the first to produce an atom bomb. Operation Freshman was an integral part of a fight against a bomb that might be able to destroy our whole universe. This demonstrated how vital the operation was, at the same time, the course of events illustrated the war's horror and sadism. The main cause of the tragedy that Operation Freshman eventually led to was the so-called "Fuhrer order" that Hitler decreed in the fall of 1942. The order instructed that saboteurs in German occupied areas should be executed if they were taken captive. Which is precisely what happened to all the captured participants in Operation Freshman.

During the trial of General Nicolaus von Falkenhorst in 1946, the Freshman story was further documented and revealed from a judicial perspective and received much attention from the general public. How the occupying force had reasoned and acted, especially came into focus.

At the start of the 1980s I began to visit people and places with a connection to Freshman. Little by little, the original area where I had begun my search for information has gradually expanded to include, among other places, Stavanger, Jæren, Forsands County, Vestre Gravlund in Oslo, and Norway's Home-front Museum, and later on, locations outside the country. All told, I've carried out 43 interviews while working with Freshman – and an additional number in connection with the sabotage missions against the German's production of heavy water that followed. Verbal sources both in and outside of Norway have weighed heavily in how I've chosen to present what took place. Also of heavy influence were the Norwegian, British and German written sources – and an extensive amount of picture material.

During the course of work, I have published parts of this story in writing and in lectures derived from the background of information I've gathered in. I now consider that this collection of material is complete and therefore I am presenting this story in its entirety.

I wish to take this opportunity to thank all the local residents who have helped me to find spores and objects from the Freshman tragedy. Discussions and an exchange of views about questions surrounding this incident with people who are interested in (war) history has also resulted in valuable insights.

Edgersund, April 2005
Jostein Berglyd

Chapter 1

Heavy Water

In the beginning of 1942, British counterintelligence received reports that indicated the Germans had tripled the production of heavy water, deuterium. Heavy water was a vital component in the production of the atom bomb, and the German's main production of this substance took place at Norsk Hydro's facility in Vemork near Rjukan. Stopping this production was given the highest priority by the British.[1]

The Norwegians chiefly responsible for furnishing the British with information about what went on in Vemork were the professors **Jomar Brun** and **Leif Tronstad**. **Brun** was a designer and head of Norsk Hydro's plant for producing heavy water in Vemork. **Brun** and **Tronstad** had founded the plant in 1934, as the world's first facility for the production of heavy water, with **Tronstad** as its scientific adviser.

After occupying Norway in 1940, the Germans immediately took control over the plant in Vemork and increased production. **Brun** and **Tronstad** saw this as a sign that Hitler's scientists were working at producing an atom bomb.

Tronstad communicated his views and information concerning the German's interest in the heavy water production in Vemork to **Commander Eric Welsh.** He was a friend of Norway and chief of the Scandinavian section in the secret British intelligence unit, *Secret Intelligence Service (SIS)*. When the Germans began to suspect that **Tronstad** was engaging in illegal activities, he fled to England in October 1941, but continued to remain in close contact with **Brun** in Norway.

Early in the spring of 1942, **Brun** received a visit from a British courier. The British were interested in information about the German's plans and technical data concerning the plant in Vemork. In October 1942, **Brun** also fled to Great Britain, a flight that was initiated by **Tronstad**.

---

1 *Operation Freshman (An account of the raid by the 1st Airborne Div. Engineers on the Heavy water plant in Norway),* By Q.M.S.D.F.Cooper, R.E., 1945, p.31

The target: The plant facility for the production of heavy water in Vemork. In the foreground is the electrolysis plant. Photo loaned out by Norway's Home-front Museum

Together, they now began planning to blow up their former place of work. They were both connected to the Norwegian Defence Command, *Forsvarets Overcommando (FO4)*, an organization that co-operated with the British (SIS).[2]

The British secret service passed on the information about German operations in Rjukan to Prime Minister **Winston Churchill.** The PM, in his turn, informed his government and, in the summer of 1942, an order was sent to *Combined Operations Headquarters (COHQ)*, the armed forces' overarching, all-embracing operations center, to execute an attack against the facility in Vemork with the aim of halting the production of heavy water.[3]

On September 8, 1942, this issue was discussed for the first time by the *Examination Committee* as a joint project for *Special Operations Executive (SOE)* and *Combined Operations Headquarters*.

Seven days later, the *Committee* held a new meeting. There, the decision was made to have *SOE*, as soon as possible, work up a sabotage-action plan against the facility in Vemork.[4] *SOE* had been grounded in 1940,

2 Brun, Jomar: *Brennpunkt Vemork 1940-1945,* Universityforlaget (University Press), 1985, p.5-7.
3 Wiggan, Richard: *Operation Freshman, The Rjukan Heavy Water Raid 1942,* William Kimber, London, 1986, *p. 23-24.*
4 *Public Record Office (PRO). Richmond, Surrey, England, Group Letter DEFE 2, Piece Number 2245, Freshman paragraphs 1 and 3.* the documents contain 70 text examples concerning the period September 8, 1942 to November 18 1942, and describe the pre-planning of operation *Freshman.* Norway's Home Front Museum has copies of the documentation, both on microfilm and as Photostat-copies

with the mission of leading, training and equipping units to execute actions against the Germans in the areas they occupied. From the very beginning, Norwegians were a part of the organization, and in January 1942, the British established a Norwegian section within *SOE,* and also an action-force to be attached to it, under the name *Norwegian Independent Company Number 1* (NOR, I.C. 1), to which *Company Linge* was later attached.[5]

On September 23, 1942, a decision was made to have the *Chief Air Planner,* head of planning for the air transport part of the attack force, go through the plan. The following day, the highest government private secretary, *the Private Secretary of the Lord President of the Council,* stated that his superior considered that the operation should be given the highest priority, On September 30, the mandate (authority to review the planning) held by the *Chief Air Planner* was expanded. As of that date, the decision to approve the project rested with him. That same day, the *SOE* submitted its first plan, but it was rejected. It wasn't possible to carry out this plan as submitted: If the military was to take part in the operation, then air-borne troopers who could land with parachutes must be used. In addition, an alternative plan for withdrawal after executing the action must be worked out. If the plan was reworked in line with these directions, the operation should be able to be crowned with success. On October 6, the *Examining Committee* adopted this standpoint.

Accordingly, representatives from the military units that would be taking part in the operation were promptly called to a meeting. The first joint meeting was held on October 7 in the *Combined Operations Headquarters* with representatives from the *1st Airborne Division and the 38th Wing of the Royal Air Force (RAF).* Six days later, the Norwegian **Lt. Colonel A. Rosher-Lund** was called to a meeting with the *Examination Committee.* That same day, the training leader, **Lt. Colonel Mark Henniker,** suggested that the operation be put off until the snow had melted in June. This suggestion was rejected and on November 14, the *1st Airborne Division* received orders to set the operation in motion. On November 16, the *38th Wing* received its orders, and on the same day, the Norwegian **General Wilhelm Hansteen** was called to a meeting to discuss questions concerning the action.[6]

In June 1942, **Churchill** travelled to the USA for a meeting with President Roosevelt. They discussed what could be done to hinder the German effort to produce an atom bomb, and came to agree that the production of an allied atom bomb would takes place in the United States.[7]

---

5   *Norsk Krigsleksikon* (Norwegian Combat Dictionary) 1940-1945, p.390, 249.
6   Footnote 4, paragraphs: 4,6,7,8,9,57,62,63,65,66.
7   Footnote 3, p.22.

In 1939, scientists in America had already discovered the secret behind nuclear fission and thereby opened the possibility of using this discovery for military purposes. It was known that the Germans were working on a similar project and, also, that British researchers were attempting to solve the problem. The American government's interest in research devoted to developing an atom bomb became significantly stronger after the USA entered the war in December 1941. Namely, such a bomb could bring about an immediate end to the war. The Americans called their atom bomb development effort the *Manhattan Project*. In 1942, *Brigadier General* **Leslie R. Groves** was appointed chief of all military activities connected to this project, and in the fall of 1943, the USA took the initiative in establishing a collaborative agreement with Great Britain and Canada. That same year a joint working committee was started, and British and Canadian scientists moved to the USA in order to participate in the project. The Americans were aware that the Germans had discovered nuclear fission in December 1938, and that this discovery could make possible the construction of an atom bomb. Three years later, the German atomic researcher, **Werner Heisenberg,** paid a visit to his old teacher and friend, **Niels Bohr,** in Copenhagen. This visit convinced **Bohr** that the Germans were intensively and successfully working at developing an atom bomb.

Some of **Grove's** scientists therefore believed in 1942 that Germany already had a reactor, and that it would only be a matter of months before the first atom bomb was a fact. This dire prediction led the USA to intensify its project to be the first to develop an atom bomb.[8]

In retrospect, we know that the Germans had definitively broken-off their effort to develop such a bomb. In June 1942, **Heisenberg** complained of his distress with the minister of armaments, **Albert Speer,** indicating that the want of money and material for atomic research had led to the German scientists now being left behind in an area of research they had been the leaders in, only a few months earlier. According to German atomic scientists, it would take three to four years to produce an atom bomb – which is to say, by a point in time when the war should have long since been over – and won.

At the start, the Germans were committed to *Blitzkrig* (lightning-war), a concept that still applied when Germany attacked the Soviet Union in June 1941. As the war began to drag out the Germans continued to lay stress on the fact that they lacked the resources to engage in a protracted war, especially after the USA had joined in the fray. With this background, according to **Speer,** the decision was made in the fall of 1942 to set aside development of the atom bomb. From the perspective of the Blitzkrig concept, it would be wrong to waste resources on such research. After conversations with

---

8. Encyclopedia *Britannica, Vol. 7, p.576-577*

Hitler on the possibility of producing an atom bomb, **Speer** perceived that conceptual considerations of such a bomb went over **Hitler's** horizon. On the other hand, **Speer** emphasized that **Hitler** would not have hesitated a second to employ the atom bomb against England if he'd had the chance to do so.[9] It wasn't until after the atom bomb was let loose over Hiroshima in Japan, on August 6, 1945, that the world first came to fully understand why the allies had put such weight on launching an attack against the plant in Vemork.

Werner Helsenberg was one of the Germany's foremost scientists, His position with regard to the question of whether Germany should produce an atom bomb, or not, is a matter of contention. Photo loan out by Norway's Homefront Museum.

---

9. Speer Albert,; *Erindringer*, Gyldendal, Oslo, 1971, p.203-205

Operation Freshman ◆ ◆ The hunt for Hitlers heavy water

Chapter 2

A risk-filled mission

On October 18, 1942, Hitler decreed what later became his so universally abhorred Fuhrer order (*Führerbefehl*). This order stipulated that all who took part in sabotage activities in areas occupied by Germany were to be executed. It didn't matter if the soldiers were uniformed and had given up without resistance. In cases where the Germans judged that the personnel in question had worthwhile information, they should be interrogated, and then shot. If the saboteurs fell into the hands of the police, such arrested personnel should immediately be turned over to the German Security Police, Sipo (SP). All detention for this sort of captive was strictly forbidden. In order to control that this order was complied with, it was required that every incident be reported to the Supreme Command in Berlin. Officially, the sabotage force was reported as having engaged in a battle, and been killed to the very last man.[10]

The same day that **Hitler** handed down this order, four Norwegian agents landed in the Hardanger wilderness at 23:30 hours (11:30 PM) in the mountain area above Fjarefit in Songadalen, approximately ten kilometers from Løkjesmyrene, north of Ugleflot – which was the location where the drop was actually meant to take place. As it happened, where they actually landed was also an uninhabited area – a fortunate and necessary circumstance if they were to avoid being detected.

The agents parachuted out, clothed as civilians, from a four-engine *Halifax* bomber, and even if they had no knowledge at that time of the *Führurbefehl,* they fully expected they would be tortured and executed if they fell into the hands of the Germans.

The four agents were the unit's leader, **Warrant Officer Jens-Anton Poulsson,** the radio-telegraph operator, **Warrant Officer**

---

[10] *Führerbefehl* or the Fuhrer Order. "The Order" is presented in both German and English in *War Crimes Trials, Vol, VI, The Trial of von Falkenhorst*, edit. E. H. Stevens, p.9 and 250.

Operation Freshman - - The hunt for Hitlers heavy water

Warrant Officer Anton Poulsson was the leader of the reconnaissance unit "Grouse" that was to meet and collaborate with Freshman. Photo loaned out by Norway's Homefront Museum.

Knut M. Hauglund, and **Sergeants Arne Kjelstrup** and **Claus Helberg. Kjelstrup** was the unit's second in command. At 29 years of age, he was the oldest. **Hauglund** was 25, and the remaining two were 24. All four agents were born in Rjukan, and with exception of **Kjelstrup,** had grown up there. The unit had been assigned the codename *Grouse,* and all were enlisted in *Norwegian Independent Company Number 1.*

The four men were to function as a reconnaissance unit prior to the setting down of British troops by gliders. *Grouse* would arrange and prepare the landing area, lead the paratroopers to the objective and reconnoiter the area with the aim of learning the German's watch routine. They had been given this mission on the shortest possible notice. Originally, the thought had been to assign them an entirely different mission to – among other tasks, organize resistance groups in their home-area.

The allied soldiers who were to be set down had the mission of destroying the Norsk Hydro plant-facility for producing heavy water in Vemork, outside Rjukan.

It was the chief of the *SOE,* **Colonel John S, Wilson,** who had, in the beginning of October 1942, selected the four agents assigned to *Grouse* and given them orders to operate as a reconnaissance unit in preparation for the coming allied sabotage action that would be carried out by airborne troops. *Defence Command* in London, *FO4,* had also been informed about what was in the works.

With regard to unit's members, in the beginning, only **Poulsson** and **Haugland** knew what the mission was about. *Grouse* already had two failed landing attempts behind them: Due, respectively, to bad weather and engine problems, forcing the planes to turn back with the mission unaccomplished.

The unit had now parachute-landed approximately 10 kilometers from the targeted objective, and were therefore forced to orient themselves and then find the food and equipment containers that had also been dropped from the plane. These equipment containers were spread out over a large area and weighed around 250 kilos. The two participants, who had not previously been informed of the mission's goal, were given that information during the course of that day, by **Poulsson.**

After two days of working at the drop site, the unit was able to continue. They agreed on the route they should follow in order to reach the cabin at Sandvatn where they would be staying for the time it took them to carry out the mission. They counted on coming across other cabins en route where they could overnight.

Every member of the unit was responsible for carrying between 60 and 70 kilos. This weight was far too heavy to carry in one trip. It was therefore divided in two. Everyday, a certain distance was covered with each man carrying a backpack weighing approximately 30 kilos. After which, they would hike back, unburdened, to retrieve the rest. All their daylight hours were taken up with this task. It was exhausting, but they were all in good

The map shows the strenuous route the members of Grouse trekked from the landing area, Fjarefit in Songadalen, to the hytta (cabin) by Sandvatn (Sand Lake). Later, they continued on to cabins in Grasdal and Svensbu.

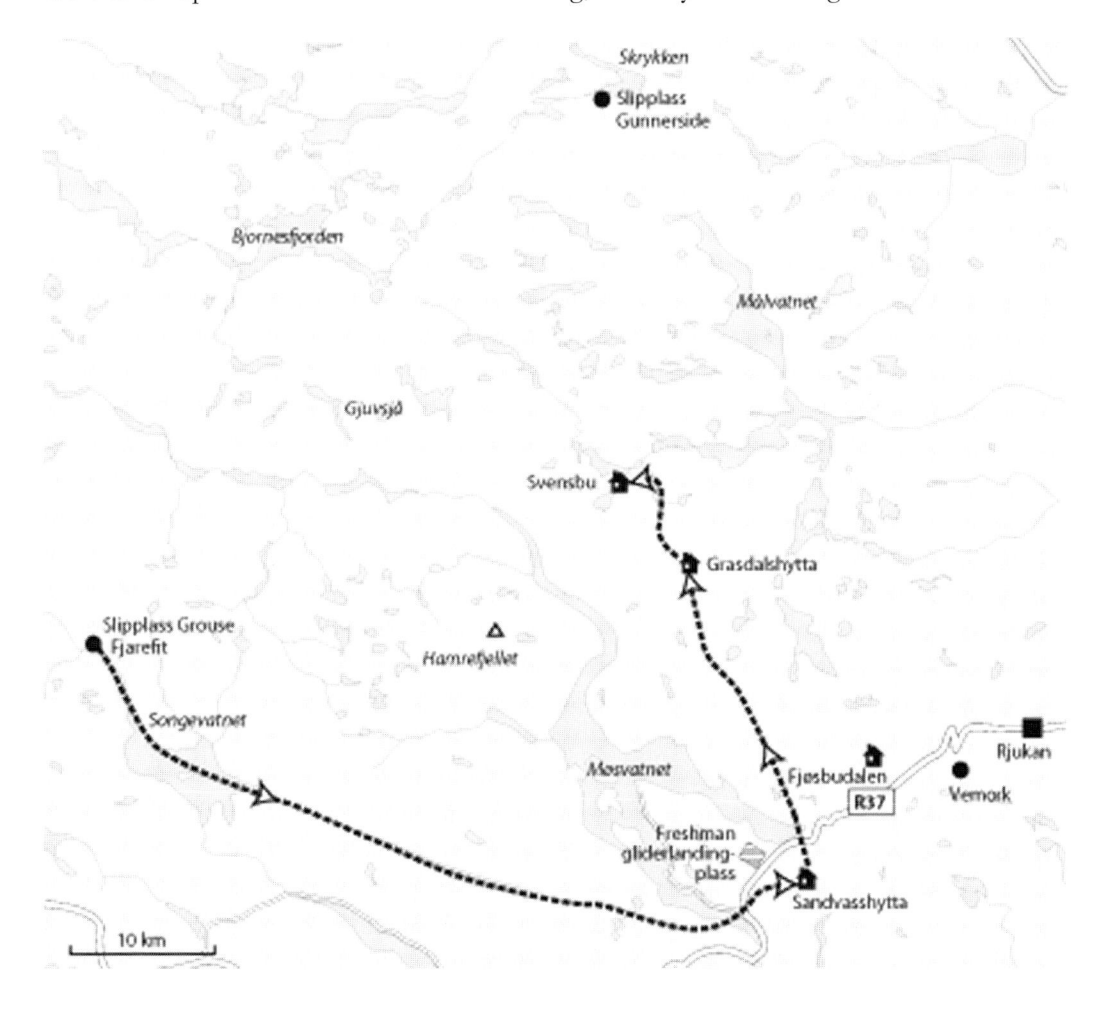

physical health and fine condition. The relied on each other and worked as a very closely knit unit.

In addition to the toll this work took on their strength, the men in Grouse didn't have much in the way of food since the provisions they had taken with them from England were limited. They therefore agreed, early on, to initiate rationing that would stretch their food supply to last a month. This meant that their calorie intake would be far short of adequate. Contained in their provisions was a type of spam, a concentrated nourishment made up of 50% dried meat and 50% fat. Its nutrient value was high and spam can be eaten either cold or hot, moreover, it can be satisfactorily blended with pretty much anything. But they didn't have much spam, which forced them to cut down its portioning right from the start.

Sometime later, **Poulsson** noted in his report that when he was with *Grouse* in Norway, a day's ration consisted of ½ cake of spam, 1 fistful of oats, 1 fistful of flour, four crackers, a little butter, cheese, sugar and chocolate. Nevertheless, during the month of October 1942, they had consumed half the food they had brought with them from England.

The stretch of distance they covered each day varied dependent on weather and snow. The snow was wet and the ice on the lakes was uncertain, a factor that on several occasions caused them to choose terrain that was harder to cross. Their situation improved somewhat when they found a toboggan they could load a large portion of their equipment on. They were bound and determined to put the struggle against the mountains in winter behind them. And after 15 days, they were at last able to take possession of the cabin in Sandvass. They had now trekked somewhere between 70 and 80 kilometers.

The cabin was located approximately six kilometers from Skoland's marshes. **Poulsson** and **Haugland** concluded that this marsh area between Møvass Dam and Rauland was the only conceivable place to land the gliders. And although there was a road close by, the area was still remotely situated. **Poulsson** suggested that here was where the glider-landing should take place, and the British military authorities approved this suggestion.

Reconnaissance patrols examined the landing area more closely and the weather was also carefully observed, with special note made of the visibility and wind velocity. In addition, they monitored Vemork and the German watch-routine and posting around the plant facility. The plant was situated on the valley's south side, protected by a deep chasm, spanned by a solitary suspension bridge. The bridge, itself, was patrolled by German guards. In October 1942, the guard force at Vemork consisted of 10 men. In addition, there was a force of ten men stationed at Møsvass Dam, and 24 men in Rjukan. The first-named lay approximately 14 kilometers from Vemork, the latter, nine.

Haugland had long had a problem in achieving intelligible radio contact with England. This put all four agents under heavy pressure, for without clear radio contact with England, it was impossible to carry out the mission. The problem was blamed on a loss of power, later diagnosed as the fault of the batteries having run down. It was a critical situation that forced *Grouse* to ignore the order about not contacting people in the area.

The battery problem was solved by locating the supervisor of the Møsvass Dam, **Torstein Skinnarland,** whom they knew to be a reliable man. He arranged to get them a six-volt car battery, and from the 9th of November on, they had serviceable radio contact with England. All messages were coded. Now, the planned sabotage operation from Great Britain could begin.

During their stay at the Sandvass cabin they made an effort to fatten themselves up and recover the strength they had lost through marginal rations and strenuous marches. They happened upon a lamb which they slaughtered and ate. The dam supervisor also helped them by providing food and needed equipment, such as boots, gloves and sweaters.

The weather was very changeable and **Haugland** sent daily reports to England. November 18 marked the start of a moon phase favourable to carrying out the operation, and the next day the telegraph operator received the code word *Girl,* which meant that the airborne troops would land the following night. Now, *Grouse* had to hustle. The last weather report sent from the landing site that day indicated that the weather was fairly good, and that there wasn't much in the way of wind. But immediately afterward, the wind picked up.

At 1700 hours (5:00 PM), November 19, all was in readiness at the landing site. The landing lamps, arranged in an L, were lit. They were battery driven pole-lamps that had accompanied the men on their flight from Great Britain – and not part of the equipment *Crouse* had managed to secure in the area. As it turned out, they were too weak for their mission, especially in bad weather.

The radio location device, *Eureka,* stood ready. It consisted of a large case, a special 12-volt battery, earphones and an antenna. A corresponding apparatus, Rebecca, was on board each tow-plane. When a *Rebecca* sent out radio waves, they would be received by *Eureka* who, in turn, answered by sending back her own radio waves. By listening in the earphones to the specific tone made by the radio waves emanating from *Eureka,* it was possible for the radio operator in the plane to determine the distance and direction to the landing zone. In a like manner, *Eureka's* signals changed tone as they were received by the planes. Consequently, by listening in *Eureka's* earphones **Haugland** could "hear" the planes drawing closer.

As the evening wore on, the weather changed for the worse. The wind picked up and a low layer of clouds covered the sky. Suddenly, **Haugland** heard the "correct" sound in *Eureka's* earphones. The time was now 21:40 hours (9:40 PM). The landing-lamps were lit and fifteen minutes later all the members of *Grouse* heard the telltale rumble of a plane. Morse code signals were sent out to make their presence known, but no glider was seen to land.

During the course of an hour, the "contact sound" was heard several times, and **Poulsson** reports that they noted airplane rumble coming from several different directions. It was hard to understand how the pilots could have missed them when the planes were so near. It wasn't until the year 2004 that **Poulsson** came to learn that one of the *Rebeccas* had ceased to function. But even so, what he still can't reconcile himself to is that the correct "contact sound" was, nonetheless, heard in the Eureka.

Grouse stayed at the landing zone until 11:30 PM. At which time, they gave up and returned to the cabin. The following day **Haugland** sent a message to England informing them that the glider had not landed as planned. This was a hard blow, and it felt especially hard to send the telegram, not least with thought to the mocking presence of exceptionally fine weather over the next several days.

In retrospect, **Poulsson** poses that the British operation was a one-way mission. The participants had no possibility of getting out of Norway after completing a hypothetically successful operation. But he takes strong exception to the assertion that the operation was predestined to fail.

Had the gliders successfully landed, **Poulsson** is convinced that *Grouse* would have succeeded in leading the British soldiers to the objective, and that they would have successfully carried out the mission. He further asserts that there are three explanations as to why the operation was not executed. Firstly, because the *Rebecca* in the plane nearest the landing site was not in working order; secondly, the pole-lamps anchored in the ground were not strong enough; and thirdly, the relatively favourable weather over the landing area had worsened, resulting in poor visibility and low lying clouds.

But fortunately, he is quick to add, the mission to sabotage the facility in Vemork was not abandoned. We were only forced to keep ourselves hidden and to keep struggling to survive until a new attempt was set into motion. "Our part in the battle over heavy water," states **Poulsson** with emphasis, "was not yet over.".

The most vital mission for *Grouse* during the period of time that followed the failed British operation was to stay alive. It was a close call because the Germans carried out extensive raids in an attempt to find people in the area who had been involved in the operation.

During one these raids, one of the men who had helped *Grouse*, **Torstein Skinnarland,** was seized as a hostage. He was imprisoned in the Grini concentration camp until the end of the war. But before he was seized, he saw to it that the battery to the radio (which *Grouse* was so dependent on) was fully charged.

The cabin in Sandvass was located entirely too near the German's radio location devices, plus there was the very real risk of some German patrol showing up the area. The members of *Grouse* therefore decided to set off in the direction of Grasdal, north of Møsvatn, where there was a shack they could hole up in, while they awaited new orders. In addition, there was also a good store of food. Thus the decision was made to make the shack in Grasdal their new base.

They took with them the food they had left, and as much equipment as their strength would allow. In the Grasdal shack they found a chest containing salted deer-meat, which was much appreciated.

Towards the end of the year, the want of food became all the more acute, and they had no choice but to stretch out the food supply with moss. Finding wood was also a problem and there weren't many deer in the area, so the 19th of December saw them moving on to Svensbu, near Store Saure. And there they remained until February 1943.

Grouse reasoned that the risk of coming upon strangers so far back in the mountains was almost nil. Therefore, they roamed over wide areas in attempts to find food, and once again, they were forced to struggle against severe winter conditions in the high terrain.

The day before Christmas Eve, **Poulsson** succeeded in shooting a deer, and now the food problem was solved. On Christmas Eve, all the unit members were full and content having eaten their fill of deer in various forms: soup and blood, boiled and fried, liver and tongue. After Christmas, they shot and ate 13 deer, and thereafter they live almost solely on meat. They absorbed vitamin C by eating the contents of the deer's stomachs. This half-digested food, which they blended with blood, was regarded as absolute haute cuisine.

On December 27, 1942, after having been on a hunting trip, **Hellberg** returned to the shack together with a younger brother of **Torstein Skinnarland.** This brother, **Einar,** joined-up with *Grouse*. Earlier that year, on March 17, he had travelled to Great Britain after having participated in an operation that succeeded in capturing the costal ship, Galtesund. In England, when it became known that he come from Rjukan, *SOE* put him through a short and intensive training course, and eleven days later, on March 28 1942, he was put on a plane and parachute-landed in the vicinity of Rjukan. *SOE* needed his services as a contact-man in the area. **Einar Skinnarland,** in fact, had been a vital link in the original plan. He was to have made welcome the members of *Grouse* when they parachute landed, but when the first plans, aimed at using *Grouse* to establish resistance groups in the Telemark area, were changed, and the unit was, instead, given the mission to prepare the way for a British sabotage operation, **Skinnarland's** mission was also changed. He was instructed to hold a low-profile and act as a "sleeper" contact who could later awake to action if either the operation of his countrymen, or that of the British soldiers, went wrong. Now he had the task of seeing to it that the batteries got fully charged. He also secured a string of contacts to get information about Vemork with respect to security-watch procedures and other German activities.

But now the unit's health began to worsen. Due to the one-dimension nature of their diet, they periodically suffered severe stomach pains. They had also suffered minor cases of frostbite, inflamed chaffing – and some of the men had developed overall body-ache. Still, all considered, they were in surprisingly good shape during the winter of 1942/43, both psychologically and physically. They lived almost wholly on meat, but the fat content in their diet was minimal. After Christmas, *Grouse* was able to compensate for this shortage over short periods, by having access to small amounts of butter, flour, sugar and even a few cooked potatoes. This largess was furnished by **Olav Skinnarland,** the third brother in the family, and by other contacts in Møsstrond. The three **Skinnarland** brothers were a godsend. They never asked any questions and tended to focus their attention on solving practical problems. In addition, they were enterprising and cheerful by nature.

Grouse could not carry out the new mission against the plant in Vemork on its own. They had neither the explosives nor the necessary information about the facility's machinery. Moreover, the Germans were constantly strengthening their security operations in the area. A bit into December, London radioed the new plans that had been devised for carrying out an operation in Vemork, and **Haugland** sent back information about the latest German troop dispositions. In January, the German force was strengthened to number approximately 200 men in Rjukan, 30 in Vemork and 40 at the Møsvass Dam.

The new sabotage attempt would be carried out by a Norwegian contingent comprised of *Grouse* and six men from *Norwegian Independent Company Number 1*. Its codename was *Gunnerside*.[11]

But before we discuss this mission, we will draw a detailed picture of what happened in the British operation.

---

11   Interview with Jens-Anton Poulsson in his home in Kongsberg, on Aug. 25, 2004. Letters from Poulsson to the author with information/comments on the subject, as follows: Sept. 2, 2004, Sept. 21, 2004, Nov. 21 2004 and Dec 28, 2004. Poulsson has also lent the following written documents to the author: the operation order that *Grouse* received on Oct. 17, 1942 – written in English. A report about the work of *Grouse* during the winter of 1942/43, written by Warrant Officer Jens-Anton Poulsson, London, Apr. 1943, Jens-Anton Poulsson: *Aksjon Vemork, Vinterkrig på Hardangervidda* (Ak Lake, Vemork, Winter combat on the Hardanger Wilderness), Facsimil, 1993, Tinn County.

Chapter 3

The Planning

In the chapter titled heavy water we saw how British and Norwegian authorities gradually worked out the planning of the sabotage operation that eventually was given the codename *Freshman*. During the ongoing work of planning, three different attack methods were considered: Bombing the facility, destroying it with the assistance of Norwegian saboteurs, or have airborne troops parachute near the target and then blow it up.

The first alternative, night-bombing, was the most common method used by the British *Royal Air Force (RAF)* at the time. But locating a target (at night) wasn't all that easy or certain, and bombing the facility would very likely cause the spilling of many Norwegian lives.[12] **Leif Tronstad**[13] strongly opposed this alternative and, to a significant degree, contributed to its being set aside.

In the spring of 1942 he was visited by two highly placed American officers. They asserted that the allies should bomb the plant in Vemork to ensure that the production of heavy water was stopped. **Tronstad** argued determinedly against this method. He pointed out that the facility was constructed of very thick, reinforced concrete and that the bombs wouldn't reach the lowest levels where the plant's machinery was located. The high mountains surrounding the facility would force the planes to fly so high that hitting the target was far from certain. He further argued that a bombing raid would risk the lives of the facility's personnel and civilians living in the area.[14]

The second alternative – employing Norwegian saboteurs in the leading role – was also dismissed. The British reasoning was that the Norwegians had as yet too little experience in this way of waging war.

---

12. *Operation Freshman (An account of the raid by the 1st Airborne Div. Engineers on the Heavy water plant in Norway)*, By Q.M.S.D.F.Cooper, R.E., 1945, p.31
13. Just who Tronstad was, is discussed in Chapter 1, Heavy Water.
14. Brun, Jomar: *Brennpunkt Vemork 1940-1945*, Universityforlaget (University Press), 1985, p.66-67.

This left the plan of using allied airborne troops as the best alternative. But which method should be employed? The first idea evaluated was seaplanes, which could set down on Tinnsjøn. But as work continued on the plan, it became evident that executing such a landing was easier said than done. The mountains around the lake were very steep, and in the event ice had already formed on the lake, a landing would be impossible.

Setting in a force by parachute was considered a workable method, but this would entail low-level flying along narrow valleys and the paratroopers could possibly be wind-driven a long way from the target. In addition, such flying tactics could easily draw the Germans' attention. In the end, it was therefore decided that gliders would be used instead.

It was also considered vital that the operation be carried out during the favorable moon phase that would appear in November. If the operation were, instead, to be carried out during the deep winter months, ski-skilled agents would be required and that was not a skill the British possessed. Another consideration was how long the reconnaissance unit could remain near the landing zone without being discovered.

The air crew on board the proposed tow-plane, a *Halifax*-model heavy bomber, consisted of seven men: two pilots, two observers, a telegraph operator, a flight engineer and a gunner.

The 1st Airborne Division, after weighing all technical factors, concluded that a force of 12 to 15 men would be required. Due to the mission's risky nature, and the importance attached to its goal, the decision was made to double the recommended size of its force. The military personnel making up this operational force would be flown over in two gliders. Each glider would transport one officer, one sergeant, 13 engineer troops and two glider pilots. The engineer troops came from the *9th Field Company* and the *261st Field Park Company* out of the *1st Airborne Division*.

All 48 participants were volunteers, even if they had no idea what the operation was about. The leaders of the respective units in the two gliders were **Lieutenant A. C. Allen** and **Lieutenant D. A. Methven**.[15]

After landing, they would meet four Norwegian agents,[16] who would lead them to the objective. The landing would take place near a road so that the sabotage operation could be carried out that very same night. How the British would get into the Vemork facility was a problem best solved by the Norwegian reconnaissance agents.

Shortly before takeoff, a plan to include foldable bicycles in the equipment was shelved. In light of a report from the reconnaissance unit

---

15. See footnote 12
16. See chapter 2, A risk-filled mission

The Planning

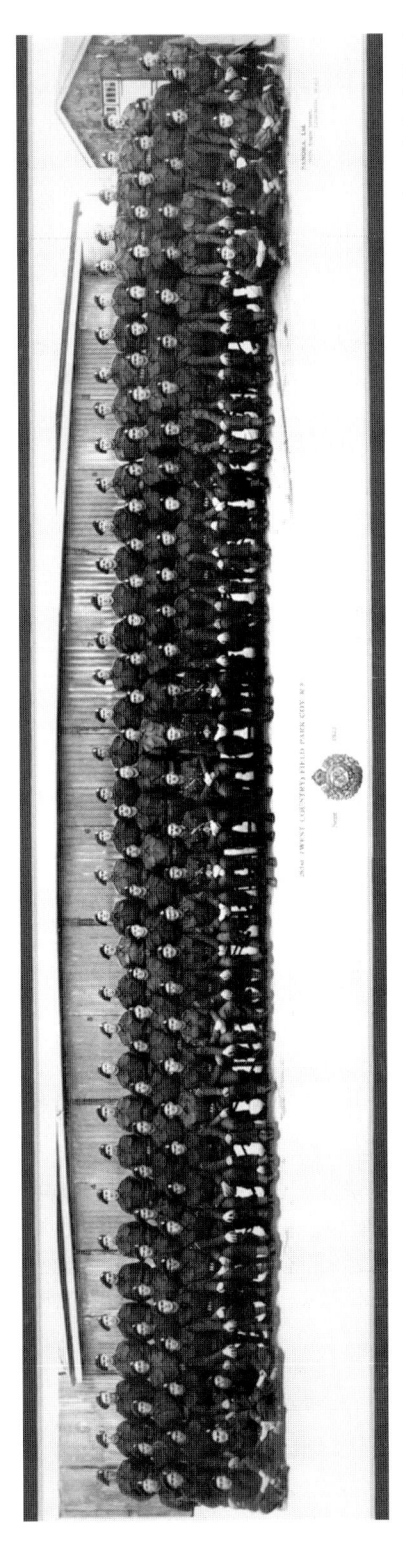

The 30 engineer soldiers came from the 9th Field Company and the 261st Field Park Company of the 1st Airborne Division. The photo shown is of the last-cited company. Photo loaned out by Kjell Skadberg.

the day before takeoff mentioning 30 centimeters of heavy snow at the landing site and 10 centimeters on road, the British reasoned that such conditions would make cycling impossible, even if the men could make use of roadways somewhat closer to Vemork to cycle to and from the objective. After the first glider had landed, the unit would wait for up to 30 minutes for the second aircraft before starting out towards Vemork. The most vital aspect of the long march towards the target was to avoid being detected by the enemy. Should a soldier be injured, he was to be given a morphine injection and left behind. The same applied to any and all who could not keep up with the unit, no matter the reason. If the troops were detected, they were not to surrender but should continue making their way toward the target, no matter what happened, to carry out the mission: "Whatever happens, someone must arrive at the objective to do the job – detection is no excuse for halting."

Two days before takeoff, this order was slightly modified: If either or both of the gliders happened to land at a location that was totally amiss, the officer, or highest ranking soldier, could decide whether it was practically feasible to carry out the mission, or should they try to flee to Sweden. Similarly, if the mission were crowned with success, it was also planned that the troops would attempt to reach the Swedish border.

Model *Horsa HK I* gliders were to be used.[17] By the end 1942 the production of this type of glider was in full swing. The model was employed as a battle-glider by the British airborne forces. The aircraft was mainly built by furniture manufacturers. It consisted of an arched, plywood body shell fastened to a more stabile wood frame construction. It was 20 meters long with a 26 meter wingspan. In addition, it was equipped with a three wheel undercarriage for takeoff/landing that could be jettisoned allowing it to land on centrally located runners. The pilot and co-pilot sat beside each other in the aircraft's nose and its instrumentation was very basic.

A fully loaded *Horsa* usually weighed close to 8 tons at the start. Half of this weight was payload, for example: 30 soldiers and a jeep, or ten soldiers and an artillery gun – six to one, a half-dozen to the other – depending. Upon landing, soldiers could quickly deplane by removing the pins from the tail, after checking that the control cables and electrical leads had been cut away – then the entire tail fell loose. But the tail component had a tendency to want to stay in place. Happily, however, a saw, an axe and an explosive charge were standard equipment, and if it was necessary

---

17. Footnote 12, much of the detailed information is taken from the *Public Record Office (PRO). Richmond, Surrey, England, Group Letter DEFE 2, Piece Number 224, See Outline plan*, dated Oct. 13, 1942 and notations about *Freshman*, dated Nov. 17, 1942, p. 117, Freshman, passages 59, 60 and 61, p. 12.

to resort to force in order to get the cargo off-loaded, these resources were at hand.[18]

The *Halifax* bomber was chosen to accomplish the heavy, long-distance tow because this model had the robust engines needed to handle this sort of mission without overheating, even in the event the glider needed to be towed back.

The problem the British confronted not only had to do with getting the saboteur force into Norway, but also with how to get the soldiers out again. Sweden was deemed the most feasible solution. And after the mission was carried out, the British soldiers would try to reach that Scandinavian country's borders.

Therefore it was vital that the soldiers had forehand knowledge of the escape routes and certain security regulations they were obligated to follow during the escape, so they could quickly leave the target area when the mission had been carried out and the order to disperse was given. They were to head toward the border in pairs since three men traveling together was conspicuous and an even larger group would surely call unwanted attention to themselves. During the very first phase of the withdrawal the British soldiers would continue to appear as combat soldiers. They were not take off their uniforms and ditch their weapons until they were at least 8 kilometers from Vemork. Moreover, they were to observe every precaution when they freed themselves of all tell-tale items that could point to them as being soldiers, and make absolutely certain that they were not observed when they threw their uniforms, weapons and equipment in one of the many bodies of water that could be found along the way. Plans for five different escape routes were provided for the first part of the march, and every route was described in detail. The men were organized into 12 pairs and every pair was designated individually by a single letter from A to L. Everyone knew in advance to which lettered pair they belonged. Some of the pairs would use identical routes, but would maintain appropriately long distances from each other. Other routes would only be followed by one pair. Five routes, it was reasoned, would in any event ensure that some of the saboteurs had a chance of avoiding capture. If a pair were taken prisoner, there was less likelihood of others meeting the same destiny. The plans were drawn up with the intent of providing each of the five routes similar natural and strategic advantages.

The geographical obstacles that had to be overcome along the routes leading to Sweden were substantial. They crossed open rivers and roads – and the bridges over the Glomma River were especially well guarded. Many of the rivers poured into inland lakes. One of these, Lake Mjøsa, formed a 96 kilometer-long barrier. The total number of roads into Sweden was therefore limited.

---

18. Dank, Milton: *Glideflygergjengen* (Glider flying), Tiden Norsk Forlag (Publishing Co.), 1979, p 43-44

Skitten was an auxiliary airfield near Wick in Scotland during 1939-1945. Map-drawing loaned out by Robin de Gency Sewell.

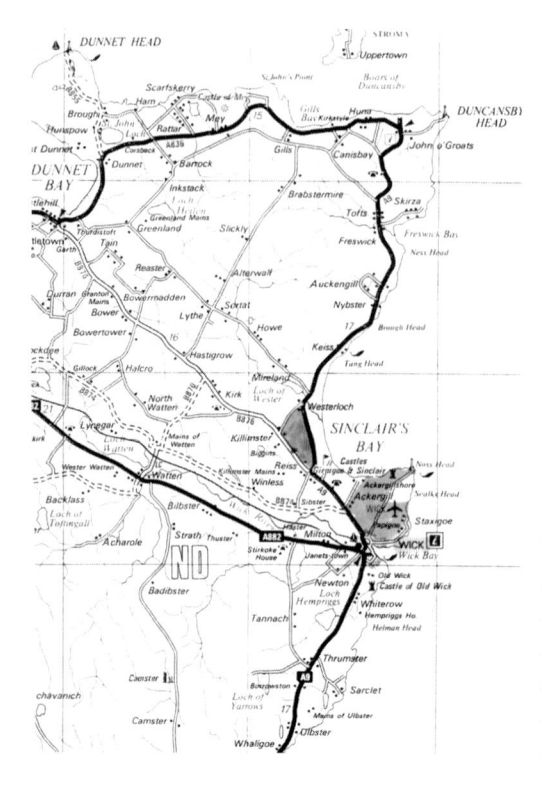

The shortest route required that a choice be made between two such bottle-necks. One of these was located between Randsfjorden (the Rands Fjord) and Tyrifjorden (the Tyri Fjord), the other between Tyrifjorden and Oslofjorden. At the first-mentioned bottle-neck, the primary obstacle was posed by the dangers attached to the presence of power stations in the area. In addition, the security watches over these stations was maximum. Therefore, of these two southerly options, the planners advised that the saboteurs following this "short" route should choose the other bottle-neck, which is to say, the one between Tyrifjorden and Oslofjorden. This stretch was shorter and the natural obstacles, in terms of topography and sudden weather changes, were not as challenging. And importantly, the Norwegians guarding the border were generally disposed to be friendly and helpful.

Those who were certain that their disguises were convincing should choose this path to Sweden. With specific regard to disguise, among other details, it was vital to remember that it was unusual to see a mustache on Norwegian men.

But there were also many dangers attached to choosing this road: It went right through the area having the highest concentration of Germans in Norway, and the border was guarded by both Germans and the Norwegian Nazi police. And not least, the Germans would surely assume that the saboteurs fleeing from Vemork had chosen this route to cross into Sweden.

According to international law, a soldier who had participated in a sabotage operation committed no crime if, subsequent to said mission, he tried to flee in civilian clothes. But, should the British be captured out of uniform and also armed, they would be regarded as spies.

The only alternative to these southerly routes was to make a detour towards the north around Lake Mjøsa. This area wasn't as heavily populated, and consequently, the German presence there wasn't especially large. But this detour was a significantly longer trek, and it was an inland area with temperatures that ranged many, many degrees lower. Those who considered themselves to be in top physical shape, should possibly choose this northerly direction.

During their flight from Norway, the British soldiers were under orders to comply with certain safety procedures and directives. It was safer to move during the day than at night, especially in well-populated areas. If they found themselves in an area where there was a long distance between houses, and if there was enough moonlight, then it might be possible to proceed at night. They were also obligated to be very restrictive in making contact with the local residents, especially during the first phase of the flight. But, if they wound up in a desperate situation, they could act on the assumption that many Norwegians were ready and willing to help them. However, the British were also obligated to keep in mind that if they were careless, they certainly could be taken prisoner – but for the Norwegians who had helped them, the consequence was death. The fleeing men should therefore seek some suitable place to spend the night before it became too dark. When they came upon lone houses, farms and sheds located in isolated areas, they were, likewise, compelled to be very watchful and alert. At several of the places where they were to cross rivers and streams, there were no bridges. But they should keep in mind that with respect to the smaller water obstacles they encountered along the way, there were most often boats lying by the shore. In the event they borrowed a boat, they should think about leaving behind some cash to the owner. With respect to the big rivers, they were most often spanned by bridges – even if these were for the most part very carefully guarded. Before crossing such a bridge, they should therefore wait at least a half-hour in order to see if there was a guard in the area. However, it was often difficult to spot the guards because they were clothed in camouflage uniforms.

If they were taken prisoner by the Germans, they were not obligated to give anything but name, rank, and serial number. Those who succeeded in crossing into Sweden would all avail themselves of the same lie about their recent history, namely: They had been taken prisoner by the Germans, but had successfully escaped. Therefore, they had now entered a neutral country and had the right to be sent home. Soldiers participating in a war

A review of the rules and regulations that applied during the withdrawal to Sweden took place two days before the mission was begun. In a closing address, it was emphasized that those who would succeed in making a successful flight, were those who had the strength to carry on though their bodies said it was time to give up. The soldiers were also informed that with respect to capture, the thing to do was to convince the enemy that you were a civilian and could gather in valuable information. In the same optimistic vein, they were also told that if luck was on their side, the chances were great that everything would work out for the best.[19]

---

19. *Public Record Office (PRO). Richmond, Surrey, England, Group Letter DEFE 2, Piece Number 224, p. 46-52. (Briefing notes on Escaping from Vemork to Sweden).*

who entered a neutral country without having first been captured by their enemy, on the other hand, were interned.

Lieutenant Colonel Mark Henniker was the man who led the training and planned the operation. But when it first began, he made known his doubts about the entire operation. In the first place, he asserted that, under the rules of war, the operation was illegal, and secondly, he argued that the distance from the central base of operations, Skitten Airport outside Wick, in Scotland, to the landing site in Hardangervidda (the Hardanger wilderness area) was too long.

Icing of the airplanes and cables could also present problems. In addition, he stressed that the RAF's personnel were not sufficiently well-trained to competently handle the navigation. And yet, he nevertheless concluded that it was possible to carry out the mission despite these reservations, but that it would be very difficult. Consequently, **Henniker** carried out the assignments stipulated in his orders, but at the time he apparently didn't know how vital the mission itself was. In 1983, he said the following on NRK, giving substance to this reasoning:

> *I was told it was extremely important. I was told it was in order to prevent the manufacture of heavy water, which I was told was connected with something far more important – though I did not know then what it was.*[20]

The head of the Norwegian section of the *SOE*, **Colonel John Wilson**, to a large degree, shared Henniker's view. From the very start, Wilson was convinced that the operation would be very dangerous: *From the outset it was realised that the operation was exceptionally dangerous.*

In point of fact, Norway was one of the European countries least suitable for carrying out an operation with gilders. Due to its characteristically steep, difficult to master mountainous landscape, it was hard to find a good location to land. In addition, the weather conditions in in the late-summer and fall of 1942 were extremely poor and hardly conducive for attempting a mission using gliders – moreover, a type of operation they had no extensive experience of.[21] By September 30, 1942, the planners had already requested the chief of flying operations to bestow the mission with a codename. Shortly thereafter, they were informed that the operation's name was *Freshman* – beginner.[22]

---

20. Radio program about Operation *Freshman*, NRK Stavanger, 1983
21. Footnote 14.
22. Footnote 12, Footnote 19, p 5, passage 7.

Chapter 4

Preparations for the mission

In order to divert attention from the mission's true purpose, the training was explained as a supposed competition, *The Washington Cup*, with an American unit. The entire training was accomplished under this cover. Security was tight, and the security police - who were constantly in close proximity of the soldiers - never heard a word from any "outsiders" about the training's true purpose. Impenetrable maximum security was a must if the mission was to succeed. If something were to leak out, catastrophic consequences could result, not only for the sabotage unit in question, but also for the initiation of any new operation if this effort failed. This cover was therefore essential.

The 30 engineer soldiers who would be carrying out the actual attack received special training lasting a month. During the first week, the unit's preparation was devoted to exercise, weapons training, map reading and long training marches. Particular emphasis was placed on training aimed at raising the soldiers' observation abilities. The second week was spent further strengthening the condition and endurance of the soldiers with mountain climbing, a training stage that was out-sourced to the northern part of Wales. Here, the soldiers also carried out long training marches through mountainous terrain where they were required to orient themselves with the aid of a map and a small scale, overnight in the open no matter the weather, and keep themselves nourished on minimum rations. The third week was focused on technical training. Among other things, the soldiers visited plant facilities in Scotland and England that were similar to Norsk Hydro's facility in Vemork. The soldiers spent the last week on the plain near Salisbury, Salisbury Plain. There, the soldiers were provided with special equipment, and, at the same time, went through the entire plan of attack in detail.

Three days before the takeoff to Norway, the special force returned to their main base. It was from here that the operation would get under way.

Freshman would fly in over Norway at Egersund, and from there continue on over the mountains to the landing site.[23] The aircraft personnel had also been given a month's training to raise their physical and psychological strength, as well as fine-tune their technical know-how.

The pilots of the tow-planes, having previously flown *Whitney*, as well as *Wellington* model aircraft, now had to familiarize themselves with the *Halifax*. They were also compelled to practice towing *Horsa* model gliders, which could only give them a little taste-sample of what it would be like to tow these planes at night, over a distance of 650 kilometers. The pilots of the gliders themselves had the added task of learning how to work their way back to base after carrying out the mission. Long-distance towing at night was a completely untested area for these gliders pilots, who, in addition, must prepare for making a night-time landing in an unfamiliar area. They couldn't escape the possibility that before, during and/or after the landing, they might find themselves in an inferno. The planes were subject to hard and notoriously changeable weather conditions, enemy anti-aircraft fire and a complicated landing. After the landing, the pilots were instructed to function as ordinary soldiers.

During the course of training, two engineer soldiers became so severely injured that they couldn't take part in the mission. One was the chauffeur, **Syd Brittain**, who broke his ankle. The other was the engineer soldiers' second-in-command, **Michael Green**. He broke his index finger in connection with an accidental shot.[24]

Aircraft mechanic **Hedly B. Duckworth** saw service in 1942 with the 138th (previously, the 161st) squadron. The squadron was intended for a special mission and stationed at the RAF's Tempsford airport, in Bedfordshire. Duckworth had, in addition to his mechanical training, experience flying short stretches as a crew member of a Halifax bomber.

Duckworth and a few other ground personnel, among them **Sergeant Gale**, were sent to the RAF's airfield near Netheravon at the end of September 1942. There, they were informed that they would be participating in a contest against American glider units. This proved not to be the case.

Duckworth and the other ground personnel were assigned the mission of servicing the *Halifax* bombers. This meant they would be helping the pilots from the 38th Wing to tow the gilders. Several airfields were used,

---

23. *Operation "Freshman" (An account of the raid by the 1st Airborne Div. Engineers on the Heavy water plant in Norway)*, By Q.M.S.D.F.Cooper, R.E., p.33; NRK Savanger, program about Operation Freshman, 1983. Over the period July 20-27, I travelled around a part of the area where Freshman was trained.

24. Mail from PeterYeates, Nov. 5, 2004. He was a close friend of Syd Brittain's and his confidant. See also: Wiggan, Richard: *Operation Freshman, The Rjukan Heavy Water Raid 1942*, William Kimber, London, 1986, p. 52, 163164.

Halifax towing a Horsa: A pattern that occurs in many variations. Photo loaned out by Kjell Skadberg.

among them, Thruxton, Tangmere and Thorney Island. The training sessions went on both day and night.

In the beginning of November, things began to move forward. A number of visitors showed up and, on the Wednesday and Thursday corresponding to the 12th and 13th of November, the ground personnel prepared to move. Attached to this unit were two Australian glider-pilots. These two had been kept to fly the gliders, while the remaining Australians had traveled home. They were both specialists in their area.

On November 18 1942, all unit personnel were in place at the Skitten airfield outside Wick, in Scotland. There, they saw soldiers wearing red berets, but their uniforms lacked insignias. **Duckworth** and **Gale** were quartered, along with other members of the operation, in small wooden houses by the edge of the airfield, completely isolated from other units. On the night of November 18, a *Halifax* plane made a reconnaissance flight in the direction of Stavanger, along the coast to Oslo and then back to Skitten. **Duckworth** recalls he was aboard that flight.

The following day, both **Duckworth** and **Gale** were informed that they might have to take part in the next training since the personnel from the 38th Wing had been assigned other missions. At the same time, they were also informed that they wouldn't be competing in a contest against the Americans, but rather their duties were required in connection with an operation codenamed *Freshman*. More than this, they were not told.

Duckworth was the man selected, but with the knowledge that his colleague's wife was expecting their first child, **Gale** volunteered to take his place – and the decision was made to follow that suggestion.[25]

Weather conditions were recognized as playing a vital role in the operations overall success. Vemork lies deep in a narrow valley, and sufficient moonlight was a must if the operation was to succeed. The meteorologists were able to confirm that the right conditions would prevail during the period of November 18 – 26. Moonlight during this period would provide sufficiently strong illumination down in the Rjukan Valley to allow the attack unit to proceed at night. The next suitable moon-phase wouldn't appear until just before Christmas.

The leader of the flight operation was a Group Captain in the air force, **Group-Captain Tom B. Cooper. Cooper**, himself, would accompany the operation seated in one of the tow-planes. The Norwegian meteorologist, **Sverre Petterssen**, had already become involved in planning the air-transport operation early on. In addition to advising on the problem of the moon's phases, he soon perceived that there were other difficulties that had to taken into consideration and addressed. During the tow-phase of the flight, a cloud-free sky was absolutely essential since the pilots of gliders had to keep the planes towing them in sight in order to keep the gliders well over the air turbulence they generated. If a glider wound up in air stream of the propellers, there was a very strong risk that the glider's tailfin would be ripped apart, followed by certain catastrophe. Moreover, clear weather was also a prerequisite for locating the landing site. **Petterssen** had extremely brief information about the weather in southern Norway, and the weather situation over the North Sea didn't come anywhere near meeting ideal conditions. Based on the prevailing airstreams, there was reason to believe that a more or less total cloud cover

---

25. Footnote 23, a written account from Hedley B. Duckworth, dated May 12, 1995: *Regarding my investment in Operation Freshman.* An undated report by Duckworth; *Freshman: Aftermath of Operation Freshman, end of September 1942 to 20th November 1942. The sequel to Operation Freshman. Up to present time.*
A Dunnett More Video (D.M.V.) This is a three-hour-long recording of the ceremony that took place when a memorial to the participants in Freshman was unveiled at the air field at Skitten, Wick, in Scotland in 1992. This recording contains several interviews, among them, one with Duckworth. It's been difficult to confirm Duckworth's information. I haven't been able to find his name in the British military documents. However, the remarkable job performed by the ground personnel under the leadership of Sergeant Gale is noted: *The admirable work cheerfully carried out by the ground-maintenance party under Sgt. Gale (DEFE 2, 221, p. 13).* In the register listing those who were onboard the tow-plane, Sgt. Gale's name does not appear, but this doesn't necessarily mean very much. Falconer, for example, is on the list, but obviously wasn't on the tow-plane since he lay buried in a churchyard in Helleland. Personnel comprising the plane's crew could have been changed at the last moment. See also: chapter 5, footnote 30.

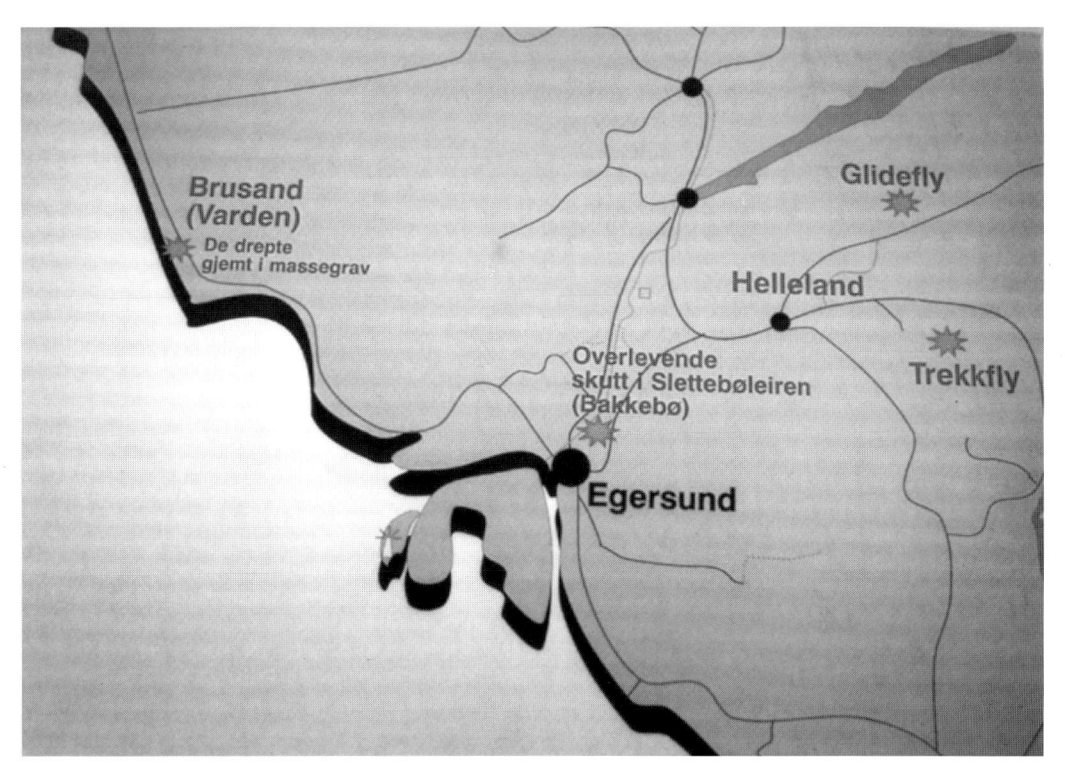

The area in Rogaland that played a vital role during Operation Freshman. The model was fashioned by Johan Aakre. Photo: Kjell Skadberg.

hung over the southern part of Scandinavia. The only encouraging sign he succeeded in coming up with was that **Cooper** had gotten a message from Grouse, the on-site reconnaissance unit in the Hardanger wilderness area, that the weather over Rjukan was fine. Petterssen was still doubtful, and on Thursday afternoon, November 19, he notified the **colonel** that in his judgment the weather situation was unfavorable. Nonetheless, **Cooper** decided that the operation should be carried out on the night of November 19, lasting into November 20. The Norwegian meteorologist, in so many words, let it be known that in his opinion the operation would require a clearer sky, than what he believed would prove to be the case that night, if it were to succeed.[26]

---

26. Petterssen, Sverre: *Kuling fra nord,* Aschehoug & Co. (W. Nygaard) Oslo, 1974, p. 158-162

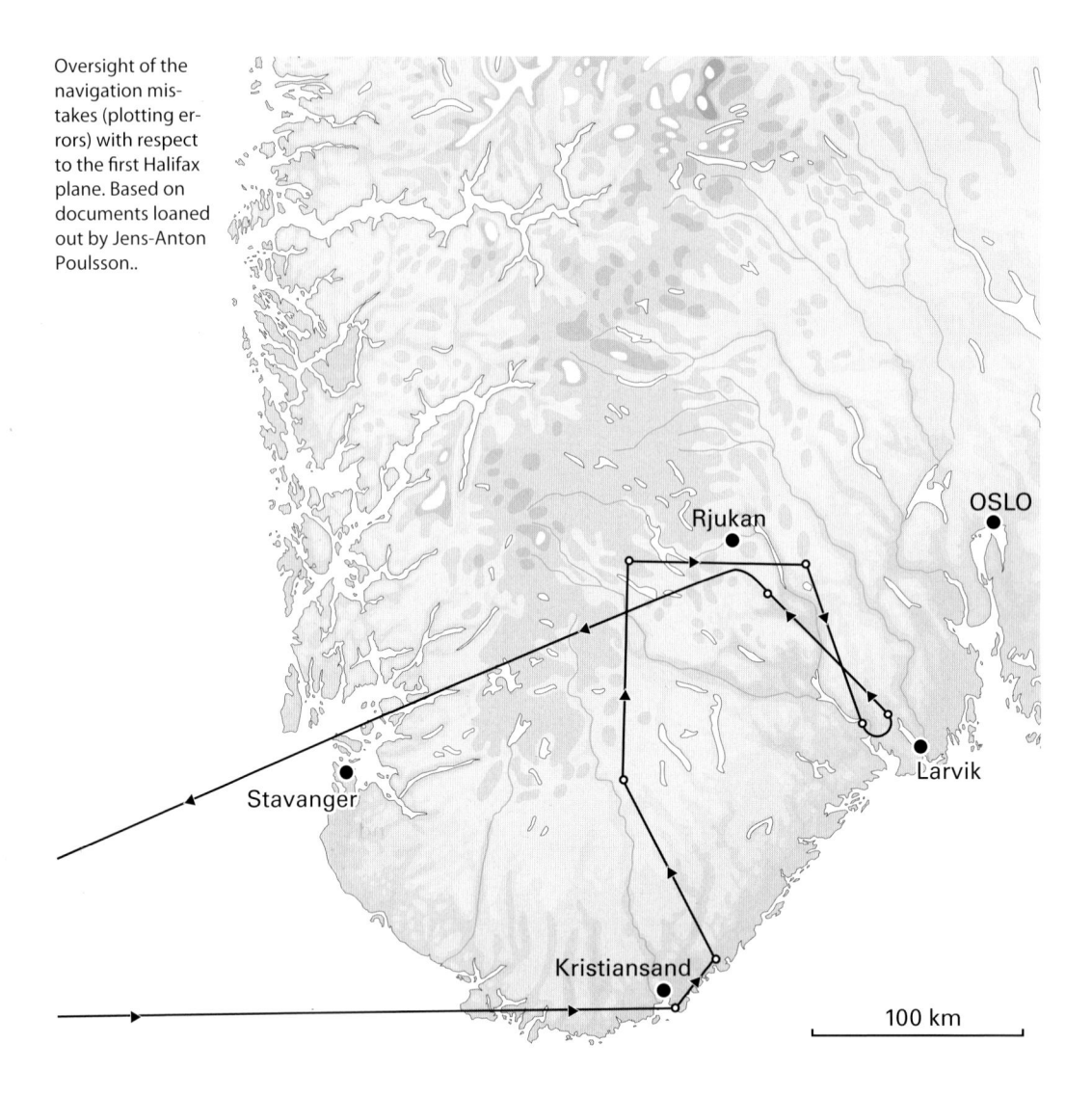

Operation Freshman ● ⌄ ● The hunt for Hitlers heavy water

Oversight of the navigation mistakes (plotting errors) with respect to the first Halifax plane. Based on documents loaned out by Jens-Anton Poulsson..

Chapter 5

The Glider crash on Benkja Mountain in Helleland

The two flying units started with a 30 minute stagger between flights. The first tow-plane and glider lifted from Skitten airfield outside Wick, in Scotland, at 17:40 hours (5:40 PM) on Thursday, November 19, 1942.[27] Squadron leader, **Major Wilkinson,** was the head pilot, and **Colonel Tom B. Cooper,** leader of the entire flying operation, was on board as an observer. The pilots of the glider were **Sergeants M. F. C: Strathdee** and **P. Doig. Lieutenant D. A. Methven** had command responsibility over the engineer soldiers aboard the glider.

The morale of the *Freshman* participants was very high, and their orders were crystal clear. After the landing, the engineer soldiers were to hook up with members of the reconnaissance unit, *Grouse* who awaited them in Hardangervidda. **Lieutenant Methevn,** two engineer soldiers and a Norwegian from *Grouse* would then quickly head out towards Vemork, as a point squad. The remaining engineer soldiers would then form up with the later-arriving unit under **Lieutenant Allen's** command. The march to the targeted objective was estimated to take approximately five hours.[28]

When the first tow-plane and glider neared the coast of Norway, the *Rebecca's* contact suddenly got worse – but the plane and the glider it towed still managed to find their way close to the landing site area, A bit northwest of Rjukan, the aircraft came into a heavy cover of clouds that was difficult to fly through. As a result, the tandem flying unit flew off-course, making a long swing that reached as far as Larvik before setting, after some degree

---

27. *Public Record Office (PRO). Richmond, Surrey, England, Group Letter DEFE 2, Piece Number 224, Freshman, p. 14, 71 passages,* dated Nov. 19, 1942. According to another British document, dated the same day, *Group Letter DEFE 2, Piece Number 221, p.5,* the first plane's take-off occurred at 17:55(5:55 PM). The next take-off was a half-hour later.
28. *Operation "Freshman" (An account of the raid by the 1st Airborne Div. Engineers on the Heavy water plant in Norway),* By Q.M.S.D.F.Cooper, p. 32-37.

of hesitation, a course towards home. Fuel gauges approaching empty became a primary concern, and icing of both tow-plane and glider steadily grew worse and worse. The very worst was that the tow-line began to ice as well. Both aircraft quickly lost altitude – Over the Norwegian coastline, the tow-plane was forced to release the glider.

At 11.55 PM, the main base's radio caught a message from the radio-operator in the first tow-plane, reporting that the glider had been released over the sea: *glider released in sea*. With the help of triangularization, intersection of bearings, experts at the base were able to determine the plane's position as it flew over the mountains of Southern Norway.

At 1:51 AM, November 20, the first tow-plane landed, unscathed, at the air base in Scotland, its fuel tanks almost completely dry. Among the passengers to disembark were **Colonel**, *Group-Captain*, **Cooper**[29], and, according to **Hedley B. Duckworth**, air-mechanic **Gale**.

According to British records, the remaining men on board were **Squadron Leader, Air Force Major Wilkinson, Air Officer Kemmis,** and **Sergeants Jones, Otto, Falconer,** and **Conacher**.[30]

The second tow-plane and glider lifted from the base in Scotland at 6:10 PM, exactly 30 minutes after the first tandem unit, while there was still daylight. The head pilot was the Canadian, Lieutenant **A. R. Parkinson.** Piloting the glider were the Australians, **N. Davies** and **H. Fraser. Lieutenant A. C. Allen** had command of the engineer soldiers.

This second tow-plane, as early as 11:41 PM, requested a course that could bring them back to the base. This message was also picked up by another British radio-listening station. With the help of information from this station, the base tried to work out the location of the tow-plane and glider when the message was sent. According to their calculations, the aircraft had been over the North Sea.[31]

How far inland the aircraft had flown over Norway, before and after the message was sent, is not known. Nor is it known how many times the tow-plane came to fly inland over Norway's southern coast.

Fourteen minutes after the message was sent, both planes crashed in

---

29 Ibid.
30 Report about the operation, dated Dec. 8, 1942, *Group Letter DEFE 2*, Piece *Number 221*, p. 8, see Chapter 4, footnote 25.
31 Footnote 28, Map, *Plotting Eries*, covering the route the tow-plane used on the return flight to Scotland: Located at the Dalane Folkemuseum (public museum), Egersund. In his letter dated Apr. 4, 2006, Jens-Anton Poulsson indicates that his present understanding is as follows: It was the 2nd tandem-flight that came into close proximity of the landing area, and the one they made contact with. His reasoning is that, in as much as flight number 1 reached the target area, there really isn't any reason to think that that the navigator for flight number 2 should not have accomplished the same. Moreover, there isn't any reason to assume that the *Rebecca* in flight number 2 should also have ceased functioning. Therefore, it must have been the 2nd flight that *Grouse* was in contact with.

the then Helleland County within Norway's Rogaland District. Helleland resident, John Munkejord, heard the plane-roar and the explosion when the tow-plane crashed. The time was 11:55 PM.

People working on the tunnel near Fidjan on the Sørland railway had also observed this sequence. The plane had come in low over Helleland Valley. The glider brushed ground near the mountain area northeast of the county, and subsequently crashed northeast of the Hovland farm near Benkja Mountain. Thereafter, the tow-plane flew over Helleland Valley at low altitude and directly into the mountain range on the other side.

The two Australian pilots in the glider died on impact, and one engineer soldier was so badly injured that he died almost at once. Of the 14 remaining soldiers, three were badly injured, while the other eleven appeared to have come through with hardly a scratch. It's quiet likely that both planes had suffered from heavy icing.

Two of the strongest men, after hard struggle, managed to reach inhabited tracts of land. They had followed the terrain down, first coming to Freden Farm by Highway 9. From there, they had continued on to Litle Hogstad, a farm located nearer the central part of Helleland. After having passed up these two farms, the two British soldiers finally arrived at the farm of the local government administrator.

When they knocked on the administrator's door, it was his son, **Trond Hovland**, who answered. The British then got to explain their perplexing situation to the governmental administrator, himself, **Theodor Hovland**, telling him that they needed immediate medical help for their comrades at the top of the hillside.

The government administrator thereafter phoned the Dahlheim School

The glider crashed by Benkja Mountain after having first scrapped ground at its top. Photo: Jostein Berglyd.

Operation Freshman ⁃ ⁃ ⁃ The hunt for Hitlers heavy water

ID tags found by Anna Sikveland, Time County. She had wandered in the near area of Benkja Mountain around two weeks after the crash. The tags are the private property of Marit Tjåland. Photo: Trond Strømstad.

in Helleland. The hour was 3 in the morning. In Dahlheim could be found a unit of the Workers' Party. This unit operated under the leadership of **Arne Lima** from Høyland in Jæren. **Lima** and the government administrator had known each other for many, many years.

The government administrator described the British plane-crash situation and requested **Lima's** help. Lima immediately set off with five men he knew personally, and trusted. The wife of the Workers' Party's doctor, **Gunvor Benestad,** herself a nurse, also came along. Her husband was ill and therefore unable to take part in the arduous march.

As it happened, there were to be several more people making the journey to Benkja Mountain besides the little rescue expedition. After the government administrator had secured Lima's promise to help, his son, **Trond Hovland,** contacted the *District Commander* of the German Security Police located in Egersund, approximately 15 kilometers distant. The British were in complete agreement with this contact having been made. Given the current situation it was impossible to initiate an effective rescue operation without outside help. Nor would it have hardly been possible to hide these survivors from the Germans, since it was difficult to hide anything in this area. The telephone network was operated manually, and the risk of calls being tapped was great.

Trond Hovland and his father, **Theodor**, who had now taken responsibility for the British soldiers' situation on their shoulders, had Telavåg still fresh in their memory. Approximately a half-year had gone by since two officers from *Sipo* were killed in a battle with Norwegian freedom-fighters. The Germans had exacted revenge by burning down all building structures in the area, approximately 300 houses, killing all the livestock and destroying the fishing boats. All women and children, and men over 65, were evacuated and interned, while all males between the ages of 16 and 65 were arrested.

Had **Theodore Hovland** attempted to keep what had happened in Helleland a secret, the entire village would have been exposed to the risk of reprisals. Given these circumstances, it was better that the British be taken as prisoners of war. The two British soldiers were in agreement with this reasoning. And when they learned how far away Sweden lay, they realized that this was the only sound alternative.

After the *District Commander* in Egersund had received the message from the government administrator's farm in Helleland, **Sergeant Karl Heinz Wiedemann** contacted the Nazi interpreter in Egersund, **Tellef Tellefsen**. **Wiedemann** told his countryman that government administrator **Hovland** had phoned him and reported that two Englishmen had turned up at his home asking for medical help. The interpreter was ordered to travel to Helleland, where he would translate what the government administrator had stated on the telephone. At about the same time the interpreter started towards Helleland, 12 men from the German camp in Slettebø also set out for the government administrator's farm. This detachment consisted of an officer, two non-commissioned officers, eight privates and a doctor. The Germans designated the detachment as a *Suchkommando*, comprised of men from *Company 11 of the 3rd Battalion* which was located in a camp at Slettebrø, several kilometers from the central part of Egersund. **Lieutenant Muecke** was the officer in charge.

The rescue expedition from Dalhiem and the Germans from the camp in Slettebrø met up at the government administrator's farm. The Germans took one of the English soldiers with them. He was to show them the

The government administrator's estate in Helleland. This house played a key role in connection with the crash involving 15 engineer soldiers and the two Australian pilots at Benkja Mountain. Photo: Jostein Berglyd.

way to the glider. In addition to the above-mentioned, **Trond Hovland** and his wife joined in the trek, along with **Severin Hogstad**. He hailed from the previously mentioned Hogstad farm. **Trond Hovland** had phoned him and asked that he join them on the trip to the mountain. **Hogstad** had lived in the USA for several years and **Hovland** thought he would feel more secure if he had someone with him who handled English better then himself. But when **Hogstad** got to hear that the government administrator had informed the Germans, he became somewhat hesitant. Hadn't the local police-authority been a little too hasty in turning over this information?

The Englishman chosen to show them the way up to the glider began to veer to the left – a direction **Hovland** soon grasped was wrong, based on what the Englishmen had previously explained. The correct direction should be towards the north. Consequently, they took that direction instead.

Eventually, they came to place where they could see flashlights blinking. At that point, the Norwegians started to run ahead of the Germans and arrived at the scene of the accident before them. **Lima** was addressed in English, and he answered in the same language. Contact was thus established. The British, all of whom were dressed in uniform, wanted to know how far they were from Sweden. When this was made clear to them, their leader, **Lieutenant Allen**, said that given the situation, he didn't see any way out, other than having to accept becoming prisoners of war. **Lima** spoke with every one of the fourteen British soldiers. He tried

Trond Hovland was among the first to arrive at the crash site of the glider. Here, he is standing at the accident site, in 1986. Photo: Jostein Berglyd.

to learn if there were any Norwegians among them, but this wasn't the case. When Lima asked, the British also assured him that they had burnt all vital documents.

The time was 5:30 in the morning when the last group, the Germans, arrived at the scene. They assembled the Englishmen on a hillside below the location of the plane crash. **Lieutenant Muecke** promised the British prisoners that they would be cared for. The British had surrendered and were now prisoners of war. The engineer soldiers, without undue problem, could have fired on and killed the Germans as they walked along the hillside, but chose not to battle against them. **Trond Hovland** was sent down to secure help and several stretchers from occupied dwellings in the area

The British were taken down to the government administrator's farm. The three deceased were laid down in the administrator's office, while the rest were detained in a farmyard, guarded by German soldiers.

Before noon that day, sometime between 10 and 11.00 AM, the British were transported from the government administrator's farm. The last time **Trond Hovland** saw of them, one of the now imprisoned soldiers raised two fingers in a V-sign, as in victory. After everyone had disappeared, he found his way back up to the wreck. There, he found a notebook. In it, stood the name **George Knowles**.[32]

---

32. Interview with Trond Hovland, Helleland, Aug. 14, 1986.
Wandering and observing with Hovland in the Benkja Mountain area, Helleland, on Aug. 8, 1986.
Rapport from Government Administrator Theodore Hovland to the police chief in Rogalund concerning the plane crash in Helleland, dated Nov. 21, 1942.
Interrogation, police investigation of Tellef G. Tellefsen (interpreter), May 24, 1945.
Report from Arne Lima concerning the crash in Helleland, dated Jan. 20, 1944, Report no. 775.
Written communication from Arne Lima to Per Johnson, Randaberg, concerning the British airborne landing attempt on Hardangervidda in Nov. 1942, dated Nov. 16, 1981
Undated memorandum by Gunvor Benestad, wife to Per Johnson, Randaberg, concerning the plane crash on Benkja Mountain, Helleland. *Public Record Office (PRO)*. Richmond, S*urrey, England, Group Letter DEFE 2, Piece Number 219, p. 59,* dated May 19, 1943.
Gescheite des Infanteriregiments 355, 1936-1945. *Eine Dokumentation, mit Auszügen aus den authetischen Verlustlisten.* Dr, Fritz Amberger, Frankfurt/M, 1973, Eigenverlag. Zum Verkauf an Buchhandlungen nicht zugelassen.
Kriegstagesbuch der 280, Infanteridivision (280th Infantry Division war diary), Nov. 11, 1942, Nov. 21, 1942.

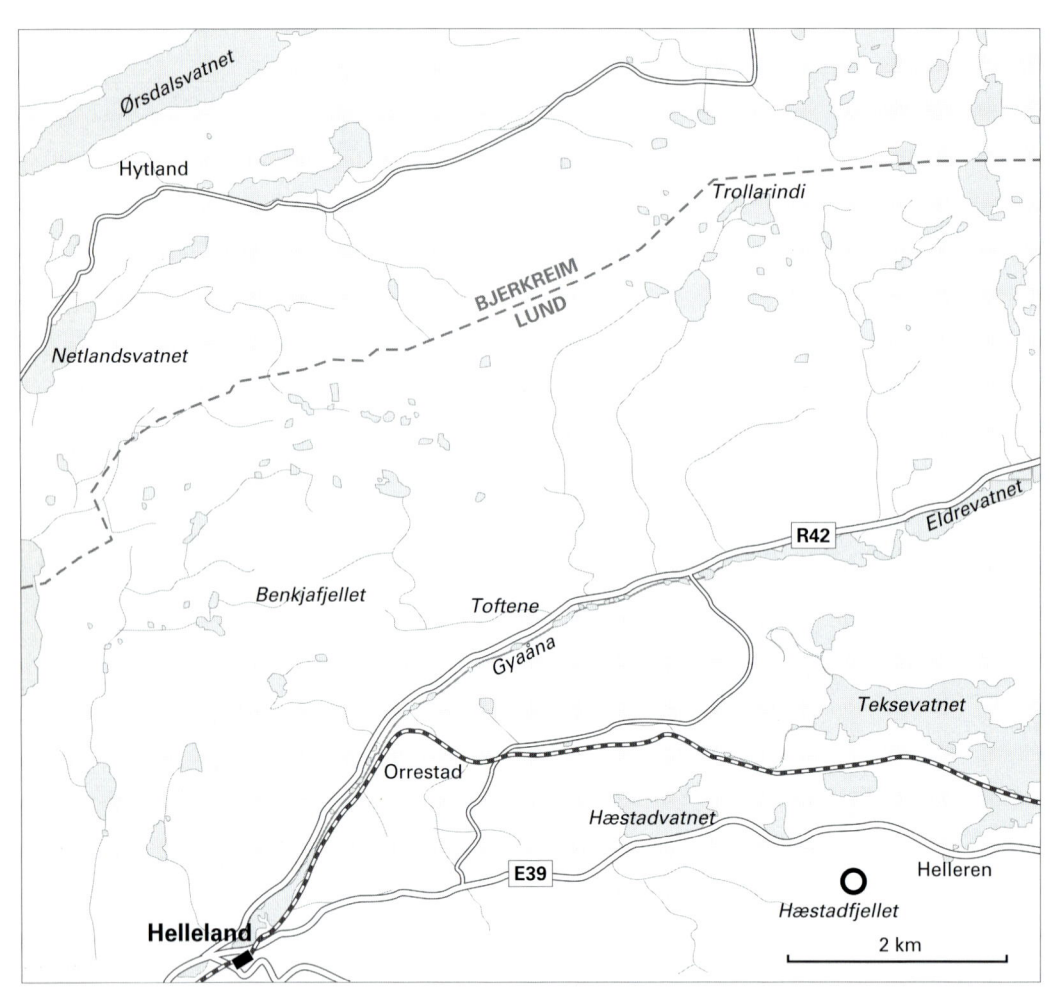

Operation Freshman — The hunt for Hitlers heavy water

The circle marks the place (Benkja Mountan) in Hovland, in the then County of Helleland, where the glider crashed.

Chapter 6

The Tragedy by the Burma Road

The guard house in the military camp at Slettebrø, which the German's used as an arrest locale, was encircled by soldiers. These men were heavily armed, and it's quite possible that the British soldiers were locked up there. There were several German civilians at the installation, and, at the district command headquarters, the interpreter, **Tellef Tellefsen**, on some later occasion, was able to overhear that an **Inspector Pedersen** from Stavanger, together with a colleague, had interrogated the British. It's possible that this **Pedersen** is identical to the German policeman by the name of Petersen, who was stationed at *Sipo's* headquarters in Stavanger during this period. The interpreter also chanced to hear other comments about someone now having a dirty job ahead of them.

The *280th Infantry Division's* war diary confirms that two men from the security police arrived at the installation at 3:30 PM and interrogated the

The main entrance to the German military camp at Slettebø. The Germans had already begun building the installation in the fall of 1940. The first soldiers stationed here came from the 3rd Battalion. Photo loaned out by Dalane Folkemuseum (the Dalane Public Museum).

Operation Freshman ◆ ᵕ ᐟ The hunt for Hitlers heavy water

The British prisoners were transported to the camp's largest barrack, the military hospital (upper building), where they were interrogated by two people from the security police in Stavanger. Photo: Ingrid Worning Berglyd. glider crashed.

British before they were shot. According to a British document, the district leader for the Nazis in Egersund, **Helge Slettebø**, acted as interpreter during the interrogation, **Helge Slettebø's** son, **Jens Martin**, maintains in two interviews, held on May 30 and June 28, 2005, that the information contained in the British report was, in his opinion, erroneous. His father could never have acted as an interpreter because he didn't understand English. While being tried as traitor to his country, **Jens Martin Slettebø**, who had been a frontline soldier in the German Army, was himself accused of being an interpreter in connection with the execution of the British soldiers, as evidenced in a document wherein a certain **Gunvald Tomstad** said he had heard this was the case. **Jens Martin Slettebø** denied this allegation.[33] All interrogation had been carried out at the military hospital, which was the largest barrack at the installation.

After short and futile interrogations, the division ordered that the "Fuhrer Order" be carried out. This order was formulated in the following words in the above-mentioned war diary:

---

33. Interrogation report, document in connection to the police investigation of the Norwegian Nazi interpreter in Eigersund, dated May 24, 1945. *Kriegstagesbuch der 280, Infanteridivision, Nov. 20, 1942. Public Record Office (PRO)*. Richmond, *Surrey, England, Group Letter DEFE 2, Piece Number 21, p.58*, dated May 19, 1943, report from G.T. Rapport to the police board in Vest-Agder, Flekkefjord, on Apr. 5, 1946.
Witness testimony from Kurt Herbert Scheulen on Oct. 23, 1945, Heinz Schneider on Oct. 23, 1945 and Werner Fritz Seeling on Aug. 20 1945. Scheulen and Schneider were both employed by the security police *(Sipo)* in Stavanger. All three confirmed that Petersen worked at the *Gestapo's* headquarters in Stavanger.

Die angeforderten Beamten des Sicherheitsdienstes sind erst um 15.30 Uhr zur Stelle. Nach kurzem Verhör durch die beiden Beamten des Sicherheits¬dienstes, wobei keinerlei Aussagen herauskommen sind, wird auf Befehl der Division entsprechend den gegebenen Befehlen verfahren.

Once this order was issued, hectic activity broke out in the military camp. In the late afternoon, the prisoners were led out from the hospital.

Outside, stood **Captain Schottberger**. He was in charge of *Company 12*. The garrison's commandant, **Major Werner von Krehan**, was away. As the garrison's next highest ranked officer, **Schrottberger** acted in his place.[34]

Schrottberger gave the order detailing how the prisoners of war were to be placed along the rim of the ditch by the side of *Burmavägen* (the Burma Road). This road had been built by the Germans, and extended from the garrison at Slettebø north towards the Teng's area and Highway 44. Along

After they were interrogated, the British soldiers were placed singly along the Burma Road. The picture shows a section of this road. The executions took place approximately 60 meters from the road to the right side of the picture. Photo loaned out by the Dalane Folkemuseum.

---

34. *War trials of von Falkenhorst*, Vol. 6, p.50-52.
Kurt Hagedorn, Erfurt, East Germany, interview on Dec. 17, 1985 and Jan. 1, 1986.
Observations made wandering through Slettebø on Dec 18, 1985.
Fritz Bornschein, Emden, West Germany, interview on June 22, 1987. Observations made wandering through Slettebø on Sep. 3, 1987. Friedrich Klippel, Mainz, West Germany, interview.

Operation Freshman ◆ ▼ ▲ The hunt for Hitlers heavy water

The person in the picture is pointing to the site of the executions near the Slettebø installation. The authenticity of this being the execution site was confirmed by the Germans Kurt Hagedorn in 1985, Fritz Bornschein in 1987, and Hans Neeb in 1992.

the first section of the road, the Germans had also built small, concrete-reinforced granite sheds for the storage of ammunition.

The set-out line of prisoners ended several hundred meters outside the camp, approximately 60 meters east of the road and next to one of the gray concrete sheds. The distance between each of the 14 engineer soldiers was about 50 meters. Every single Englishman was guarded by two German soldiers. All the Norwegians who worked on the Burma Road had been ordered to disappear.

Earlier in the day, while the Germans were eating lunch in the canteen, one of the men from the security police had shown up. In brusque language, he announced that needed volunteers for an unpleasant, but extremely vital mission. The German soldiers realized that he needed people who were prepared to execute the British.

But several of the Germans were nonetheless surprised. They had witnessed the British having been dressed in uniforms. Shouldn't they, then, be treated s prisoners of war? For although they had, in fact, heard their superiors describe them as saboteurs who had come there in an attempt to poison the garrison's drinking water, were they actually going to be executed? In any event, some 20 Germans reported as volunteers. Of these men, 12 were chosen from *Company 12* and one from general staff. A German NCO, **Wagner**, would be in charge of the execution platoon.

One man at a time, the Englishmen were led to the place of execution, a little grassy slant below a grass covered hill. The order "Ready – Aim – Fire!", "*Hoch – Legt an – Feuer Frei*!" was voiced, and one after one the prisoners fell to the ground. After every execution, **Wagner** approached the victims and gave them a *Gnadenschuss* (mercy shot) in the head. The dead bodies were then thrown in a large hole that had been dug in close-by bog.[35] According to the British documents cited in footnote 33, an engineer soldier suffering a broken foot was made to sit on a chair when he was executed. After each execution, the execution platoon hid behind one of the ammunition sheds, only to reappear again when a new victim was brought up.

On the evening of November 20, 1942, the Germans showed up at the Polish prisoner of war camp in Egersund. They collected ten Polish prisoners of war and transported them to the military camp in Slettebø. **Roman Zetelski** was among these transported prisoners. They were taken to a location outside the military camp at Slettebrø and were confronted with the sight of 14 dead British soldiers. All of them were clothed in British uniforms. The dead bodies were not yet cold, and blood still ran from them. The Poles were ordered to place the corpses on two trucks. After which, the Poles were driven to a garage where they collected three more corpses which lay in sacks. All the corpses were then driven to Jæren and buried in the sand at Ogna. **Zetelski** stood at the bottom of the grave and took in the dead bodies. **Captain Corsepius** had command of the Germans who oversaw the burial.[36]

In the late evening, around ten o'clock, **Kristoffer Varden**, a farmer and chauffer from Jæren, came cycling from the railway station in Brusand which lay to the north. Just at the entrance to what is now a camping area in Ogna, he was stopped by an edgy German sentry who ordered him to turn around. At first, **Varden** declined, pointing out that he was only 200 meters from his house – but the German was not in a mood to listen. In the end, **Varden** was forced turn his bike around and cycle back north.

But after cycling only little while, he snuck unobserved over the railroad overpass, just as the moon disappeared behind a cloud. He hid his bike in a little wooded area right by the train rails, climbed up a small hill and found a likely vantage point to lay down.

---

35. Kurt Hagedorn (1920-1986) East Germany, interview on Dec. 12, 1985, Dec. 18, 1985 and Jan. 30, 1986. Observations made wandering through Slettebø on Dec. 18, 1985. Fritz Bornschein, Emden, West Germany, interview on June 22, 1987. Observations made wandering through Slettebø on Sep. 3, 1987.
Friedrich Klippel, Mainz, West Germany, interview on June 22, 1987. Hans Neeb, Hanau, West Germany, interview on June 10, 1992. Observations made wandering through Slettebø on June 10, 1992.
36. *War trials of von Falkenhorst*, Vol. 6, p. 53-54

Operation Freshman ▲ ▼ ▲ The hunt for Hitlers heavy water

Kristoffer Varden saw what happened down on the sand below from the top of a slope. Photo: Josten Berglyd

Back then, the terrain was rather different ~~than~~ *from what* it is today. The foot-bridge over the railway tracks near the hill was somewhat further away, and the hill itself was higher relative to the surrounding area. The greater part of the round sand-duned area outside the current camping place was just flat sandy ground. In short, **Varden** had a good view over the road and flat sandy ground. Moreover, there was moonlight on that November night.

Two German trucks were parked by the hill. Two large tarpaulins were dropped from the bed of the trucks, making a heavy thud when they hit the ground. **Varden** didn't see what lay hidden in the tarps, but from the sound and judging by the situation in general, he guessed that they contained corpses.

The tarpaulins were dragged down to the sand embankment. He saw that a large grave had already been dug there. With apparent jubilation and scornful laughter, the Germans emptied the contents of the tarpaulins into the grave. **Varden** realized that the traces of something not meant for public knowledge was now buried in the sand.

A short while later, he therefore sought out **Jørgen Tengesdal** from Egersund, who was forced to work for the Germans at Ogna during the war, and said: *I know you have a camera, and I want you to take a particularly special picture for me, now.* Then he described how the corpses had been buried in the sand. The two men started out towards the grave site, and

Tengesdal photographed the area. Both **Tengesdal** and **Varden** had brought along a crowbar, and they shoved them down in the sand to see how deep the dead bodies lay. They both concluded that the British soldiers' grave was relatively shallow.[37]

In the war diary of the *280th Infantry Division* it reads that at 1700 hundred hours, on 11/20/42, the command of the Slettebø garrison in Egersund determined that the British should be executed: *Um 17.00 Uhr erstattet Unterabschnitts-Kommandeur Egersund Vollzugsmeldung*. Therafter, in a short phone call, the division officially notified the Supreme Command in Berlin of the events that had taken place. *(Dem Höh. Kdo. LXX wird daraufhin fern¬mündlich kurz berichtet.)*[38]

On November 21, German radio broadcast that during the night spanning the 19th and 20th of November, two British bombers had flown over southern Norway, each bomber towing a glider. One of the bombers and both gliders were forced to land. The saboteurs on board the planes were engaged in battle and annihilated to the very last man. This report was

The place where the British soldiers were buried in the sand near Jæren was photographed shortly after the war by Jørgen Tenges, after Kristoffer Varden revealed where the grave lay. Photo loaned out by the Dalane Folkemuseum.

---

37. Kristoffer Varen, Sievåg, interview on Aug 11, 1986. Observations made wandering through Ogna that same day.
Jörgen Tengesdahl, Egersund, interview on July 7, 1987.
38. Egersund's resident, Hans Andreassen's witness testimony according to the *Dalane Tidende*, in an article published on June 7, 1946 about the investigation of the German commander in the Stavanger area, Karl Maria von Beeren (Behren).
Interview with Per Rasmussen, Egersund, on July 10, 1999.

In Geirulf Albrethsen's Krigsdagboker (War Diaries) 1935-1947, pp. 1496 b, 1497 b, 1506 and 2928 are observations about the plane crash that were made at the time. The destny of the British soldiers is also noted. These diaries are stored at University Library, Oslo, and on microfilm at the Dalane Folkemusem in Egersund.

repeated without comment on November 22 in the English newspapers. And the following day, it was published in the Norwegian press.

On the 21st of November 1942, Egersund resident, businessman and draft-enlisted **Captain G. Albrethsen** noted in his diary:

Rumor has it that the Englishmen who were rescued from the crashed plane have been shot to death by the Germans.

Three days later he wrote:

*It's now reported that the Germans have shot **all** the prisoners. Nonetheless, this can't be represented as anything but outright murder*

In retrospect, **Albrethsen** considers that he hadn't been …

…wrong in his diary concerning the crashed plane.[39]

---

39. In Geirulf Albrethsen's *War diaries 1935-1947*, p.1496 b, 1497 b, 1506 and 2928 are observations of the plane crash. The fate of the British soldiers is also mentioned. These diaries are in the University Library, Oslo, and on microfilm in the Dalane Folkemuseum, Egersund.

The 14 men from the glider who were executed by the Germans were;
Lieutenant (OC) Alex Charles Allen, 24 years old
Sergeant (second in command) George Knowles, 28
Private Ernst William Bailey, 31
Private John Thomas Vernon Belfield, 26
Private Howell Bevan, 22
Lance Corporal Frederick William Bray, 29
Lance Corporal Alexander Campbell, 24
Private Thomas William Faulkner, 22
Private Charles Henry Grundy, 22
Private Herbert J. Legate, age unknown
Private Leslie Smallman, age unknown
Private James May Stephen, age unknown
Corporal John George Llewellyn Thomas, 23
Private Gerald Stanley Williams, 18

The three who died as a direct result of the plane having crashed were:
Pilot Officer (chief pilot) Norman Arthur Davies, 28 years old
Pilot Officer(co-pilot) Herbert John Fraser, 28
Private Ernst Pendlebury, 25

The two pilots in the gliders came from the Australian Air Borne Glider Force. The rest of the men were British soldiers belonging to the *Royal Engineers*.

In December 1942, the *3rd Battalion* at the camp in Slettebø was re-stationed in Jæren. The two companies in this battalion that had been drawn into the destiny that befell the engineer soldiers from the crashed glider, that is, *Company 11* and *Company 12*, were ordered to Hognestad and Bryne, In the fall of 1944, the batallion was sent to the Oslo-district, and in February 1944, units of the batallion were detached to Narva in the Soviet Union. Thereafter, the batallion fought in Ukrania, Poland and in the eastern part of Germany, until the *3rd Battalion* and the Regiment it belonged to were disbanded at Breslau in February 1945. Not many of the soldiers from the *3rd Batallion* survived the war.[40]

---

40. *Gescheite des Infanteriregiments* 355, 1936-1945. *Eine Dokumentation, mit Auszügen aus den authetischen Verlustlisten*. Dr, Fritz Amberger, Frankfurt/M, 1973, Eigenverlag. Zum Verkauf an Buchhandlungen nicht zugelassen, p. 49-50.

Operation Freshman — The hunt for Hitlers heavy water

Map covering the Slettebø area near Egersund, the circle to the left on the lower half of the map shows the building the Germans used during the war as a hospital. After the British prisoners had been incarcerated there for a time, they were transported north along the Burma Road and shot to death at the place marked by the circle on the upper half of the map.

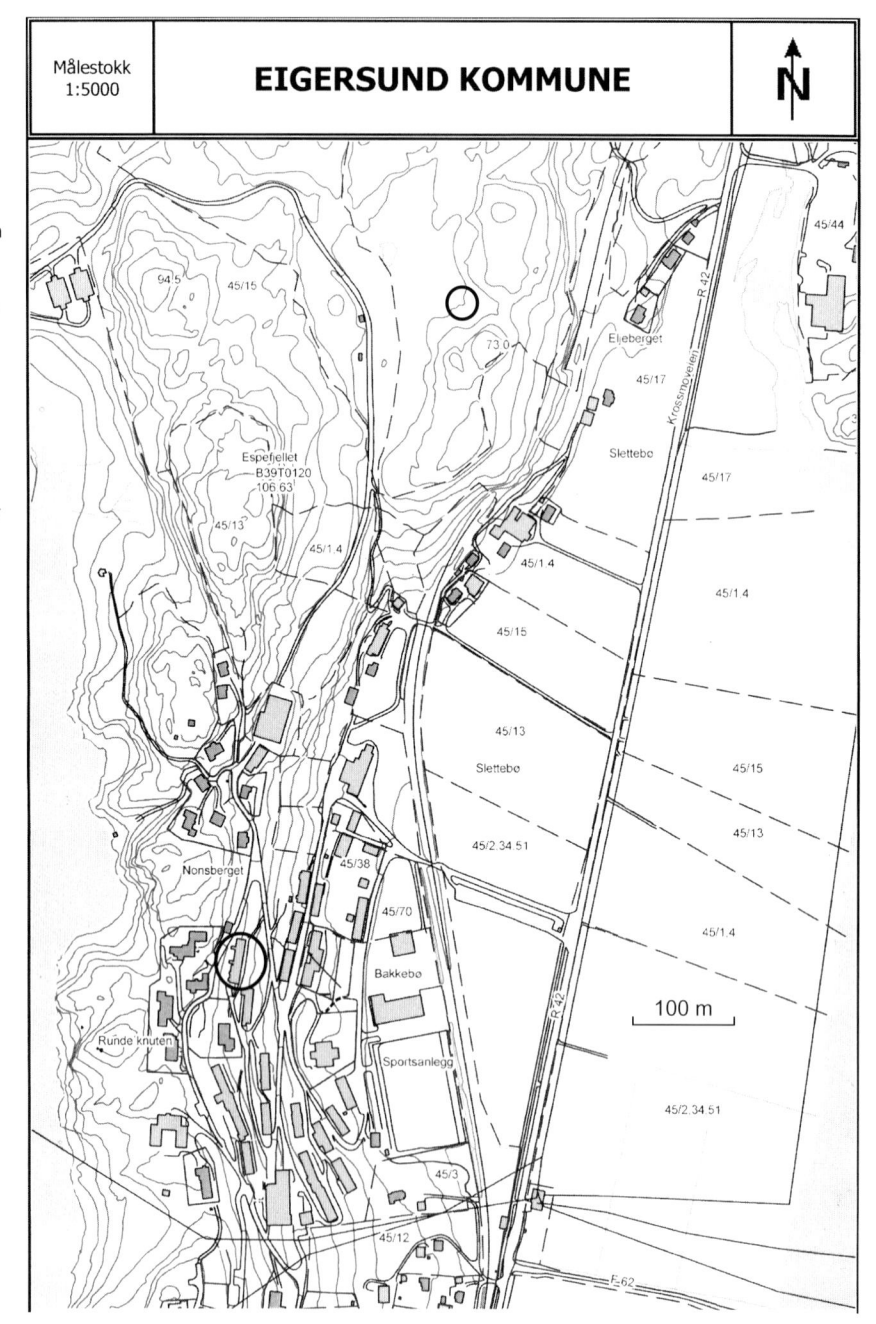

EIGERSUND KOMMUNE

Målestokk 1:5000

N

Chapter 7

The Tow-Plane's Fate

After the glider had crashed, the tow-plane continued to fly over the valley at low altitude and right into the mountains ranged on the other side. It crashed at Jønsokknuden in Hæstadfjellet (the Hæstad mountain area, editors note).

In Hæstad, no one noted what had happened, In Øgried, however, the loud rumble of a plane flying at low altitude in a southeasterly direction was heard. Shortly after, a very bright light was seen. Construction workers on the railway's night-shift also heard the rumble of the plane.

That same night, several people from Øgreid, equipped with lanterns, attempted to reach the site where the plane had crashed to see what had happened, but they didn't succeed. The first to reach the site of the accident were people from the farms of Hæstad and Øgreid, in the early morning

Even though the place where the plane crashed has been "vacuum cleaned" by souvenir-hunters over the years, remnants of the Halifax plane are still found in the Hæstad Mountain area.

Operation Freshman – – – The hunt for Hitlers heavy water

of November 21. They hurried down again and by 7 o'clock reported what had happened to the goverment administrator **Theodor Hovland**. The government administrator and some other men started out towards the accident site, Martin Ramsland drove them as close to the location as possible. And then a local man with good knowledge of the area led them up to the accident area by the best route.

Once there, there wasn't anything they could do, other than confirm that the information they had been given was correct. The government administrator got in contact with the *District Commander* in Egersund. The time was then 8:15 AM, and another group of Germans was sent off. This group was recorded in the *280th Infantry Division's* war diary as a *Hunt* (seek out and destroy) *Commando* Unit.

Martin Sandstøl of Hæstad farm got word of what had happened that very morning. Before noon, he treked up Jønsokknuden together with his wife and a young girl, aged 10-12, who lived with them. They were greeted

The circle on the map marks the place, Jønsokknuden, in the Hæstad Mountain area in the then County of Helleland where the tow-plane crashed.

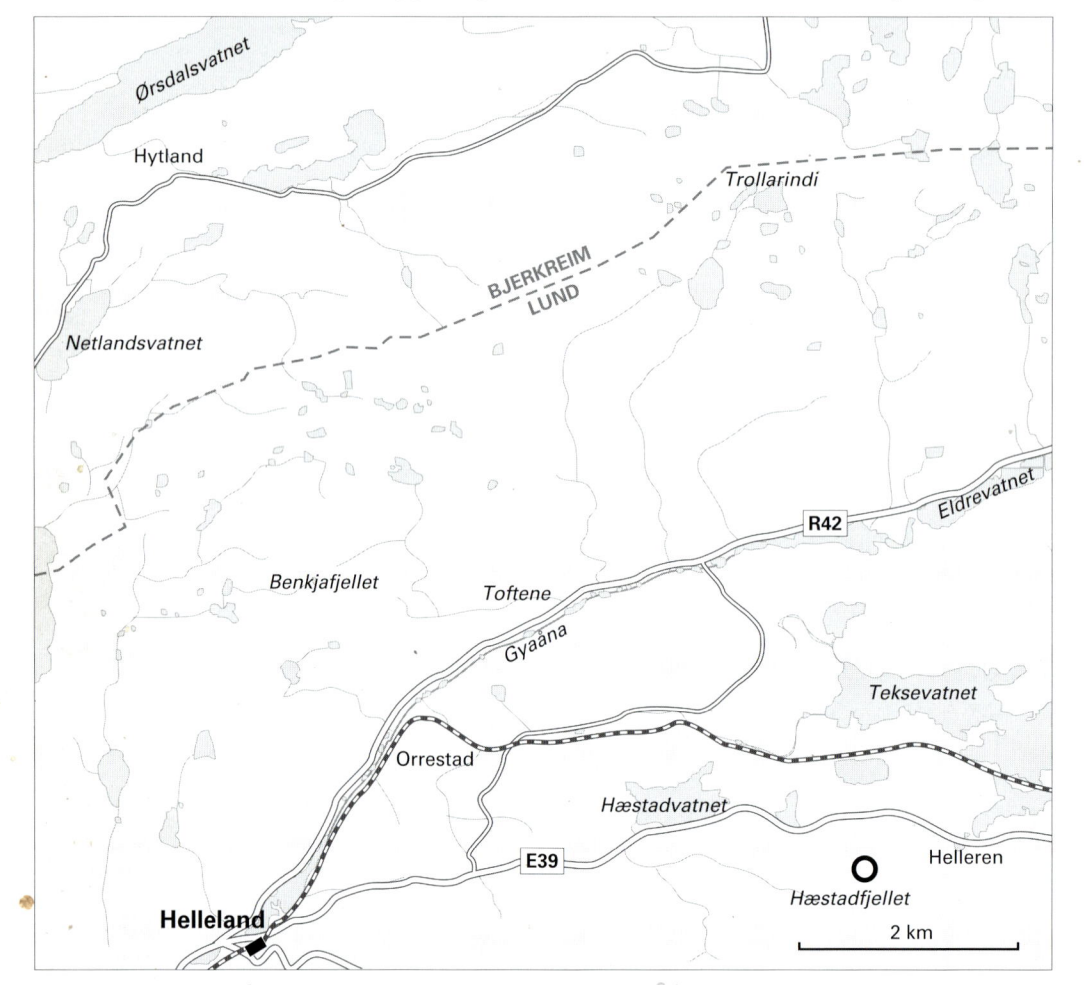

THIS PICTURE IS A REPEAT OF THE ONE ON P. #8

by a terrible sight: A deep depression in the ground made it very clear where the plane had initially crashed. After which, the main body of the plane had traveled over the top of Jønsokknuden, and continued several hundred meters further onto a plateau made up of large stones, ending where the mountain again became steeper. During this horrendous trip, with the plane's fuelsilage scraping stone, mountain and earth, the tow-plane had been ripped apart. But the four fueltanks were not especially damaged, and there was plentyof fuel left in them.

A large portion of the tow-plane's equipment was taken by the local residents before the German's arrived at the site. Here, Martin Selmer Sandstøl stands wearing a jacket that belonged to one of the pilots. After Sandstøl's death, the jacket was donated to the Dalane Folkemuseum. Photo: Jostein Berglyd.

Near the spot where the plane had first contacted ground lay the corpse of a colored man. **Sandstøl** assumed it was the rear gunner, who would have been seated farthest back in the plane. He had few external injuries. **Sandstøl** was convinced that six men had died in the crash. Bodyparts, like the plane parts – and weapons, ammunition, leaflets, and sundry equipment – were spread over the whole area. **Sandstøl** observed that the tow-cable was torn apart: Something he presumed was caused by icing. He returned to the site of the accident several times, and on one these occasions he found yet another dead Englishman between some stones. He informed the Germans that there was yet another corpse up on mountain. He didn't mention the three photographs he had found in the victim's jacket.

The first objects the Germans seized and took down from the mountain were the fuel tanks. In their war diary, the Germans made special note that a colored man was among the deceased. They further reported that the plane was towing a glider, which the torn cable attested to.

The Germans tried to bury the corpses up on the mountain by scrapping away the moss and heather from a suitable spot. However, they very quickly ecountered primal rock and were forced to give up on this method of burying the British. Subsequently, they tried to bury them in a grave dug in a bog right below the mountain's plateau. The grave worked out to be quite shallow, and the farmers asked the Germans if they would give permission for a proper grave to be dug – a request the Germans at first rejected. The farmers then turned, through the auspices of the government administrator, to the district medical physician in Egersund, **Műnster Mohn.** The doctor then explained to the Germans that the corpses must be burned, otherwise they could begin the spread of disease. This motivation was better understood. At the behest of the goverment adminstrator, the neighboring residents were now asked if they could carry up two armloads of wood, which they stated they were quite ready to do.

But then a contraorder arose. It was reported that a German priest had expressed the view that the corpses should be laid in coffins placed in a becoming and orderly grave in dry soil. So, at a high elevation, the neigbors dug a deep grave in a fine and dry location. The Germans came and took care of the rest.[41]

Martin Selmer Sandstøl was one of the first to arrive at the site of the accident in the Hæstad Mountan area. Body-parts where strewn everywhere. He is pointing to one of those places with his cane.

The deceased were:

Captain, chief-pilot, Arthur Roland Parkinson, 26 years of age
Lieutenant, co-pilot, Garard Walter Sewell de Gency, 20
Captain, observer, Arthur Edwin Thomas, 32
Pilot Officer, observer, Arnold Thomas Haward, 28
Sergeant, radio-operator and gunner, Albert Buckton, 23
Sergeant, gunner, George Mercier Edwards, 24
Sergeant, aircraft mechanic, James Falconer, 20

The chief pilot belonged to the *Royal Canadian Air Force (RCAF)*; the rest came from the *Royal Air Force (RAF)*.

41. Martin Selmer Sandstøl, Helleland, interview on July 7, 1986. Observations made while wandering on Hæstadfjellet that same day.
I was also present when the American author, Dan Kurzman, interviewed Sandstøl at his home in the fall of 1943. See the last chapter. Also see the magazine, *Hellelands buen*, November 1992 and *Kriegstagesbuch der 280, Infanteridivision, Nov. 20, 1942.*

Chapter 8

The Glider Crash in Fylgjesdalen

The glider that was towed by the first *Halifax* fell victim to a different destiny than the plane that towed it, which had barely succeeded in returning to Scotland by the skin of its neck. The glider had been set loose over the mountainous area of southern Norway, more precisely, over Fylgjesdalen (Fylgjes Valley) in Forsand County, and crashed approximately 150 meters north of Fylgjesdal's-farm. This farm lies towards the north end of Fylgjesdal's Lake and, at that time, two families were living there. Long past midnight, **Martine Fylgjesdal** was suddenly awakened by a loud boom. She thought it was a mighty thunder clap and so she went back to sleep. The following day, **Martine** and her cousin **Torvald Fylgjesdal** became the first people to make contact with the survivors from the crash.

On the morning of Friday, November 20, **Martine Fylgjesdal** looked out the window. It was nine o'clock, and outside the window stood three complete strangers. Three men who had sought protection under the rowanberry tree only a few meters from the house. She hurried to her cousin and told him what she'd seen. He looked out the window and motioned the men to come in, but they apparently didn't want to. So he went out to them in order to learn what they did want.

Torvald Fylgjesdal didn't understand English, but the word *doctor* – which they repeated over and over again – he understood. With the help of mime and sounds he understood they were trying to say something about an airplane, and that there were several men who needed medical help. He also understood that the soldiers before him weren't German because their uniforms were different – and, of course, it wasn't German they were speaking. Long knives hung from their belts, but otherwise, he didn't see any weapons.

After inviting them for coffee, he led them down a steep cliff by the unoccupied Sagbakken farm, and then continued in a westerly direction along the mountainside over rugged terrain towards Håheller, where there was larger, lived on farm. On the Hållheller farm lived **Jonas Håheller** together with his sisters, **Ola** and **Kristi Sagbakk**. The farm was located about eight kilometers west of Lysebotn and some hundred meters from the shore. At the Håheller farm there was a telephone from which **Torvald Fylgjesdal** rang the government administrator's office in Forsand at one o'clock. He reported that he had come into contact with some foreigners up on the mountain. He didn't understand what they said, and they didn't understand what he said either, but there was no mistaking that they needed help. It wasn't the government administrator, **Thorvald Espedal,** who answered the telephone but rather his daughter, **Hjørdis Espedal,** who was the fully empowered administrator while her father was on vacation. Until 1940, **Thorvald Espedal's** son, **Leif Espedal,** had functioned as his

The circle on the map shows the area in Fylgjesdalen where the glider crashed..

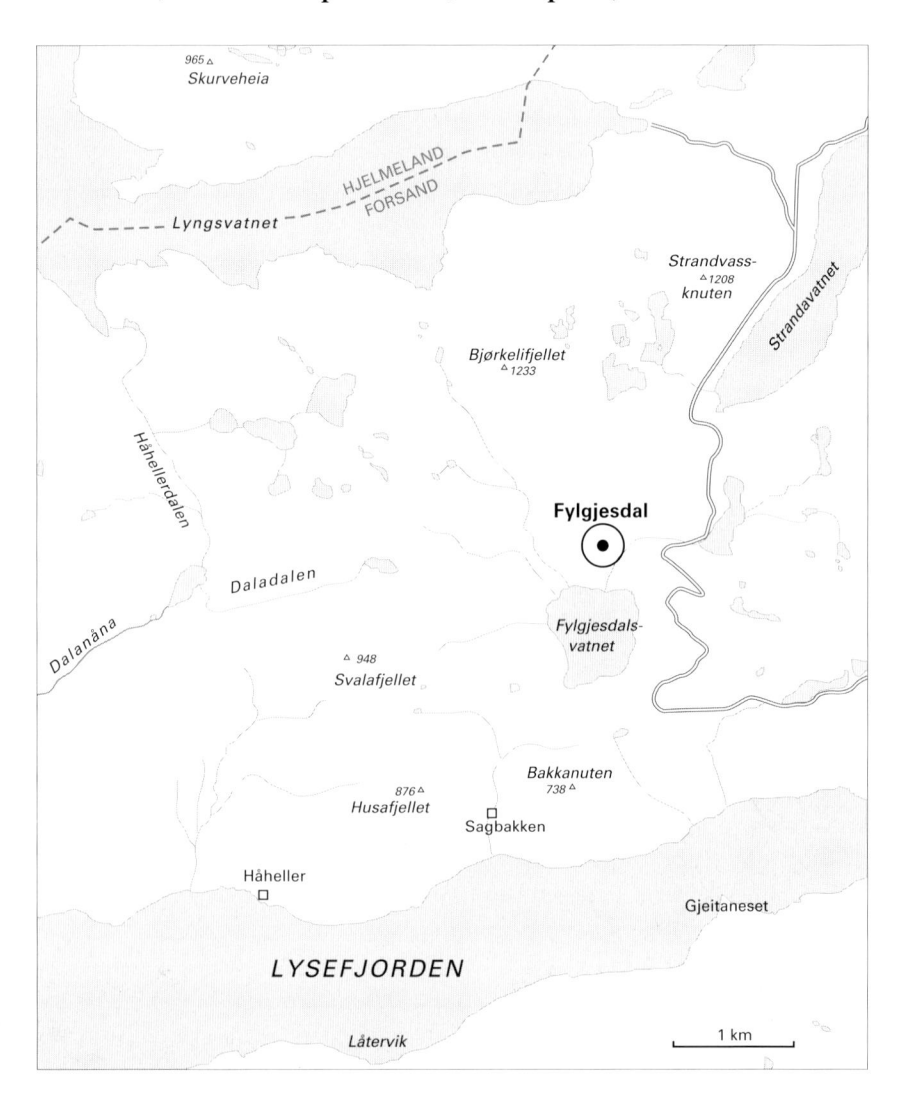

father's assistant, but the son had fallen afoul of the Norwegian Security Police, Stapo, and thereby had lost his job. (Stapo was the Norwegian equivalent of the German Security Police, the *Gestapo*).

The county had given **Leif Espedal** a new job as head of the Rationing Authority (a governmental organ created in June 1939 to oversee all issues related to rationing), which he now worked at full time. As it happened, the government administrator's office and the Rationing Authority had a common telephone line in Forsand. As a result, **Espedal** overheard the conversation between his sister and **Torvald Fylgjesdal. Espedal** closed the office and sought out the district doctor, **Finn Bjønnes,** who was his closest neighbour and man he knew well. When **Espedal** met with **Bjønnes,** the doctor had already been informed by **Hjørdis Espedal** who had also contacted the police in Rogalund to which the governmental district authorities of Høle and Forsand belonged. She had done this with the realization it would be totally impossible to keep secret a rescue effort that included a physician and hospital care, and not least, because the telephone line was most probably tapped.

After a brief discussion, it was decided that **Espedal** would accompany the doctor up to the Håheller so that the doctor could administer first aid to the three foreigners there, and at the same time, they could both get a clearer picture of what had happened. **Espedal** and the doctor took the ferry directly to Håheller, arriving late that afternoon,

At Håheller, they met **Torvald Fylgjesdal,** the three foreigners, and some neighboring farm people. The foreigners turned out to be British. The doctor re-bandaged them – after which, they had little choice but to wait and see what developed.

Fylgjesdal's farm, to the right is the farmhouse. Photo: Tor Ødemotland.

Representatives from the authorities were already en route. Among them was **A, Lahlum,** the police commissioner in Rogaland's police district, which had been informed over the phone by the government administrator's office. The following sequence was described by Police Legal-Officer (law-schooled policeman, in certain instances with the prosecutor's authorization), **Knut Leirvåg,** in a 1982 report. The police commissioner called him and Police Officer **Tollef Ravn Tollefsen** into his office and informed them of the message he had gotten from the government administrative offices in Høle and Forsand. The commissioner had then informed the German Security Police, who asked that the police in Rogaland take custody of the foreigners. The police commissioner then gave **Leirvåg** and **Ravn Tollefsen** orders to carryout this assignment, and the two policemen started out shortly thereafter.

After working out meeting arrangements with the government administrator's office, they drove down to the boat pier in Høle. There, they were met by **Hjørdis Espadal** who had been waiting for them in the harbour with a motorboat. They motored over to Håheller, arriving in the late evening. They were oriented about the situation by **Leif Espedal** and **Finn Bjønnes,** a situation that proved to be completely different, and significantly more serious, than simply taking three foreigners to Stavanger: The British had been on board a glider that had crashed up on a mountain. Seventeen men had been aboard that plane. Some had died in connection with the crash, others were badly injured and needed immediate help. Clearly, a full-scale rescue operation was needed if everything was going to be effectively sorted out and dealt with. After having discussed the situation and its immediate demands, **Finn Bjønnes, Hjørdis Espedal, Leif Espedal,** and **Ravn Tollefsen** started up the steep, ice-covered hillside towards Fyljesdalen, while **Leirvåg,** who was dressed in a suit and street shoes, stayed with the Englishmen. From Håheller farm, he was to co-ordinate the rescue operation, while simultaneously trying to get hold of people who could lend a hand. In addition, it was essential that he contact the police in Rogaland to request additional help. These tasks he carried out during the evening.

During the course of the night, several help-crews showed up in Håheller, from both Flørli and Lysebotn. After being familiarized with the situation, they started off to the site of the accident. When a measure of calm at last settled over Håheller farm, **Leirvåg** had time to talk with the three foreigners. They were dressed in normal brown uniforms. One of them had two military stripes on the sleeve of each arm. If there were any other indications of rank, he didn't see them. One of the soldiers limped due to a foot injury. Otherwise, they were unhurt.

When the British realized that the Norwegians didn't pose a threat to them, they relaxed and began talking about all sorts of things – but especially about the accident and their concern for their comrades who lay injured up on the mountain. It was fairly evident these men were part of a sabotage force, but the Norwegians didn't interrogate them about it. In any event, **Leirvåg** got the impression that the plane had crashed sometime around midnight, either on Thursday night, or in the early minutes of Friday, November 20. The soldiers asked if it was a long way to Sweden, but when they understood they had crashed in an area where they could neither cross the Swedish border nor the sea back to Great Britain, they foresaw they would be taken prisoner by the Germans. They were anxious to know what the Germans would do with them, and the Norwegians answered that, since they were English soldiers in full uniform, nothing could happen to them, other than being incarcerated as prisoners of war until it was over. They appeared to become more at ease after that summation. The conversation gradually ended, and everyone lay down to sleep.

In the middle of the night, the telephone rang. The caller turned out be a representative of the German Security Police. He was enraged and screamed out of control. He dressed-down the Norwegians for not having informed the security police about the crashed glider. He further stated that the security police would be arriving in Håheller on Saturday, and that he held **Leirvåg** personally responsible, with his life at stake, for seeing to it that the foreigners did not escape. The British had awakened during this conversation, and **Leirvåg** told them the gist of what the German had said. That night's sleep was destroyed.[42]

---

42. Per Johnsen, Randaberg: *The Fylgjesdal Glider*, 1982, unpublished work.
Interview with Leif Espedal, Sola, on Nov. 19, 2002.
Reports from Knut Leirvåg, Stavanger, on Mar. 23, 1982 and Sep. 16, 1982, lent out by Per Johnsen, Randaberg.
Kriegstagesbuch der 280, Infanteridivision, Nov. 21, 1942, p. 10-12.
Witness testimony, Martine Fylgjesdal on Aug. #, 1945.
Report, Tollef Ravn Tollefsen on Nov. 23, 1942
Witness testimony, Finn Bjønnes on Aug. 7, 1945 and Oct. 27, 1943

Operation Freshman ⬆ ⬇ ⬆ The hunt for Hitlers heavy water

Leif Espadal, son of the then government administrator in Høle and Forsnad, Together with Dr. Finn Bjønnes, he arrived quickly at the crash site. Photo: Jostein Berglyd.

Chapter 9

The Tragedy in Fylgjesdalen

For the four Norwegians, who had begun their journey up towards Fylgjesdal's farm much earlier in the day, the prospect of getting a comfortable night's sleep that night was likewise little. They arrived at the farm in the early night, to find that three "new" British soldiers had shown up. Two of them were severely injured, while the third had come through the crash relatively unscathed. They had made the trip down from the accident site with the aid of stimulants and pain tablets. **Hjørdis Espedal** and **Ravn Tollefsen** immediately took them into the house and tried to help them. The man who was in the best shape explained how to get up to the site of the accident, which lay a couple of hundred meters east of the farm, to **Finn Bjønnes** and **Leif Espedal.**

By the time they reached the plane wreckage and the crash victims, it was eleven o'clock at night – but there was moonlight. A large pine tree loomed over the crash site, and over a stony bog area with a radius of about 200 meters where plane debris, weapons, explosive material, backpacks,

The glider crashed near a large pine tree in a wooded grove in the middle of this picture. Fylgjesdalen and Fylgjesdalen Lake are in the foreground.

Operation Freshman ⬥ ⬥ ⬥ The hunt for Hitlers heavy water

and clothes could be found. The planes forward section and wings were totally demolished. But the aft section was largely intact. **Bjønnes** and **Espedal** were forced to go very carefully as they walked around the crash sight.

They could hear groans and shrieks coming from inside the plane. In addition, several soldiers lay outside of what remained of the fuselage. The doctor went inside the glider and, with a lantern in hand, he tried to orient himself and give three badly injured men as much medical and humanitarian assistance as he could under the circumstances. Inside the wreckage he found a large store of medical necessities he was able to make use of. Among other items, he came across small injection-ready vials, each of which contained a dose of 0.25 GR (grain = 0.0648 gram) morphine. The two Norwegians succeeded in helping the injured into sleeping bags and gave them something warm to drink. Besides the sleeping bags, **Espedal** found bags of tea, sugar, powdered milk and an alcohol stove. Using snow that he'd scraped together and melted, he also accumulated sufficient water. Much of the help given was owed to the morphine which had relieved the worst of the pain, allowing the men to calm down and even fall asleep.

The two Norwegian men both realized that it would be impossible for them to move the three injured men down the relatively short stretch to Fylgjesdal's farm in a satisfactory way. The slope was quite simply too

Objects from the plane wreckage: Even in June 2000 such objects cfrom the crash could be found. Photo: Tor Ødemotland.

steep. They agreed that this task was something the rescue crew could better sort out later. The district doctor walked down to Fylgjesdal's farm in order to catch a little sleep, while **Espedal** remained and stood guard the rest of the night by the glider.

The weather was continuously changing, something that helped create a very special, mystical feel to the night. The wind blew in from the west and dark clouds raced over the sky. But every now and then, the moon would break through, lighting up the area. Two centimeters of snow had fallen and a light snow-cover hid some of the terrible tragedy. But in the moonlight, **Espedal,** to his considerable horror, discovered that he hadn't been setting his teacup on a rounded, flat stone – as he had idly thought – but on the back of a corpse. Some meters from the plane he caught sight of a dead soldier who sat with his back against a stone. The soldier had broken the lower part of his leg. It appeared he had tried to set his foot in a splint, for right beside him lay some sticks and a scarf.

When the first stretcher-bearers arrived at Fylgjesdalen, they carried the three injured soldiers down to the farm. More than anyone else, it was **Hjørdis Espedal** who took care of the soldiers. In a radio program broadcast on *NRK* in 1983, she tells of the time the British took out their maps and showed them to her. It was apparent that Rjukan was the intended target area. They had thought they were much closer to the border with Sweden, but once she showed them where they actually were on the maps, they realized they weren't going to reach Sweden. They also understood that for the moment they were with friends, a fact they set large store by. The soldiers had suffered frostbite injuries, especially to their legs. **Hjørdis Espedal** massaged their frozen limbs, gave them hot tea and tried to take care of them as best she knew. They got along well together, but the situation was hopeless – and she didn't have the strength to pursue what was to become of them more deeply.

The Germans were going to arrive soon. **Leif Espedal** and **Finn Bjønnes** had no desire to have anything to do with them, and therefore left for Håheller farm early Saturday morning. Once down in Håheller, **Espedal** rang up an acquaintance in Flørli who came by boat and took them home.

Ravn Tollefsen had walked up to the accident site early that Saturday morning. He wanted to remove all compromising objects before the Germans arrived, as well as seeing to it that all maps and documents were burned. Soon he was joined by several others, and then more and more Norwegians showed up looking to help. One of them began to fiddle with an explosive charge that detonated. The ensuing fire spread to what remained of the glider and the area around it. The wreck burned for 24 hours, but the Norwegians were able to extract the dead from the flames.

The first troublesome carriage of the injured began sometime during Saturday morning, the shortest, but most difficult, route was from Fylgjesdal's Lake and along the ravine down to Sagbakken farm, and from there another 600-700 meters over extremely rugged and steep terrain to Lysefjorden (the Lyse-fjord) at Bakkeånå, which was the name the locals gave to the location where Fylgjesdal's Lake runs out into Lysefjorden. It was here the first two British soldiers were carried on stretchers.[43]

The eight soldiers who died when the glider crashed were:
Lieutenant, unit commander, David Alexander Methven, 20 years of age
   Sergeant, second in command, Frederick Healey, 29
   Private John Glen Vernon Hunter, 22
   Private William Jacques, 24
   Private Robert Norman, 22
   Private George Simkins, 30
   Lieutenant (chief pilot) Malcolm Frederick Strathdee, age unknown
   Sergeant (co-pilot) Peter Doig, 25

---

43. Per Johnsen, Randaberg: The Fylgjesdal Glider, 1982, unpublished work.
Interview with Leif Espedal, Sola, on Nov. 19, 2002.
Reports from Knut Leirvåg, Stavanger, on Mar. 23, 1982 and Sep. 16, 1982, borrowed by Per Johnsen, Randaberg.
Wandering around the crash site on June 24, 2001 and Aug. 8, 2002. On the last-cited date, the author, along with people from the area, continued to walk in a southerly direction , down along lake Fylgjesdal towards the ravine at Sagbakken, and then turned west at the side of the mountain along the Lyse Fjord towards Håheller.
Witness testimony, Finn Bjønnes on Aug. 7, 1945 and Oct. 27, 1943.

Chapter 10

The Red Cross is drawn into the drama

During the first years of the war, **Police Officer Per Roth** of the Stavanger police was responsible for the civil air-defence's hospital facility. On Friday morning, November 20, 1942, the head of the German army's medical service in the district, **Doctor Fritz Koch,** requested that two men be placed at his disposal, along with a sufficient number of stretchers, to assist in retrieving the dead and injured from a plane crash. Roth said he would see to it, at once. He immediately contacted the hospital orderly, medical student **Johan Fredrik Thue,** who was on duty at the air defence unit's center, and asked him to follow along. After securing supplies from the unit and other medical equipment, they met at Skagenkajen (Skag Pier) at ten o'clock the following morning. Then they went on board a German coastal patrol ship which got underway after about an hour.

Both Norwegians wore Red Cross armbands. The police officer was dressed in his blue uniform, while the other man was dressed in civilian clothes. Before leaving the pier, the ship also took on people from *Sipo* and several armed soldiers. The security police were dressed in their characteristic uniforms with skeleton-skulls on their uniform jackets and brimmed military caps. An additional three men from the German Security Police *(SD)* also boarded the ship: Interrogation Leader **Arnold Hölscher,** and **Criminal Investigators Erwin Stelter** and **Eugen Hartmann.**

Hölscher played the leading role in the fight against the Norwegian resistance movement in southern Rogaland. On his uniform jacket's underarm stood the letters *SD*, indicating that he was a member of the security police. Despite his low rank, he had a strong influence on his superiors and those under his command. **Hölscher** was strong, and he often used this strength to manhandle resistance movement members who had been arrested by the Germans. For these reasons, he became a symbol for the *SD* and all its abominations. But there was a more significant reason than **Hölscher's** brutality and physical strength that made it possible for him to uncover several resistance cells in Rogaland, namely: He had previously worked within the criminal police in Hamburg.

The coastal patrol ship transported its passengers to Håheller on Lysefjorden (the Lyse Fjord). They arrived between 1:00 and 2:00 AM. The ship lay near the pier for a while and waited until a fast-moving German torpedo-boat turned up and put in east of Håheller. A high-ranking officer from the air force, **Major General Karl Koechy,** and a group of armed soldiers wend ashore.

Koechy claimed he followed along to Håheller as an observer. As chief commander of the German Air Force in the Stavanger district, he wanted to avoid being involved in this story concerning the British airborne troops. He was well aware of the Fuhrer Order, and he knew that if the Norwegian authorities had been the first to come into contact with the foreign saboteurs, it then rested with the Norwegians to hand over the prisoners to the German Security Police. Therefore, he neither gave any order nor did he talk to the three British soldiers.

The costal patrol ship that **Roth** and **Thue** were on, put in shortly after the German torpedo-boat. All the Germans aboard the ship went ashore – which the two Norwegians also wanted to do. But **Hölscher** told **Roth** that he was to remain aboard. **Thue,** however, was permitted to go ashore after the German soldiers had debarked *disembarked*.

The Germans ran rapidly up the 200 meters to the farm, encircled it with weapons loaded, and then stormed the house where the three British were being held in the custody of Police Officer **Knut Leirvåg**. He reasoned that his job was now over and he left to go aboard the coastal patrol ship. The three unarmed British were taken to the ship in Håheller. Two of them went aboard themselves, while the third was carried aboard on a stretcher. The two uninjured men were speedily settled under the main deck, watched over by armed guards. It proved to be impossible, however, to fit the stretcher through the ship's hatch. Therefore it was set on the main deck. The injured soldier, who lay in a sleeping bag, told **Roth** that some damage had been done to his hip. **Hölscher** heard them talking to each other, and angrily told them that talking to prisoners was forbidden. **Roth** was going back to Stavanger on the ship, but the Norwegian medical orderly was ordered to journey with Hölscher and the other Germans up to the site of the accident. There were several injured up there, and now the stretchers were needed.

The German coastal patrol ship returned to Stavanger, arriving later that evening. On the way there, the ship put in at Bakkenånå and took custody of the two British soldiers who had been carried there on stretchers earlier that morning. Seeking to make the boat trip somewhat more tolerable for the soldier who lay in a stretcher on the main deck, **Roth** and one of the Germans tried to screen off the cold wind, making use of down comforters. In Stavanger, the English soldiers were taken to Tollboden, while **Roth** proceeded to "Døves Hus" where the civil defence unit was housed in the cellar.

As soon as the coastal patrol ship had departed land with the injured on board, the Germans, including the three *SS*-men, got ready to go up the mountain together with **Thue**. A Norwegian interpreter and a German engineer also joined them. It had snowed and the way was icy, making the steep climb up to Fylgjesdalen a slow affair. This suited **Thue** to a tee, since he was carrying a large backpack containing medical items, along with two stretchers. No one offered to help carry this heavy load.

Gradually, the terrain began to flatten out, and they caught sight of Fylgjesdal's farm in the distance. It had begun to darken, but the sky was almost completely free of clouds. A few of the Germans went ahead with sub-machineguns set to fire, while the rest of the detail trailed a little further back. The Germans feared the British would begin opening fire on them. At half-past six in the evening, they stormed the farm. Doors were kicked open, and with loud shrieks the Germans charged in. The four British soldiers, who lay on mattresses arranged on the floor, were subjected to rough treatment. **Hjørdis Espedal** and **Ravn Tollefsen** saw there was no more they could do, and so they left the house.

The medical orderly who had just arrived, on the other hand, was very sure of his mission. The Germans shouted and screamed, and when **Thue** witnessed **Hölscher** on repeated occasions kicking one of the injured soldiers, he protested making it clear that this was not the way men treated their enemies. **Thue** was present as a representative of a humanitarian organization and his mission was to ensure that the prisoners got the help they needed. Thue's outburst got the Germans to stop, after which, insofar as **Thue** was able to observe, no further direct violence was inflicted by the Germans.

Thue was given an opportunity to examine the British. All the men were between the ages of 20 and 30, and almost all of them were injured. The most serious injuries were a broken shin bone, skull injuries and cracked rids. **Thue** tried to help the soldiers to the best of his ability. He also realized that he was being allowed to bring back a good portion of excellent supplies from the plane: woollen blankets, sleeping bags, chocolate and canned goods, including corn beef. Again, insofar as **Thue** could see, the Germans did not carry out any interrogations with the prisoners.

The Germans, the British and the Norwegians were scheduled to spend that evening and night and into the following day – which was a Sunday – together. **Thue** asked **Höscher** when they would be returning down the mountain with the prisoners. It was quite apparent they needed immediate medical help. The German answered that he had more important things to consider. Hurrying back for the prisoners' sake was not going to happen. First, the Germans must make a closer examination of the glider and the equipment the British had brought with them. They also planned to investigate the area around the crash site. It was very possible that explosive material was spread-out over the terrain in connection with the crash.

    Thue also overheard that a German soldier had fallen and injured a foot. One of the *SS*-men asserted that, now, the Norwegian could demonstrate that he was a worthy representative of the Red Cross and attend the German soldier as carefully as he had attended the British. **Thue** examined the injured German and was able to conclude that the ligament on the outside portion of the ankle was damaged. The Norwegian banded the German with an elastic support bandage, advised him to stay in bed and gave him pain-killing pills. The German was also told not put weight on the injured foot. It appeared the German was delighted with the help he had received.

    Thue asked the German engineer if he might have permission to look at the glider. The engineer asked one of the *SS*-men who answered that it would be fine. The glider had landed on its fuselage which, in itself, was a standard practice, but under the light snow-cover the ground was stony and uneven. The wings had been ripped off, and the central body of the plane was torn in several places. The wreck lay with its nose pointed towards the south. On the slope immediately below the plane, the eight lifeless bodies of the British fatalities had been laid side by side, after they had been extracted from the burning wreck.

    Thue learned that the Germans had sent a request to the government administrator's office asking that a sufficient number of men be sent up the following day in order to carry two men who required stretcher transport down the mountain. One was the Englishman with the broken shin bone – the other was the injured German. The three other British soldiers could make it on their own. Chauffeur **Kristian Berge** from Forsand recounted that on that particular Saturday evening a bazaar was held in the prayer-house. The government administrator had showed up at the bazaar and made a request for twelve men to act as stretcher-bearers.

    At seven o'clock, on the Sunday morning of November 22, a large crew of men showed up at Bakkeånå. They had sailed there on the freight- and-fishing boat, *Karin,* owned by **Ingvald T. Fossan**. The boat put in a bit west of Bakkeånå. From there, they directly proceeded up towards Fylgjesdalen, arriving there at 9:00 AM. **Berge** relates that they had to wait quite a while outside the prayer-house. The reason was that **Thue** needed this time to make the two injured man as comfortable as possible on the stretchers. The German soldier was not in exceptional pain and pain-killing pills were enough to see him through. **Thue** gave the Englishman ten milligrams of morphine in order that he could hold out during the trek down the mountain.

After the first stretcher was carried away, the three Englishmen, guarded by Germans, walked down the mountain. The next stretcher and the *SS*-men followed soon after. **Berge** accompanied the first stretcher-bearers. Four men carried while two acted as reserves. As the bearers became tired, they were replaced two men at a time. Since it was still daylight, the trips went off relatively easy, and the *Karin* was ready to set out when they arrived at the shore. **Berger** recalls it was at this juncture that **Hjørdis Espedal** turned up. She lit a cigarette and set it in between the lips of the most severely injured Englishman. He smiled his thanks, but the German guards pointed up towards the mountain and shouted: *Offizier, Offeizier!* The guards feared that the officers would make it down to the fjord momentarily and discover this indication of humanity.

The four British soldiers were placed in the cargo hold, guarded by German soldiers armed with sub-machineguns. **Thue** let it be known that he wished to be with the prisoners, and the Germans said yes.

The boat put in again at Flori where the local residents had put together a little lunch in a parish house in honor of the British soldiers, but this the Germans were adamantly opposed to. **Thue,** however, got permission to go up there, and he came back with milk, cakes, chocolates, canned fruit and variously filled sandwiches. He passed out the food to the British soldiers and the German guards when the boat set out for Stavanger.

During the boat trip, one of the German soldiers broke away and approached **Thue**. The soldier told him he should take good care of the prisoners and that he could talk freely with them: The British soldiers were also human beings who had simply done their duty. **Thue** was deeply moved by having heard such a statement coming from a German soldier. For the remainder of the trip, **Thue** talked with the prisoners about everything under heaven, but they were still unwilling to discuss what their mission in Norway was all about. All the prisoners expressed their gratitude to **Thue** for the care he had shown them. One of the Englishmen presented him with a fountain pen. **Thue** would come to keep it in memory of them – a present that has been well taken care of.

The boat tied up in Stavanger late that afternoon. The sky had already begun to darken. They debarked long out on Skag Pier, a little bit west of the Stavanger Damp Shipping companys offices. German cars and ambulances awaited them. **Thue** said his goodbyes by shaking hands with each and every British soldier. And then he said the following words in farewell: *Gud vare med dig!* (God be with you!). This was the last **Thue** saw of the Englishmen.

On Monday, November 23, several people from Flørli and Songesang were assembled, at the behest of the Germans, to carry out a new task up on the mountain. They were to bury the eight deceased Englishmen. The appointed location where the graves were to be dug was about 200 meters behind the Fylgjesdal farm's outhouse. The local residents thought this was completely wrong. They wanted the British soldiers to have a proper burial.

Three of the central witnesses to the tragedy in Fylgjesdalen would eventually suffer very badly at the hands of the Germans. The affects of these experiences on them would totally overshadow those of the drama that took place during November 1942, even though, in the view of **Roth** and **Espedal**, they had a direct connection to the *Freshman-* affair.

On December 3, 1942, **Roth** was arrested. The reason was that he had arranged for a radio apparatus hidden in a room at "Døves Hus" to be removed. The Germans had learned that a radio could be discovered there. They had successfully unearthed this information by manhandling one of **Roth's** co-workers. As the person responsible for the operation of the air-defence medical facility housed there, he was arrested and incarcerated in the prison on Lagårdsveien (Lagårds Road) in Stavanger. In addition, he was interrogated at Sipo's headquarters on Eiganesveien (Eiganes Road).

There, he again met with **Hölscher,** who wanted to find out if **Roth** had learned some vital information from the Englishmen during the rescue operation. **Hölscher** began by heavily manhandling **Roth,** but then he changed tactics, stating: *It hurts me to beat a colleague.* **Roth** took this to mean that it didn't take a hero to beat someone wearing handcuffs. **Hölscher** slowly unlocked the cuffs and removed them.. **Roth** readied himself for being repeatedly smashed in the face since **Hölscher** now began swinging them back and forth in his hand – but as it turned out, **Hölscher** wasn't thinking of assaulting him. Instead, he said: *Please, take a seat. Will you have a cigarette?*

Afterwards, **Roth** was transported to Prison B by the central square in Stavanger. This prison was administered by the Germans. Approximately three weeks after his arrest, a number of German soldiers were transported to the prison. They had been arrested for having discovered, during the course of carrying out their guard duties at the site where the glider had crashed in Fylgjesdalen, that twenty dollars in gold coin had been sown into the dead Englishmen's uniforms. The guards had then stolen the coins and sold them to two entrepreneurs who worked for the Germans in Stavanger. The two entrepreneurs had also been arrested and found guilty of having participated in the plundering of corpses for which they were sent to concentration camps in Germany. The German soldiers, meanwhile, were sent to a "punishment company" on the eastern front.

Criminal Commissioner Eugen Hartmann, for some unknown reason, showed the gold coins to **Roth** during his incarceration at Prison B in Stavanger. For the remainder of the war **Roth** was imprisoned in Grini, in the Sachsenhausen concentration camp, and in other installations throughout Germany. Severe physical assault and other forms of physical abuse have set deep wounds in **Roth's** soul, but he did survive the war and was taken away from this horror by the white painted, Red Cross busses in the spring of 1945.

Thue, who was arrested somewhat later in connection with a student protest in 1943 and sent to the concentration camp at Buchenwald, also survived the war. He experienced a different sort of treatment during his imprisonment than **Roth,** due to the fact that students, in general, were handled well. For example, they had permission to take subject-oriented literature with them and could continue studies on their own in the camps. They were served the same food as the *SS*-soldiers since their food came from the German soldiers' own kitchen. The aim of student internment was to induce the students to adapt themselves to the "new" era, a goal the Germans in no way realised.

On September 14, 1943, yet another witness from Fylgjesdalen was arrested. **Espedal** was incarcerated in prison by the Germans, had the misfortune of encountering the interrogation leader, **Hölscher,** and was subjected, as had happened to so many others in Rogaland who found themselves in the claws of this German, to violent assault. After having become acquainted with the prison on Lagårdsveien and *SS*-headquarters on Eiganesveien, he was transported to Oslo and imprisoned in *Sondercelle* (isolation cell) on Møllergata 19 for the remainder of the war. In the beginning of May 1945, he returned to Forsand and was employed, once again, in the government administrator's office.[44]

---

44. Interviews with Per Roth, Hafsfjord, on Nov. 19, 2002, and with John Fredrik Thue, Sandnes, on Nov, 19, 2002.
In addition, further confirmation is found in the accounts of several information contributors; written in 1982, and lent to the author by Per Johnsen, Randaberg.
Also see Trygve Wyller and Knut Stahl: Av Stavangers historie under okkupajonen, 1940-1945. De lange arena (The long years 1940-1945, Stavanger's history during the occupation), Stavanger, 1964, p 13 ff.
Witness testimony, Johan Fredrich Thue on Oct 7, 1945.
Witness testimony, Sigurd Stangeland (interpreter) on July 7, 1945.

Operation Freshman • – • The hunt for Hitlers heavy water

Chapter 11

The Brutality of the Security Police

The head of the security police in Stavanger, **SS-Obersturmbannfűhrer Friedrich Wilkens,** was between a rock and hard place as to how he could resolve the situation concerning the nine British prisoners he had responsibility for. Therefore, he got in contact with the *Gestapo* headquarters in Oslo. The order they gave him was abundantly clear. The German authorities in Stavanger were to comply with the Fuhrer Order: The injured were to be executed – the rest sent to the headquarters in Oslo.

We've earlier seen (Chapter 2) that on October 18, 1942, Hitler had an order sent out to all his commanders in the occupied areas. The main instruction this order dealt with was that all saboteurs the Germans came upon in their areas were to be annihilated to the last man. If the situation so allowed, prisoners were to be taken. These, without delay, should then be turned over to the security police *(SD, SicherheitsDienst, editors note),* who would attempt to extract information from them – after which, the prisoners were to be executed,

The problem **Wilkens** now confronted was that his subordinates were not especially inclined to carry out this order. **Kurt Herbert Scheulen,** Criminal Secretary with the security police and the security service in Stavanger, sent word that he, in common with his colleagues **Kuhn, Pedersen, Hartmann, Günther** and **Wangerin** refused to shoot the injured prisoners.

Wilkens therefore got in touch with **Dr. Werner Fritz Seeling** who was a military doctor in the German Air Force. A short time previous to this, **Seeling** had examined and treated five British soldiers from the crash at Fylgjesdalen, Just then, these men sat incarcerated in the prison on Lagårdsveien. They lay on stretchers in a cell on the second floor.

Seeling had examined all the soldiers, given them pain-pills and told them they required hospital care, otherwise, without further medical treatment, their injuries could only become worse and worse. Most of the injuries concerned fractures, but one of the men had a head pain that indicated a possible brain concussion. **Kuhn,** who had been nearby during the examination, had said that transferring the prisoners to a hospital wasn't possible since they were to be interrogated. **Seeling** made no protest against this, but directly left the hospital and drove home. Ten minutes after he'd arrived home, **Wilkens** rang. He ordered **Seeling** to present himself at the *Sipo*-commander's office. This, **Seeling** did, and **Wilkens** further informed him of the crash in Fylgjesdaen: The soldiers from the glider were saboteurs and must be shot. This was the Fuhrer's order. **Seeling** protested against executing the injured prisoners. As he had earlier stated, they should be placed in the hospital. Wilkens then said he thought to once again contact his superiors in Oslo and directly question if this order must be carried out.

A day later, Seeling was once again summoned by **Wilkens. Seeling** wasn't assigned to work under the purview of the security police, but as the *SD* in Stavanger lacked a doctor of their own, he presented himself. **Wilkens** said that he was forced to obey the Fuhrer's order. The saboteurs must be shot and the execution would take place out by the coast. **Seeling** reiterated that the Englishmen were far too ill to be moved, and even if they were saboteurs, he insisted that they first should be transferred to the hospital in order to receive adequate care. **Wilkens** said no, and then asked **Seeling** if he could see his way clear to poisoning the British soldiers.

Seeling declined, and during the heated discussion that followed, **Wilkens** let it be known that in his opinion all doctors were too weak and effeminate. The injured British soldiers would be shot, and this decision was definitive. **Seeling** then offered to give the injured morphine. His intent was that in this way the British would avoid experiencing the horrendous destiny that awaited them, due to the Fuhrer Order, in a fully wakened state.

During the course of the night, **Seeling** gave each and every one of the injured Englishmen four morphine injections in the left upper-arm. **Criminal Commissioner Petersen** of the German Security Police was present. Petersen had informed the prisoners that they would be getting a shot against typhus. While this was going on, the German prison guard, **Fritz Feuerlein,** showed up, along with a colleague and another criminal commissioner.

After receiving the first shot, the prisoners became very tired. After the second injection, which they received 45 minutes later, two of them became anxious and nervous but they weren't fully conscious and were removed to the prison office. After a further 95 minutes had passed, **Seeling** gave the prisoners their third morphine injection. **Seeling** wasn't sure how big a dose would prove deadly, but he took care to vary the amount between 0,01 gram and 0.02 gram, doses he knew would not take the prisoners' lives under normal circumstances.

When **Seeling** was instructed to give the prisoners a fourth injection, he became certain that the security police intended to poison them. To prevent this, he told them he didn't have enough morphine with him. He returned to his patient clinic, where he filled a bottle with distilled water. The time was then somewhere between 11:00 and 12:00 PM. **Seeling** administered the fourth injection to the Englishmen, but this time there was only water in the vials. In his affidavit after the war he asserted that if his intent had been to poison the prisoners, he would not have used morphine, but rather some one of the quick-working poisons he had access to in his patient clinic, such as strophanthin, evipan natrium, scopolamin-eukodal or -ephetonin forte. He had administered the morphine injections in order to help the prisoners, and no one had died as a result of them. The prisoners had died either through strangulation or of gunshot wounds and these executions he had no part in.

Late that evening, he saw that a leather strap had been placed around the neck of one of the prisoners. The other end of the strap was fastened to a radiator. A German lifted the prisoner up, pulled him tight and released him, repeatedly, until the man died. Another Englishman, who lay on the floor, also had a strap around his neck but he was already dead. The third Englishmen, he too lay on the floor, wheezed and moaned. He was murdered by a German stomping full force on his exposed throat.

Well into the night, **Kuhn, Hartmann, Hölscher, Günther** and **Scheulen** drove to the prison in a truck. They had received orders to sink the three corpses in the sea. At the prison they met **Seeling, Petersen, Wangerin** and **Sachse,** who showed them the dead bodies. Two were located in a cell, and the third lay in a small room. The detail who had responsibility for disposing the corpses, laid the naked bodies in caskets and lifted them onto the floor of the truck bed. Then they drove down to the harbor. But now the wind had picked up and a full storm was in progress, making it impossible to put out to sea. Consequently, they drove back to their office. The caskets remained on the truck until the following day. Before they went home for the night, they learned that the fourth Englishman was to be shot the next day. He lay with his eyes open and he could move, but his speech was slurred.

The next morning, Tuesday, November 24, 1942, found the fourth Englishman still alive. **Petersen** and **Seeling,** along with the **Chauffeur Fahrdiendtleiter und**

SS-Hauptscharführer, Erich Hoffman, transported the Englishman to *Sipo's* headquarters on Eiganesveien. At the headquarters, the men from *Gestapo* forced the Englishman down the stairs to the cellar. As the Englishman went down the stairs, **Hoffman** shot him in the back of the head. **Petersen** also fired a shot at the defenceless Englishman who wound up lying at the foot of the staircase. **Seeling** pronounced him dead.

When the men from Gestapo assigned to dispose the corpses came to work the following day, they were instructed to remain home after their workday was over. Via telephone they would be informed of the time arranged for them to retrieve the corpses, drive them away and sink them out at sea.

It was **Petersen** who rang up **Günther** and **Scheulen** that evening and told them they should report to headquarters. There, they met the duty-guard and **Hoffman**. Directly after that, **Kuhn, Hartmann** and **Wilkens** also showed up.

The Englishman who had been shot to death at headquarters lay fully dressed at the bottom of the cellar staircase. His head was completely bloodied. The shoes were removed from the corpse which was then stuffed in a sleeping bag. The three corpses, which been lying in caskets the previous day, were now also transferred to sleeping bags. After which, they were driven down to the harbor and taken aboard a boat. The men who took part in this assignment were **Hartmann, Hoffman, Kuhn, Scheulen** and **Petersen.** Large stones were fastened to the corpses with the aid of steel wire before they were cast into the sea off Kvitsøy, sinking to a depth of 395 meters. With this sinking accomplished, Scheulen concluded that the corpses had disappeared for good. Those responsible feared the consequences of their actions.

Two weeks later, **Hoffman** gave a sack containing blood-stained clothes to **Karl Dawe,** chauffeur at *Gestapo's* headquarters in Stavanger. **Dawe** was ordered to burn the clothes. Hoffmann noted that they had belonged to some injured Englishmen.

SS-Hauptscharführer Arthur Wolfgang Heinz Schneider worked with the *Gestapo* in Stavanger. **Hoffman** had told **Schneider** that it was he who had shot the Englishmen, since no one else in *Sipo* in Stavanger was willing. Schneider regarded Hoffmann as a morally objectionable individual. **Schneider's** understanding is that neither **Wilkens** nor Petersen could have ordered **Hoffman** to shoot a prisoner. His military occupational task was to function as head of the chauffeurs at the installation. In other words, he must have freely volunteered himself to carry out the mission of executing the British soldiers.

Later on, the **Kriminalsekretär** of the SP and SD in Stavanger, **Georg Schomacker,** was also to say that, in his presence, **Hoffman** clearly and distinctly said that it was he who had shot the Englishmen. **Schomacher** had nothing good to say about **Hoffmann,** who he thought to be both a dishonest and egotistical person.

The four who met the hideous fate described here in the prison on Lagårdsveien, and in the Sipo headquarters in Stavanger, were:
Corporal James Dobson Cairncross, 22 years of age
Chauffeur Peter Paul Farrell, 26
Lance Corporal Trevor Louis Masters, 25
Private Eric John Smith, 24

And how did things turn out for the five British soldiers from the glider-crash in Fylgjesdalen who were transported to the *Gestapo* Headquarters in Oslo?

Kriminalrat Welhelm Esser, who was attached to *Gestapo* Headquarters, was able to give a partial account of what happened. Towards the end of November 1942, *Sipo's* commander in Stavanger, **Wilkens,** had informed the head of the security police in **Norway, Heinrich Fehlis,** about the plane crash in Fylgjesdalen. In that same conversation, **Wilkens** inquired if the prisoners were to be treated in accordance with the Fuhrer Order. He also wanted *Gestapo* Headquarters in Oslo to arrange that an investigator be sent to Stavanger to inspect the situation. Headquarters sent **Kriminalsekretär Herbert Stehr.**

A few days later, **Stehr** reported that, after having interrogated the survivors of the crash in Fylgjesdalen and inspected the glider wreckage, he concluded that the Englishmen were saboteurs. **Fehlis** decided that some of the prisoners should be transferred to Oslo. As a result of this decision, **Esser** was assigned to interrogate the five English prisoners now held at Grini. The prisoners had been involved in a sabotage effort directed against the heavy-water facility in Vemork. After having been imprisoned, their uniforms were taken from them, and they were given blue civilian clothes to wear instead. This was done on orders from **Fehlis.**

The prison on Lagerdsveien (Lagerds Road) in Stavanger. Photo: Ingrid Worning Berglyd.

The following afternoon, **Esser,** along with his assistant **Brüggemann,** travelled to Grini. Also following along were the German interpreter, **Hans Edmund Behncke,** and **Esser's** stenographer. There, **Esser** interrogated the five English prisoners. The interrogations were held over the course of five to six afternoons and evenings. The prisoners stated that on the evening of November 19 they had flown from a location in northern Scotland. Other than the pilots, the men onboard were soldiers from the *Royal Engineers.* Their mission had been to destroy the heavy water plant at Rjukan.

When the interrogations were completed, the Germans wrote a protocol covering what the British soldiers had said. This protocol was submitted to **Hellmuth Reinhard,** head of the *Gestapo* in Norway. From that point on out, **Esser** was no longer involved in all that transpired.

He was not informed of any details concerning the executions, as for example, the time or place. Everything was shrouded in secrecy. Nor did he know if the executions were carried out by the SP or the *Wehrmacht.*

A report written by the Norwegian, **Corporal Erik Dahle,** provides some further puzzle-pieces as to what happened to the five British prisoners. **Dahle** was arrested by the Germans and imprisoned at Grini. For a period of time, the five British prisoners were locked in a cell alongside his. They told Dahle that they hadn't been subjected to physical torture, but the Norwegian got the impression that, on the other hand, they hadn't received the medical attention they needed. They were first questioned by a person from the security service. He had threatened the prisoners and

Sipo's headquarters on Euganesveien in Stavanger.
Photo: Ingrid Worning Berglyd.

stated that they would be shot. Subsequently, they were heard by an air force pilot. He spoke excellent English and was very friendly. He assured the prisoners that they would be sent to Germany as prisoners of war.

During the night of January 17, 1943, the five Englishmen were removed by the Germans, handcuffed, and driven away.

After the war, **Behnke** reported in a hearing with Norwegian and British authorities that he had twice acted as interpreter for **Esser** during interrogations of the five Englishmen. On these occasions the prisoners had been collected from Grini and transported to *Gestapo's* headquarters in Oslo. He also acted as interpreter on several occasions when **Esser** interrogated them at Grini.

On the night of January 17, 1943, he was again summoned to Grini and was driven there by car. The five British soldiers had been taken from their cell and **SS-Hauptsturmführer Otto Hans** ordered **Behnke** to inform the prisoners they were to meet a high-ranking German officer at an air field. Therefore, it was necessary that they be blindfolded. **Behnke** remained with **Otto Hans** and his detachment of soldiers as the prisoners were being driven to Trandum. Once there, the prisoners were immediately taken into the woods and shot to death. **Behnke** attested that he, himself, did not see the executions.

The five were:
Private James Frank Blackburn, 28 years of age
Private Frank Bonner, 25
Lance Corporal Wallis Mahlon Jackson, 21.
Private John Wilfred Walsh, 26
Private Thomas White, 22[45]

---

45. Beginning in 1939, the German Security Police, *Sicherheitspolizei (Sipo)*, all the German police forces, the *Gestapo* (secret police), and the security police – *Sicherheitsdienst (SD,)* were all part of the same organization. This organization was Hitler's most vital tool for crushing all opposition to the regime.
Norsk Krigsleksikon (Norwegian War-Dictionary) 1940-1945, J.W. Cappelens Publishing, 1995, p 398.
Witness testimony; Fritx Seeling, Aug. 20, 1945 and Nov. 6, 1945
Witness testimony: Fritz Feuerlein, July 6, 1945 and Aug. 16, 1945
Witness testimony: Arthur Wolfgang Heinz Schneider, Oct. 23, 1945
Witness testimony: Georg Schomaker, Oct. 23, 1945.
Witness testimony: Kurt Herbert Scheulen, Oct. 23, 1945
Witness testimony: Karl Dawe, Aug. 17, 1945.
Witness testimony: Erich Hoffmann, Sep. 9, 1945, Oct 23, 1945, and Oct. 22, 1945
Witness testimony Ohan Esser, July 17, 1945.
Also see: *War Crimes Trials, Volume VI, -The Trial of von Falkenhorst*, 1949, and Richard Wiggan: Operation Freshman, William Kimber, London, 1986.

Operation Freshman ⬆ ⬇ ⬆ The hunt for Hitlers heavy water

The plant facility in Vemork from two perspectives. Photo loaned out by Norway's Home-front Museum

Chapter 12

Gunnerside arrives

A short time after the *Freshman*-tragedy became known, British **Major General Colin Gubbins**, head of the *SOE*, requested permission to undertake an attack attempt with his own men. **Gubbin's** request was granted, and so it was with this background, anchored in command initiative and responsibility, that *Gunnerside* was launched. The training began immediately, and was carried out via the co-operative efforts of **Major Leif Tronstad** of the *Defence Central Command Headquarters, FO4*, and British officers. This co-operation made it very difficult for the equipment section to anticipate all that would be required, both as to the training and the operation iself.[46]

A complete model of the highly concentrated facility for producing heavy water in Vemork had all ready been built. The model was constructed based on the drawings that **Professor Jomar Brun** had taken with him when he fled to England. Moreover, the *Freshman*-force had trained in this model, so in a sense *Gunnerside* arrived at a table already set.[47]

With the aid of photographs and drawings, **Tronstad**, together with *Gunnerside*, planned the sabotage attempt in minute detail. It was of the most vital importance that this operation went-off as planned, because if the Germans succeeded in producing an atom bomb before the allies, they would win the war.[48]

Joachim Rønneberg received an order from *SOE*/London that he was to lead the operation against the heavy-water plant in Vemork, and he was further instructed to select five men for *Gunnerside* as soon as possible.

---

46. Major General Colin Gubbins forward in Knut Haukelid's book *Kampen om tungtvannet* (roughly: The battle over heavy water) Ernst G. Mortensen's publishing A/S, Oslo 1983.
47. Letters from Joachim Rønneberg to the author, Nov. 9, 2004, Nov. 24, 2004 and Dec. 9, 2004. *Operation Gunnerside*, Warrant-Officer Rønneberg's report. It's written in English and is in Norway's Home-front Museum.
48. Knut Haukelid: *Kampen om tungtvannet*, Ernst G. Mortensen's publishing A/S, 1983, p. 12.

The force, fully manned, consisted of Warrant Officer Joachim Ronneberg, second-in-command **Warrant Officer Knut Haukelid, Warrant Officer Kaspar Idland, Sergeant Fredrik Kayser, Birger Stromsheim** and **Hans Storhaug.** At this point, no one at the headquarters in Scotland knew the operational target. Therefore, **Ronneberg** was forced to travel to London to become more familiarized with the operation down to its details, as well as being able to take part in the planning. He was also responsible for selecting the winter equipment the force would be provided with. The Norwegian Brigade's workshop in Dumfries handled certain special equipment: sleds, weather-proof clothing, ski-masks, and backpacks. The remaining members of *Gunnerside* were already in training. Time was short. In barely three weeks, the 17th of December would mark the beginning of a new moon-phase. Weather permitting, the goal was to have the force ready to set the operation in motion at a moment's notice beginning as of that date. It had been decided that the airborne force would parachute-land at Store Saure.[49]

After *Gunnerside* had been oriented about its vital mission, all the participants devoted their time to target practice and a program of intensive physical training. A month later all force-members were in top physical shape. In addition, they were accomplished skiers, a prerequisite skill for taking part in the mission.

Tronstad and the head of the Norwegian section of the *SOE,* **Colonel John S Wilson,** favored having all the participants in *Gunnerside* proceed together as a unit towards Sweden after carrying out the sabotage. In the event they wound up in battle with Germans along the way, a larger Norwegian force, it stood to reason, had a better chance of successfully dealing with it. A precondition of this plan was that everyone wore uniforms. Many regarded this suggestion as far too risky. It opened the door to a situation that could quite conceivably become extremely dangerous, particularly up in the Hardanger wilderness area subsequent to an operation against the facility in Vemork. The British had already lost 30 specially trained engineer soldiers, four glider-pilots and a seven man glider crew in its first attempt at this operation. All 23 plane-crash survivors had been executed by the Germans. There no reason to believe that the Norwegians would be treated any differently if they fell into German hands.

Every saboteur was therefore equipped with his own little rubber-covered capsule containing calcium cyanide. If someone of them became injured or was taken prisoner, the best alternative was to commit suicide as soon as possible. When the capsule was crushed by a bite, death followed

---

49. Footnote 47.
50. Footnote 48, p. 51 and p. 55.

in three seconds. The use of cyanide capsules was completely normal. All agents had them on their person.[50]

The weather during the month following the *Freshman* tragedy was very bad. This made it impossible for *Gunnerside* to be launched in December, as had been hoped. The first attempt to parachute the force in Hardangervidda (the Hardanger wilderness) was made on January 22, 1943. The weather was perfect during the entire flight.

They flew in over Norway, east of Kristainsand. The plane came in over the southern part of Norway, but the pilot didn't succeed in finding the air drop location. In fact, the plane circled over the area for several hours but still wasn't able to locate *Grouse*.

Ronneberg finally requested that they be dropped over Bjornesfjorden, but the pilot, citing the fact that no contact had been made with *Grouse*, said no. And the plane returned to Great Britain, mission aborted.

Yet another long wait followed for the members of *Gunnerside*. It wouldn't be possible to hop out over Hardangervidda until the next suitable moon phase, providing, of course, that the weather was likewise suitable. Several times the men were given the order to be ready to take-off that same evening, only to see the operation called off at the last moment,

On February 16, 1943, however, the weather was fine, and there was a full moon as well. *Gunnerside* was given a preliminary order that it was time to set things in motion, and that evening they were driven to an air field in southern England. This particular air field, as it happened, was often used for secret missions. **Tronstad** was there and wished them good luck.[51]

Before take-off, *Gunnerside* had requested permission to hop out over Bjornesfjorden. From there, they would make their way to Grouse, just then housed in a cabin near Svensbu. The flight in went as planned, and at midnight they hopped out from an altitude of 1000 feet. The airdrop and landing went well and everyone came through in good shape. The equipment also came through as hoped – with the exception of one container. Its parachute had drifted some two kilometers away before stopping in an open channel. And it wasn't until then that they were able to retrieve it. It contained three sleeping bags and backpacks for half the group – In other words, it was absolutely necessary to recover this equipment if they were going to accomplish the mission.

All the equipment that was to be used for the attack on Vemork was repacked in the backpacks and put on the sleds. Anything not necessary in connection with the actual sabotage itself was buried and could laterbe dug up for the withdrawal to Sweden. The spot was marked-out with stakes. Not long thereafter, all traces of the landing and burying had

---

51. Ibid., p.54-56

disappeared in a fresh snowfall. All indications were that they had landed in the Bjornesfjorden area.

As dawn broke, they saw a cabin in the distance, which they soon made use of for protection and a chance to rest up. During the course of the day, they prepared for the trip to Svensbu. Backpacks and sleds were readied, and at 5:00 PM they were able to get underway. Each man carried 30 kilos and 50 kilos was packed on each sled. After an hour's journey, the snow fall had become so heavy that **Ronneberg** ordered a return to the cabin. By then, it was becoming bitter cold and the snow storm continued unabated blowing in from the west. Now they were forced to struggle back through hard wind and blinding snow by compass. Fortunately, luck was on their side and they walked right onto a road – and after checking their location more closely – it turned out the road belonged to the cabin they had just left. It was a good cabin and it had a good store of firewood. Given the course of the weather, this cabin quite probably saved the lives of the group's members – not to mention, that had they not returned to the cabin, the entire operation would have been aborted. If they had continued their trek, they would have wandered in the wrong direction and they could never have found their way back to the cabin. The entire operation would have ended in catastrophe.

Gunnerside parachuted nearby Skrykken Lake. From there, they hiked to Grouse, that had once again located in the cabin near Svensbu. The route is indicated on the map.

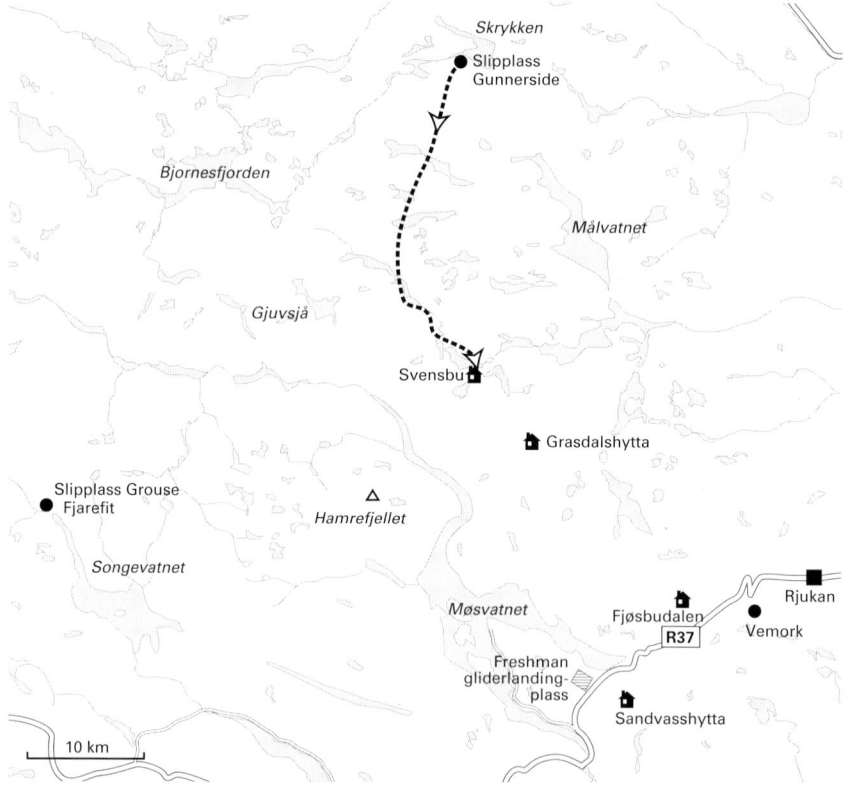

Gunnerside arrives

During the night, the wind gusted even harder, and a hellish storm let loose. It lasted several days. Nevertheless, on the third day of the storm they attempted to leave the cabin to retrieve more food. This attempt was cut short. The risk of them not being able to find their way back was too great.

The following day the wind let up some, and a new attempt was made. But the storm had altered the landscape and they weren't able to locate the stores. After three hours they gave up.

Warrant Officer Joachim Rønneberg was the leader of Gunnerside. Photo loaned out by Norway's Homefront Museum.

That evening they chanced yet another attempt, and this time they found a container in the snow. They realized the buried stores must lay somewhere very near. Due to the storm, it wasn't possible to dig up the food, but now they could at least re-stake the area.

During their first expedition they had noted signs in the landscape indicating that they may not have landed in the Bjornesfjorden area, which was the assumption they had made at the start. The vegetation was not what they had expected. After examining the map more closely, **Ronneberg** came to the conclusion that the cabin they had been occupying lay near Skrykkenvatn. The cabin's guestbook confirmed his supposition.

When they left the cabin on February 22, they had revised the marchroute to accord with the new information. The weather was fine, and **Ronneberg** gave the order that they would set out at noon.

The swift and drastic climate change they had been exposed to upon landing in Norway had caused two of the group's members to come down with severe colds. The bitter cold also took other tolls on the body, especially on the hands. The storm had raged for several days, and beyond forcing delay, it had further worsened *Gunnerside's* situation.

By this, **Ronneberg** had in mind that the overall health of his men was not the best. Therefore, the load of every pack was somewhat lightened. Each pack would now weigh 25 kilos, and the weight of equipment tied on the two sleds would be 40 and 30 kilos respectively.

The tracks the men had left that morning between the storage site and

Operation Freshman ◆ ◣ ◆ The hunt for Hitlers heavy water

the cabin were discovered by a hunter. He walked up to the cabin where he was immediately subjected to a thorough interrogation. *Gunnerside* concluded they had no choice but to take him with them.

The hunter was familiar with the area, and *Gunnerside* therefore let him function as a guide to Kallungsjå. He led them over a route that **Ronneberg** characterized as "first class." At Kallungsjå, Gunnerside caught site of two skiers. **Haukelid** was instructed to change into camouflage clothing and a civilian ski-hood. He was to meet up with the two skiers, and if necessary, present himself as a reindeer-farmer who was out and about seeing to his deer. The rest of the group sought protection. Shouts of joy indicated that **Haukelid** had met-up with *Grouse*. The two skiers were **Helberg** and **Kjelstrup.**

The hunter was then separated from the group and was held in Slettedalsbu under guard. He wasn't released until *Gunnerside* had arrived at Svensbu by Lille Saure. The distance *Gunnerside* had covered totalled approximately 45 kilometers.

In Svensbu, the guests shared the good food they had brought with them. The *Grouse* unit was also supplied with uniforms and *Gunnerside* was able to inform their hosts that they now had a new name. Beginning as of then and there, they would be known as *Swallow*. But the members of the reconnaissance unit more-or-less chose to ignore it, and continued to use the name they'd grown accustomed to.

This sketch shows the facility in Vemork from the entry gate across the railroad tracks where Gunnerside broke into the area in February 1943. This pen-sketch was drawn by Harold Olsen, Vemork, 1946. Photostat copy loaned out by Norway's Homefront Museum.

52. Footnote 47.

Grouse related the facts of their long wait for *Gunnerside:* On January 23, 1943, they received a message from London saying that *Gunnerside* would land that night. Thereafter, Grouse had begun preparing for their arrival. The *Eureka* was set-up on a height outside Svensbu, and **Helberg** was assigned to monitor its receiver. **Haugland** sat inside the cabin and listened to the radio in order to hear if any new orders came in. **Kjelstrup** and **Poulsson** waited out on the ice, on the northern end of Lake Store Saure, ready to light up the lanterns as soon as **Helberg** heard that the plane was approaching. When this happened, he would signal by blinking his flashlight.

The plane arrived deep into the night, but disappeared to the west and never returned. The men stayed on watch until 3:00 AM before giving up.

On February 16, they once again received a message saying that *Gunnerside* was to land, but again, they never showed. The day after, the same thing happened, yet again. On February 19, London sent a message allowing that the previous alert (2/17) had been a misunderstanding. The parachute-landing had taken place, as had earlier been reported, on February 16.

If this message was accurate, the question was: Where had *Gunnerside* landed and how had they survived during the horrendous weather? According to the report they had received from England, *Gunnerside* had hopped-out over Bjornesfjorden. If this was so, then Gunnerside would be forced to get past Kallungsjå (Kallung Lake) and then continue on through Slettedalen (Slette Valley) in order to make their way to Grouse.

On February 23, the weather was fine, likewise the snow for skiing. **Helberg** and **Kjelstrup** set off for Kallungsjå seeking to find *Gunnerside* – which they did, and late that afternoon the sabotage group from England arrived in Svensbu.[53]

---

53. Interview with Jens-Anton Poulsson at his home in Kongsberg, on Aug. 25, 2004. Letters from Poulsson to the author with information and comments concerning complications, Sep. 9, 2004, Sep. 21, 2004 and Dec. 28, 2004. Poulsson has also lent the author the following written source material: the operation-order that *Grouse* received on October 17, 1942; Report concerning *Grouse's* work in the Norwegian winter of 1942/43 written by Jens.Anton Poulsson, London, April 1943. Also see Jens-Anton Poulsson: *Aksjon Vemork, Vinterkrig på Hardangervidda,* Faksimil, 1993, Tinn kommune.

Operation Freshman — The hunt for Hitlers heavy water

Chapter 13

The Sabotage is successful

After the parachute-landing, *Grouse* and *Gunnerside* became a combined force with **Ronneberg** as commander. They spent a day together in Svensbu and used much of that time to go through the operation. The members of Grouse, who knew the terrain, would, among other things, act as guides during the planning stage. The saboteurs would operate in two units. One, designated as the support unit, was made up of **Haukelid, Helberg, Kjelstrup** and **Poulsson.** . Their mission was to neutralize the German security force in Vemork. The second, the demolition unit, consisted of **Ronneberg** and **Stromsheim** – with ready to set explosive charges – along with **Kayser, Idland** and **Storhaug** acting as support.[54]

Poulsson recounts that he had suggested a forward fire-base be set up in Fjøsbudalen. There, they should be able to find a suitable cabin. And during the course of a march to that area, they should, likewise, be able to brake into cabins along the way. **Poulsson** and the other men from Grouse considered Fjøsbudalen as the only conceivable starting point for the attack. There, the saboteurs could stay close-by the objective and make their final preparations. In addition, from this location the final stretch down towards the objective in Vestfjorddalen was relatively easy. **Rønneberg** accepted this reasoning. He relied on the reconnaissance unit's local knowledge.

After the failed Freshman-action, the German's had strengthened their security strength in Vemork. In Vemork itself, there was again a 15-man force, and an additional watch had been posted on top of the ridge overlooking the facility. Today, **Poulsson** knows that a German security guard and two Norwegians were supposed to have been patrolling inside the entryway, but their presence was made notable by their absence.

---

54. Letters from Joachim Rønneberg to the author, Nov. 9, 2004 and Dec. 12, 2004. Operation *Gunnerside*, Warrant-Officer Rønnegberg's report. It's written in English and is in Norway's Home-front Museum.

Operation Freshman — The hunt for Hitlers heavy water

Poulsson is also now aware that the Germans hadn't sent any troops to Vemork from Rjukan after the explosions, even though there were many Germans stationed there. Two Germans guarded the suspension-bridge.

The information *Grouse* needed had been discussed several times. After the disaster of *Freshman*, they had made up a list of such questions which **Einar Skinnarland** took with him when he and **Helberg** set off for Møsvatn on February 19. This list was then turned over to **Seläs**. He was the president of the union in Rjukan. An arrangement was made whereby the answers would be handed over to someone at Krosso railway's lower station (the lower of the mountain train stations). This would take place on February 25, and the person designated to hand them over was engineer **Rolf Sørlie**. He and **Helberg** knew each other, which meant that no password would be necessary. All went according to plan. And **Helberg** was already in Fjøsbudalen when the saboteurs landed.

The weather was cloudy, slightly windy, and the temperature rested a few degrees under zero-centigrade, when the nine saboteurs began the first stage to the cabin by Langsjø (Long Lake). They made good use of **Poulsson's** local knowledge of the area and arrived at the cabin by 5:00 PM. The doors and windows were secured with bolts, but since they had

The Norwegian saboteurs set out for the plant facility in Vemork from the cabin in Fjøboda. The approach route is marked on the map. In addition, the first stretch of the withdrawal from the objective is also indicated.

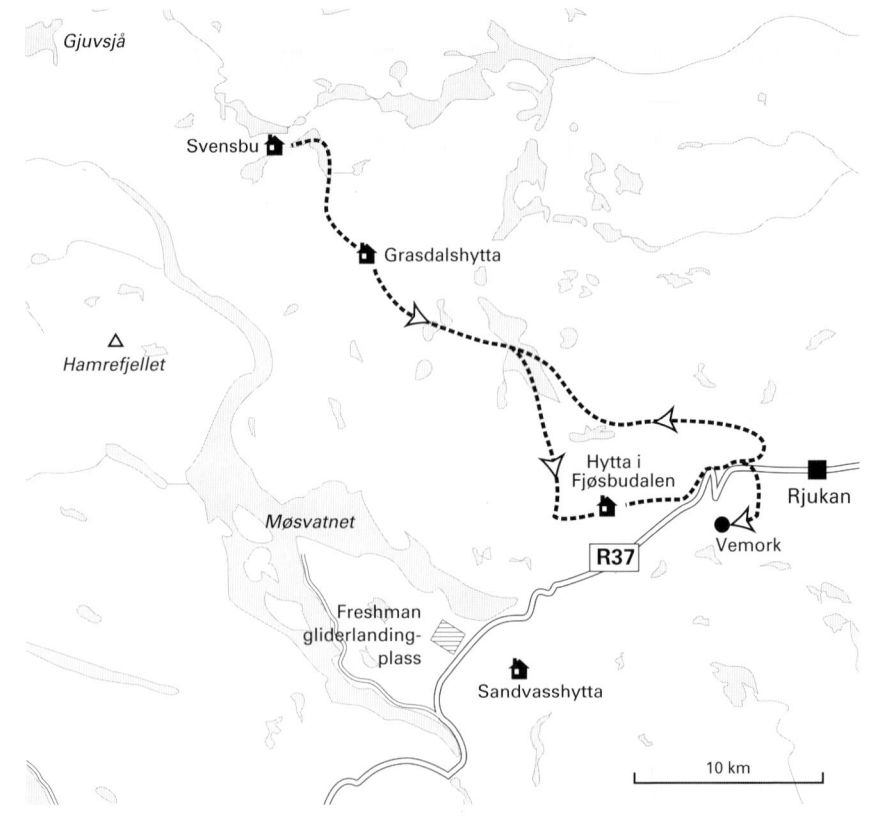

strong bolt-cutters with them, they were soon inside. **Rønneberg** had brought the bolt-cutters with him from England – having just purchased them from a hardware store in Cambridge. They found food in the cabin, and therefore avoided having to make inroads on their own stores.

The next day, at one o'clock in the afternoon, Saturday, February 26, nine white-clad and well-armed soldiers again forged ahead. They were careful not to be seen, and once in Fjøsbudalen they did as planned, and set-up home in a cabin where they joined-up with **Helberg.** What remained of the day was used to prepare for the attack.

After digesting the information they got from **Helberg,** they became even more certain that it would be best to cross the Måna River somewhere between Rjukan and Vemork. **Helberg** was now given the mission of finding a likely place, which would obviously be sufficiently away towards Rjukan so as not to be discovered from Vemork/Vaer. On the morning of February 27, **Helberg** investigated the situation. When he returned, he was able to tell them that crossing the river undetected was fully possible.

The cabin they were staying in was located some 800 meters above a remotely situated valley floor by the edge of a steep mountainside with an excellent view over Rjukan. Over weekends, however, cabin owners celebrating them in nature could definitely be found – a drawback **Poulsson** had overlooked. For this reason, they didn't dare to go outside.

Three hours before they would begin the journey to Vemork, the posted watch reported that he had seen a skier in the near vicinity of a cabin. They took the skier into custody and interrogated him. He turned out to be a school-friend of two of the saboteurs. He was one of four people to enjoy weekends in the neighboring cabins, and he had specifically gone out to "investigate" what sort of folk were living in the cabin by the side of the mountain. He was given strict orders not to talk about this meeting, and was then released since he was deemed to be reliable.

The two units started out from Fjøsbudalen at 8:00 PM, the 27th of February, 1943. All the participants wore uniforms: specifically, British combat uniforms under white windproof attire. They were armed with sub-machineguns, pistols, and hand grenades. In the beginning they use skies, but later on they proceeded on foot, down to the main road from Rjukan to Møsvatn above Våer, then followed along this road, but took care to avoid the built up area in Våer.

The two units arrived at te river's ravine as planned. They chose to cross over to the Vemork side of the ravine at a location below Våer. The areas of surface water had grown, but crossed over to the other side without a problem, having found a suitable ice-bridge (i.e. a stretch of weight-bearing ice). Since it was **Helberg** who was familiar with the area, it was he who led the units down into the ravine and over to the other side. It was difficult to climb up to the railway tracks. After which, they followed them until they reached entry gate stretched over the rails, cut off the chains and then proceeded into the fenced-in area.[55]

The demolition-unit with its support crew headed towards the electrolysis plant, and the support unit drew closer to the German guardhouse and other installations, ready to do whatever was needed with the not unlikely appearance of security guards and patrols.

Since the vertical distance between the yard-area and the cellar was approximately 15 meters the demolition-unit members, to one degree or another, were forced to execute their missions independent of each other. **Rønneberg** and **Kayser** located the cable tunnel leading to the plant itself. Crawling through this tunnel they entered the plant area where the apparatus for producing heavy water was located. Their sudden appearance nearly scared the life out of the elderly Norwegian watchman on duty. He was neither a soldier nor an armed security guard, but only a common civilian hired to watch over the production.

While **Kayser** took charge of the watchman, **Rønneberg** started to set-out the explosive charges. These had already been custom-constructed for the various machines. The model they had trained on in England was almost identical with the actual facility. While they were going about their mission, a window was suddenly smashed. It was **Strømsheim,** who very much wanted to make contact but hadn't been able to locate the tunnel. He was dragged through the broken window and helped set-out the explosives. The placement of the explosive charges was controlled twice before **Rønneberg** lit the fuses.

The original plan had called for using two minute fuse-lengths. But, with thought to how well everything had gone so far, **Rønneberg** didn't want to risk someone coming in at the last moment, and making waste of all the effort that had been put in. He therefore set two extra fuse-lengths into the charges, each with a 30 second burn-time. Thereafter, he first lit the two minute fuse and then the cords timed for 30 seconds. Then everyone ran out of the production room. Despite the shorter timed fuses, they all got out of the building in time.

The boom sounded like a muffled explosion. A German stepped out of the guardhouse. He illuminated the area around him with a flashlight

---

55. Ibid. Interview with Jens-Anton Poulsson at his home in Kongsberg, on Aug. 25, 2004.
Letters from Poulsson to the author with information and comments concerning complications, Sep. 2, 2004, Sep. 21, 2004 and Sep. 29, 2004. The operation-order that *Grouse* received on October 17, 1942; Report concerning *Grouse's* work in the Norwegian winter of 1942/43 written by Jens.Anton Poulsson, London, April 1943. Also see Jens-Anton Poulsson: *Aksjon Vemork, Vinterkrig på Hardangervidda,* Faksimil, 1993, Tinn kommune.

and concluded that it most probably came from the production facility, but he nevertheless went back into the guardhouse: The Germans were accustomed to explosions in connection with electrolysis production facilities. The two sabotage units met-up outside the entry gate. Spirits were high. Thus far, all had gone well.[56]

The withdrawal, which had been planned down the smallest detail, also went as hoped; down over the power-line road to the Krosso railway, up Rye's Vei and then on towards the mountain. By following this route they avoided the main road to Rjukan, and in addition, they took a detour to avoid being detected from the railway's lower station.

Morning had caught up with them. There was frost in the air and they travelled facing a strong wind. The weather was miserable but they managed to reach their first goal, the cabin by Langsjø. They were totally convinced that the horrendous weather had destroyed all signs of their passing, thus making it more difficult for the pursuers. Therefore they decided to overnight in the cabin and rest up.

The following morning, the snowstorm was so strong that venturing outdoors was not an option. But in the afternoon, the weather improved to the point where they were able to continue on towards Svensbu. When they arrived there, it felt as though they had come home. **Rønneberg** placed a report saying the operation had been carried out in a canned goods container. This was then buried in the snow at a pre-agreed upon spot, so that **Haugland** would be able to find it and forward the message to England.

Today, **Poulsson** knows the Germans found signs of the saboteurs trail along the train rails and down into the ravine. They even discovered traces of blood, and **Poulsson** says he recalls that **Rønneberg** had scraped his hand. But on the ravine's north side, all signs had disappeared – and up on the mountain, the crusted snow had frozen so hard that not even the marks of ski poles could be detected.[57]

---

56. Footnote 54.
57. Footnote 55.

Operation Freshman ▲ ▼ ▲ The hunt for Hitlers heavy water

The memorial stone with the names of the main participants in the Norwegian operation against the plant facility in Vemork.

Chapter 14

The Withdrawal

After the sabotage explosions, there followed a huge stir in Vemork. Both **Josef Terboven, Hitler's district commissioner** in occupied Norway, and the highest commander of the German forces in Norway, **General Nicolaus von Falkenhorst**, were involved. **Von Falkenhorst** considered the sabotage to be the best executed operation he'd ever seen.[58]

Grouse and *Gunnerside* had been incredibly lucky. The action had been 100 percent successful. Now the objective was to get themselves to safety. The demolition unit and its support crew were to start making their way towards the Swedish border as soon as possible. At 2:30 PM, March 4, 1943, the five men were ready to go. Their escape was calculated to take ten days. They would be wearing uniforms and if they ran into opposition on their way through Norway, they were instructed to fight. The march to safety was estimated to take 10 days, but as events unfolded it became apparent that18 days would be required. Before crossing the border, they were to ditch their weapons and uniforms.

During the day, they scanned the area they were about to cover with binoculars, and at night they hid in cabins and shacks. The food they came upon was greatly appreciated because the distances actually covered during the day were shorter than had been estimated.

Fourteen days after the start, they had completed the trek through Norway, and on March 18, 8:15 PM, they passed over the border into Sweden. They continued walking several kilometers into Sweden before making camp and starting a fire for the first time under the open sky, since the day they had landed in Norway.

The backpacks were almost empty. All that was left was a little ski-wax, extra socks, cup, spoon, sleeping bag, weatherproof clothing, a little

---

58. Jomar Brun: *Brennpunkt Vemork* (Burning Point, Vemork), 1940-1945, Universityforlaget (University Publishing) 1983, p. 73.

Operation Freshman ▴ ▾ ▴ The hunt for Hitlers heavy water

spam and money. As to attire, whether underwear, boots, socks, shirts, or weatherproof outer clothing, it made no difference – they were all clad alike. Everything that could point to them as soldiers had been discarded – in fact, everything of English origin.

Want of food made it necessary for them to seek out inhabited areas as soon as possible.

They located a few woodsmen floating timbers at a log-jam. There, they were given food and information as to where the district police superintendent was.

They were given a lift in a lumber-sled down to the main road where they were stopped by a Swedish patrol, which then informed the government administrator. Three hours later, this gentleman showed up and fetched them. The government administrator became a little suspicious when he noted they were all dressed identically. But for whatever reason, he saw to their being taken in by a hospital at Likenäs where they were able to bathe and be deloused. Their clothes were disinfected and dried.

The next day they were taken to the police station. After a short interview, they ate at a nearby hotel. In every instance and in every way they were well-treated.

They had to remain in Likenäs until March 22. Then they travelled, without guards, by car and train to Kjesäter where they underwent a routine secutity check. Thereafter, **Rønneberg** had to travel to Stockholm in order

General Nicolaus von Falkenhorst (in the white coat) and National Commissioner Josef Terboven (pointing) in Rjukan. This photo was taken during their visit following the destruction of the facility in Vemork. The Germans cordoned-off the entire Hardanger wilderness area and fine-combed it, seeking to catch the saboteurs. Photo loaned out by Norway's Home-front Museum.

to report to the British legation. All the offices of the official Norwegian authorities were closed.

The formalities were soon taken care of, and on March 28 they took-off from Bromma Airport, destination Great Britain, where they landed, safe and sound, the following day at !:30 AM.[59]

But there was one person from *Gunnerside* still left in Norway: The force's second-in-command, **Knut Haukelid. Haukelid** had, for both the Norwegian and British authorities, stated that having carried out the mission, he wished to remain in Norway. He was familiar with living up the mountain area and could survive off of nature. Moreover, he was located in his home territory. The Germans would never be able to seize him. He would do just fine.

About the same position was forwarded by the second-in-command in *Grouse,* **Arne Kjelstrup.** After blowing up the production facility in Vemork, he got together with Haukelid to begin working together in ØvreTelemark.

After spending a while there, **Haukelid** and **Kjelstrup** looked westward to Røldal and Suldal, where they tried to establish contacts with the local residents. The winter was very harsh. The snow lay deep and the reindeer – which they had planned on hunting – couldn't be found. In addition, wood was hard to come by. Hunger, cold and harsh weather were their constant companions.

Hunger necessitated their seeking the help of local residents, but as it turned out, there were German troops in the area. They also learned that the Germans had, mildly put, fine-combed the entire Hardanger area. As a result, they were forced to consider returning to the mountains, and one day, over snow-crusted ground, they set out. It turned into a battle against severe weather and starvation. For five days they were forced to lay still in their light sleeping-bags out on the snow.

When they reached the cabin at Langesæ, west of Haukeliveirn, it was quite apparent that the Germans had been there and conducted a thorough search of the entire area. After the sabotage of the facility in Vemork, the Germans concluded that there were sizable allied forces in the Hardangervidda. Consequently, they had sent out 3,000 men to search the area.

Spring was approaching, and it was time to try getting in touch with the two radio-telegraph operators, **Hauglund** and **Skinnarland.** The day after **Haukelid** and **Kjelstrup** reached the cabin near Svensbu, **Haugland** and **Skinnarland** also showed up. Their mission was to continue maintaining radio-contact between Hardangervidda and London. They had been worried that **Haukelid** and **Kjelstrup** had been seized by the Germans.

---

59. Operaton *Gunnerside*, Warrant Officer Rønneberg's report.

While the German's were conducting their search of the area, the two telegraphers kept hidden on a mountain top near Møsstrond.[60]

In May, **Haukelid** and **Kjelstrup** journeyed to Oslo, staying there a month. In the beginning of June they returned to the mountain area, and lived a peaceful life. They also tried to establish contacts around the area with thought to setting up resistance groups, but in the fall of 1943, **Kjelstrup** decided to return to England while **Haukelid** was content to stay-on in Norway.

The members of the support unit were allowed to decide for themselves what they would do after the sabotage operation was carried out. If they wished to follow the others into Sweden, they were compelled to do so in uniform. But they didn't care to escape to Sweden.

Poulsson traveled to Oslo and went underground for several weeks. While in Oslo he met with **Helberg** to talk over their future plans. This meeting had been arranged beforehand. **Helberg** decided that he would stay in Norway and found his way to the mountain area. **Poulsson** made his way into Sweden, and from there he flew to Great Britain and joined up with his unit.

The German's kept an eye on **Helberg** and he was arrested, but succeeded in escaping. The resistance movement helped him flee to Sweden and from there he continued on to England. And in May of 1943, he once again saw **Poulsson,** in London.[61]

---

60. Letters from Joachim Rønneberg to the author, Nov. 9, 2004 and Dec. 12, 2004 Knut Haukelid: Kampen om tungtvannet, Ernst G. Mortensens Forlag A/S, 1983, p. 96-105..
61. Interview with Jens-Anton Poulsson at his home in Kongsberg, on Aug. 25, 2004. Letters from Poulsson to the author with information and comments concerning complications, Sep. 2, 2004, Sep. 21, 2004 and Sep, 29 2004. The operation-order that *Grouse* received on October 17, 1942; Report concerning *Grouse's* work in the Norwegian winter of 1942/43 written by Jens-Anton Poulsson, London, April 1943. Also see Jens-Anton Poulsson: *Aksjon Vemork, Vinterkrig på Hardangervidda,* Faksimil, 1993, Tinn kommune.

Chapter 15

Mission Accomplished

The apparatus required for the production of heavy water in Vemork, which had been blown apart, was speedily repaired. A delay of only six months was incurred before production was again in full swing. This necessitated that a new sabotage effort be carried out.

Now the American military and scientific authorities were in the picture. After going through the issue with the British, Vemork was given the highest bombing-target priority.

Vemork was bombed on November 26, 1943. The raid was executed by the *US 8th Army Air Force* using *B-17* and *B-24* bombers. Other air force units, having had Kjeller designated as their main target objective, were re-directed to Rjukan/Vemork due to unfavourable weather conditions. The combined force, now totalling 161 planes, bombed the power station and electrolysis plant in Vemork. Twelve other planes from the force originally meant to bomb Kjeller, now went on to attack the plants in Rjukan instead.

The extent of destruction in both Vemork and Rjukan was extensive, and 20 civilians died. But the production facility itself, which was located several floors underground and protected by reinforced concrete, came through undamaged.

The Norwegian authorities had not been pre-alerted about the bomb-attack, and strong protests were made. *Forsvarets overkommando* (Norwegian Defence Command) in London and *SOE* had just been in the middle of planning a new sabotage action. The Norwegian governmental representatives in London wanted, as much as possible, to spare Norwegian lives and industries, and bombings raids were hardly the right way to fulfil this goal.

The Germans reacted to the bombing raid by making a decision to transport its accumulated store of heavy water to Germany. When this report reached England, a decision was made at the very highest levels that this must be prevented, a decision which the Norwegian representatives in

American bombers en route towards Vemork. Photos loaned out by Norway's Home-front Museum.

England approved. Every possible approach to destroying this stockpile under transport must be utilized.

The task of carrying out this mission went to **Knut Haukelid,** who was still in Norway. For the second time he was to execute an attack against the facility. Since there was a high probability that this sabotage would claim civilian lives, prior approval was obtained from the Norwegian government. This was done in accordance with a contract between the government and SOE. When the approval was granted, **Haukelid** was ordered to sink the ferry that would transport the heavy water storage over Tinnsjøen (Tinn Lake).[62]

Engineer **Kjell Nielsen** was the man in Vemork who had informed Rjukan resident **Rolf Sorlie** that the heavy water was due to be transported to Germany. **Sorlie,** in turn, forwarded this information to **Einer Skinnarland,** who then reported it to London. Thereafter, **Haukelid** received orders to carry out a new sabotage operation. Both before and after this last operation, **Kjell Nielsen** was an extremely vital contact within the facility itself.[63]

---

62. . Archive Box NHM10B – This box contains a number of documents concerning the bombing of Vemork, and is in Norway's Home-front Museum.
63. Letter to the author from Jens-Anton Poulsson, Nov. 29, 2004. Also see: The report written by Warrant Officer Knut Haukelid concerning the sinking of the ferry "Hydro" on Tinnsjøen (Tinn Lake) at 10:15 AM on Feb. 20, 1944, and engineer Kjell Nielsen's account about the sabotage mounted against the ferry in Rjukan in February 1944, dated Nov. 9, 1983.

The Germans had planes stationed along Tinnsjøen, and they were constantly out on reconnaissance missions. The only possibility of carrying out the ordered sabotage was to sink the ferry transporting the train cars loaded with heavy water over Tinnsjøen. Very likely, Norwegian lives would be lost, and German reprisal had to be anticipated. Nevertheless, whatever the cost, the operation must be executed! The orders from London were explicit. Preventing the Germans from having access to heavy water was of great import to the outcome of the war.

Sørlie got in touch with **Knut Lier-Hansen** who arranged a car and driver for the mission. **Lier-Hansen** had earlier moved to England but had since re-entered Norway illegally and was now living in Rjukan. This history led to his becoming involved in the sabotage operation against the Tinnsjøen ferry.

At midnight, February 19, one day before the transport was scheduled to leave, **Haukelid** snuck on board the ferry. **Sørlie and Lier-Hansen** would act as **Haukelid's** support crew while he reconnoitered the target. There was no German security force on board, but a group of Norwegians had arranged to have a party below decks.

Now **Sørlie** and **Lier-Hansen** came aboard. Suddenly, the ferry's security guard was standing in front of them. The three men explained that they needed to hide and he didn't raise an alarm. He told them that

Railroad-ferry "Hydro" on Tinnsjøen (Tinn Lake). When the ferry was blown-up by Norwegian saboteurs, it apparently set an end to the production of heavy water in Norway. Photos loaned out by Norway's Home-front Museum.

the ferry had harboured illegal cargo on a number of occasions. He showed them a hatch on the deck and **Haukelid** and **Sørlie** crept down and began adapting a timed explosive charge. **Lier-Hansen** continued to talk with the guard. According to the plan, the charge should detonate when the ferry was in Tinnsjøen's deepest water. To be on the safe side, they used two alarm clocks and electrical firing-caps to ignite the explosion. The train cars containing heavy water were scheduled to drive on board Sunday, 8:00 AM.

Everything went as planned and the explosive charges detonated when the ferry was out in the middle of Tinnsjøen. The ferry with the heavy water on board sunk. In all, 14 Norwegians and 20 Germans lost their lives. This took place one year after the first successful operation had been carried out.[64] According to the *SOE's* highest commander, **Gubbins,** that organization had sent out another small unit to Skien in the event that Haukelid was unable to carry out his mission. This alternate unit later signalled that *the ball had been snapped up later on,* from this *Gubbins* was able to verify that **Haukelid's** operation was one of the most daring and

64. Footnote 62.

most effective actions to be carried out in Norway during the war. In his four page report submitted in 1944 on the sinking of the ferry, **Haukelid** writes: *I'm grateful for the confidence shown in me by having entrusted me with this mission, which I, to the best of my ability, have attempted to carry out.*[65]

---
65. Ibid., p. 13. Report written by Warrant Officer Knut Haukelid concerning the sinking of the ferry "Hydro" on Tinnsjøen (Tinn Lake) at 10:15 AM on Feb. 20, 1944. This report is letter-dated "Stockholm, Mar. 3, 1944" and is undersigned by Knut Haukelid.

Operation Freshman — The hunt for Hitlers heavy water

The picture presents a majority of the Norwegian saboteurs. The back row, starting from.the left; Hans Storhaug, Fredrik Kayser, Kasper Idland, Claus Hellberg, Birger Strømheim. Front row, again from the left: Jens-Anton Poulsson, Leif Tronstad, Joachim Rønneberg. Photo loaned out by Norway's Homefront Museum.

Chapter 16

The Germans' way of doing things

The events that took place in the *Freshman*-affair as a consequence of the Fuhrer Order[66] were not accurately mirrored in the news report that was broadcast on German radio on November 21, 1942, the day after the tragedy. Translated, this message reads as follows:

> *On the night spanning the 19th and 20th of November, two British bombers flew-in over southern Norway. Each of the planes had a glider in tow. One bomber and both gliders were forced to land. The saboteurs onboard felt compelled to enter into battle and were annihilated to the last man.*

This announcement was repeated several times, without comment, the following day, November 22, in the English newspapers, and the day after that in the Norwegian press.[67]

Its content also had little in common with the telegram **General Wilhelm Redeiss,** head of the *SS* and the German police in Norway, immediately sent to his superiors in Berlin concerning what had happened. Translated, his message reads as follows:

---

66. The British soldiers' fate should be seen against the background of the Fuhrer Order, dated Oct. 18, 1942. Hitler formulated this order, personally. Subsequently, it was then distributed to the chief commanders of a list of occupied nations by *Field Marshall, General* Wilhelm Keitel. Nicolaus von Falkenhorst, the chief commander of the German forces in Norway, was among those who received this order, and he further forwarded it to his sub-commanders at the various military installations. The order's content is given at the beginning of chapter 2. The Fuhrer Order is presented in German, p. 8ff and in an English-version translation on p. 250-255 in the *War Crimes Trials, Vol. VI, The Trial of von Falkenhorst. Edit. E.H. Stevens,* Edinburgh, 1949.
67. Radio program on the topic of Operation Freshman broadcast in 1983 by NRK Stavanger. Knut Haukelid: *Kampen om tungtvannet,* Ernst G. Mortensens Forlag A/S, 1983, p. 48.

On November 20, at approximately three o'clock in the morning, a tow-plane with a glider in tow crashed near Egersund. The cause of the crash is, as yet, unknown. As far as we have been able to determine, the entire crew onboard the tow-plane died, among them a negro. There were seventeen men onboard the glider, very likely agents. Three of them had died, six were seriously injured. All the men onboard the glider had large sums of money in Norwegian currency. Unfortunately, the Wehrmacht (regular army) executed the survivors, which makes further clarification impossible.[68]

The German patrol that came to Benkja Mountain in Helleland, did not annihilate the British soldiers to the last man. They accepted the British soldiers' capitulation, and possibly weren't aware of the Fuhrer Order. If they had been made aware of this order, perhaps they had forgotten it, or perhaps they chose not to act on it in light of the tragic situation the British found themselves in. The patrol's choice to deal with the situation in a correct manner would, in the short run, cause the *Wehrmacht* in the Slettebø camp to be drawn into a very uncomfortable and difficult situation. The acting battalion commander, **Schrottberger,** was well-aware of his responsibility as it related to the Fuhrer Order.[69] Therefore, he contacted the military command authority in Stavanger and reported that a British plane had landed in the Egersund area. Nowhere in the source material is there evidence that he felt the need of seeking the advice of his immediate superior, battalion Commander **Major Werner von Krehan,** who was on authorized absence attending an officers' meeting in Haugesund.

With the British suddenly in **Schrottberger's** custody,

Major Werner von Krehan, battalion commander in the Slettebø military camp near Egersund. German soldiers recall him as being a very stern commander, Major von Krehan died in the summer of 1989, 92 years old. Photo loaned out by the von Krehan family.

---

68. *An Feldkommandosteele*, BDS *in Oslo berichtet, 21.11.1942* (roughly: A Field-command Installation (BDS) in Oslo, Feb. 21, 1942) Also see Richard Wiggan: *Operation Freshman, The Rjukan Heavy Water Raid 1942*, William Kimber, London, 1986, p. 81.
69. Interview with Hans Neeb on June 10, 1992.

he once again got in touch with Stavanger. On both occasions he spoke with the next highest commander in the Stavanger district, **Colonel Erwin Probst.** During the last contact, he reported that the British were, beyond any doubt, saboteurs. **Probst** then gave orders to comply with the Fuhrer Order. After both telephone inquiries from **Schrottberger, Probst** informed his superior, **Major General Karl Maria von Beeren,** about the conversations. **Von Beeren** saw no reason to question the information concerning the mission of the Englishmen.

Based on a written communication sent to the *Gestapo* three days after the executions, it's apparent that the district commander in Egersund also considered the Englishmen to be saboteurs. Among other items contained in this writing is the following

> (By reason) *of the maps and diverse winter equipment, such as white overalls, skies and snowshoes that were found, there is reason to believe that the mission of the British sabotage force was to explode and destroy a building in Rjukan in Telemark. A number of other objects were also found, conceivably weapons of some unknown type, and a number of poison capsules, radio transmitters, and sub-machineguns. The aforementioned objects of unknown type, and items that can possibly be used as material evidence, have been sent to the Gestapo, Victoria Terrasse, Oslo, today.*[70]

This writing also documents that the responsible parties in the Slettebø military camp lied when they informed the battalion that the British saboteurs' mission was to poison the installation's drinking water. They possibly came up with this fabrication in order to make it easier to enlist men in the execution platoon.

The all but instant execution of the British also brought about many problems for the battalion's leadership in the Slettebø camp and for the Wehrmacht-elite in general. This can be drawn from the report that **Rediess** sent to Berlin.[71] The Nazi's interpreter (see page 50) claimed in a hearing after the war that the Gestapo had already been in the Slettebø military camp on the morning of November 20, 1942. The interrogation of the British prisoners conducted by a **Commissioner Pedersen** from Stavanger did not produce the hoped for results. The aforementioned **Pedersen** is possibly identical to the **Criminal Inspector Petersen** who was stationed

---

70. Ibid. Report from the *Ortskommandantur* (District Commander) in Egersund concerning seizure of objects from the British glider, dated Nov. 23, 1942, this document is at Norway's Home-front Museum.
71. See footnote 68.

Corporal Fritz Bornschein was present during the lunch and witnessed what occurred at Slettebø in 1942. Photo loaned out by Fritz Bornschein..

at *Sipo's* headquarters during this same period.[72]

Fritz Bornschein, who was stationed at the Slettebø military camp that very day, clearly recalls there were two individuals from the German Security Police, *SD*, who came to the camp. They interrogated and photographed the British prisoners.[73]

If the information indicating that the German police were in the Slettebø installation and interrogated the prisoners is correct, it would mean that the *Wehrmacht*, on the whole, operated in compliance with the Fuhrer Order. This didn't come out during the trial against **von Falkenhorst** where he claimed that the *Wehrmacht* in Slettebø had operated counter to the prevailing order since they hadn't handed over the British soldiers to the security police.

Which military or security authority was responsible for executing the prisoners, after they had been interrogated by the *Gestapo*, was not clearly spelled out in the Fuhrer Order.

When the security police at Victoria Terrasse in Oslo executed people, they used their own execution platoon under the command of **SS-Hauptsturmführer Oscar Hans.** This platoon was also used on isolated occasions outside of Oslo.[74]

Afterwards, the German soldiers were reluctant to talk about the executions that had taken place outside the military camp in Slettebø, possibly because it was a case of cold-blooded murder inflicted on uniformed prisoners of war. As late as the 1980s, the two former soldiers,

---

72. Interrogation hearing with the Nazi's interpreter on May 24, 1945. This document is in the Dalane Folkemuseum, Egersund.
73. Interview, Fritz Bornschein, Emden, West Germany on Sep. 9, 1986.
74. Berit Nøkleby: *Gestapo, German politics in Norway 1945-50.* p.120.

Kurt Hagedorn and **Fritz Bornschein** stated that bearing witness to the British soldiers' final fate had been a horrifying experience. The picture of this awful event had forever been burned in their minds, and something they thought must also be true for the other German soldiers who had followed the tragedy.[75]

The survivors of the glider that crashed in Fylgjesdalen spent a significantly longer time in Norwegian hands than had the survivors of the crash in Helleland. It appears as though both **von Beeren** and **von Falkenhorst** tried to take advantage of this situation. They energetically worked to prevent a repeat of what had happened in the Slettebø military camp – to, at the very least, keep the *Wehrmacht* out of the proceedings.

By ringing **Field Marshall General Keitel** at Supreme Command in Berlin and requesting a review of the Fuhrer Order in this instance, **von Falkenhorst** made an attempt to help the British in Fylgjesdalen. But **Keitel** denied **von Falkenhorst's** request.

Falkenhorst and **von Beeren** regarded the British in the glider as belonging to the air force. Therefore, they did not fall within the *Wehrmacht's* jurisdiction. The responsibility rested with the German air arm, the *Luftwaffe*. This conclusion was passed on by **von Beeren** to the German who was head of the air force in the Stavanger district, **Major General Koechy**. **Koechy** was also well-aware of the Fuhrer Order, an order that he by no means championed. According to his testimony, he therefore followed along with the *Gestapo* to Fykgjesdalen in order to witness, with his own eyes, the Norwegian police hand over the prisoners to the German police. From that moment on, it was the *Gestapo* that had the responsibility. **Koechy** heard nothing more concerning the prisoners' fate, nor did he ask any questions.[76]

Why the order *Sipo's* commander in Stavanger gave to his underlings, instructing them to shoot the prisoners, was not obeyed is hard to understand. **Wilkins** put heavy pressure on the executioners, and especially on **Dr. Seeling,** to kill the prisoners during the night. The following day, **Wilkens** reported to the *Gestapo* headquarters, Victoria Terrasse in Oslo, that the prisoners had been executed as ordered. Having then had the corpses sunk in open water several hundred meters deep shows that this act had been regarded as an atrocious misdeed that was best kept secret.

The British soldiers who got to live the longest, about two months, were those from the gilder that crashed in Fylgjesdalen. They were interrogated on a number of occasions both by the *Gestapo* and an officer from the

---

75. Footnote 8, interviews with Kurt Hagedorn, Egersund, earlier resided in Erfurt, East Germany, Dec. 17, 1985, Dec. 18, 1985.
76. *War Crimes Trials, Vol. VI, The Trial of von Falkenhorst*. Edit. E.H. Stevens, Edinburgh, 1949.

air force. According to the Fuhrer Order, they should have been shot immediately after interrogation. Instead, the order for their execution dragged on for a significant period of time, which constituted a direct contradiction of the Fuhrer Order. This delay – at least at first glance – appears even more peculiar in light of the other British prisoners having been executed with such notable dispatch and wholly in accord with the Fuhrer Order. Had this relatively long imprisonment been a Fuhrer Order-exception authorized by Berlin? – Or had the *Gestapo* in Oslo acted on its own? In either event, this long postponement indicates a desire to extract more information from the British. The first interrogations hadn't gone to the Germans' satisfaction, and these five British prisoners were only the only ones left. The British had tried, all else aside, to covertly land over 30 soldiers in German occupied territory, and the question "why" must have concerned the occupiers. When the five British soldiers were at last executed, the Germans had not become that much more informed. Because, as it happened, the five prisoners of war didn't know very much about the operation's ultimate purpose. After the executions, the five prisoners were secretly buried in Trandum. As we have learned, the British who were executed earlier came to be buried in the sand at Ognastrand, or were dumped and sunk into the sea off Kvitsøy. Regardless of when the prisoners were executed, the Germans attempted to cover all traces of what had happened to the survivors of the crashes.

Most of the Germans in the Eigersund area were stationed at the Slettebø military camp. The pictures show some of the occupying German troops in the area. Photos loaned out by the Dalane Folkemuseum.

Chapter 17

The Wehrmacht is brought to account

After the war the Norwegian and British authorities attempted to locate and bring to account the Germans responsible for the inhumane treatment inflicted on the survivors of the glider crashes in Helleland and Fylgjesdalen. This proved to be a difficult and time consuming process.

The 3rd Battalion, which had been stationed in the Slettebø military installation in November 1942, was transferred to the east front the following year. To make the assumption that this relocation was an effort to conceal the executions outside the Slettebø camp is perhaps too far a stretch. Hitler needed soldiers for the battles in the Soviet Union where losses were very heavy, and many witnesses to the tragedy in the Slettebø camp came to be killed in action. Among those to die on the eastern front were **Captain**

Operation Freshman — The hunt for Hitlers heavy water

Corporal Kurt Hagedorn witnessed the executions at Slettebø, and in 1945 he left a sworn description of it in connection with the trial of Nicolaus von Falkenhorst. Photo loaned out by Kurt Hagedorn.

Schrottberger, acting commander of the Slettebø military camp, and **Sergeant Wagner,** leader of the execution platoon, as well as several execution platoon members. The installation's highest commander, **Major Werner von Krehan,** remained a prisoner of war in Russia until the 1950s. And since he had not been acting in the capacity of chief commander of the installation on that particular day, he was never brought to task for having any responsibility for the tragedy. The British military authorities did succeed in locating seven men who had earlier served in the *3rd Battalion*. And even though these Germans had nothing more to do with the tragedy beyond having been stationed the Slettebø camp, they were nonetheless sorted from the other prisoners and regarded as war-criminals. Concept-formulations such as "collective guilt" were expressions that were weighed against them, and all seven were gradually transferred to the former concentration camp, Esterwegen. They were not released until 1947, long after the trial against their division commander, **Karl Maria von Beeren,** had been adjudicated.

The British had also succeeded in locating **Sergeant Kurt Hagedorn** – as an eyewitness to what had happened in Slettebø, the British transported him the Great Britain. There, he was put in prison and remained incarcerated until the trial against the command in Stavanger was completed in 1946.[77]

On November 20, 1942, **Colonel Probst** was the officer who had the highest responsibility for the Germans in the Stavanger district. He was deputy commander and adjutant to **Major General von Beeren,** who on that particular day had leave. **Probst** was the general's right hand, an officer and a man who, according to his superior, had earned a very good reputation. The colonel was a conscientious staff-officer and was very effective when it came to carrying out an order.

According to another description of the colonel, he was a person committed to the Prussian school of blind discipline: An order should always be followed in its every and smallest detail. When he received the

---

77. Information via letters from Hans Neeb, Hanau am Main, West Germany, on Feb. 3, 1986 and May 6, 1986.
Gescheite des Infanteriregiments 355, 1936-1945. *Eine Dokumentation, mit Auszügen aus den authetischen Verlustlisten.* Dr, Fritz Amberger, Frankfurt/M, 1973, Eigenverlag. Zum Verkauf an Buchhandlungen nicht zugelassen.

report concerning the 14 engineer soldiers, he didn't hesitate a second. He ordered that they be shot, immediately.

When the British glider crashed in the vicinity of Egersund around midnight, November 19, **Probst** was the first to be informed by the acting-commander of the Slettebø military camp, **Captain Schrottberger.** The report was based on information provided by the government administrator and was extremely brief. The patrol that had subsequently been sent out to take the British into custody was unable to report what had happened to higher command, as they didn't have the necessary radio equipment with them.

This was a source of deep irritation to the command headquarters in Oslo. It wasn't until several hours later, when the patrol had returned with the prisoners that the necessary information was provided. On behalf of **von Bereen, Probst** got in touch with the highest German authorities in Oslo, inquiring if the Fuhrer Order was still in effect and whether it should be acted on in accord with its original instructions. This was confirmed. After several hours, **Probst** was notified from Egersund that the British had been executed.

On November 20, **Probst** had twice gotten in contact with his superior, **von Beeren,** concerning the glider. The first contact occurred at 9:00 AM, to report that a Norwegian government administrator had telephoned information about a glider having landed, and that a German patrol had been sent out from the military camp in Slettebø to search for it. This information contained nothing about the glider being British, or a crash, or that there were survivors, much less British soldiers.

The second contact took place that evening. By that time **Probst** was certain, beyond any doubt, that the British men onboard the glider were saboteurs. This was made evident from recovered documents, maps, and other equipment. He also reported that he had given the commanding officer of the Slettebø military camp the order to proceed in compliance with the Fuhrer Order. **Beeren** did not question **Probst** as to whether or not prisoners had been taken, or whether or not the British survivors were still alive. What the division commander knew after this last telephone conversation was that the enemy had been on a sabotage mission, and that his deputy commander had given the order to the acting battalion commander of the Slettebø military camp to act in compliance with the Fuhrer Order. Based this knowledge and **von Bereen's** understanding of the Fuhrer Order, this meant that the prisoners were to be handed over to the security police. At a later occasion, he was to learn that **Probst** had talked with the highest placed German leadership in Oslo about the matter, but he didn't know who.

That night, **von Beeren** received a call from **Friedrich Wilkens,** head of the security police in Stavanger. Wilkens reported that another British glider had landed, and during the course of this conversation **von Beeren** got the impression that five or six British saboteurs had been executed in the Slettebø camp which deeply upset him. He became even more upset when he came to learn that the actual total was 14.

In the morning that followed the day of the murders in the Slettebø camp, **von Beeren** went through what had happened with **Probst,** where he took the occasion to bring up what he saw as a problem with what had been done. Specifically, **von Beeren** knew that **Probst** had seen the Fuhrer Order when it flowed into the Stavanger headquarters in October. The Fuhrer Order had then been further distributed to the commanders in the district, and **von Beeren** had gone on to comment and discuss the order with them. **Probst,** moreover, had been present during these discussion sessions. **General von Beeren** had impressed upon them that in the event a Fuhrer-Order situation occurred, those responsible for dealing with it should do so in soldierly and honourable manner. Captured saboteurs were not to be shot, but rather handed over to the German Security Police. He had, in fact, repeated these instructions for **Probst** over the telephone

The German's top Commander in Norway, Nicolaus von Falkenhorst, visiting the Slettebø military camp after Operation Freshman. Here, he is seen conversing with the camp's commandant, Major Werner von Krehan. Photo loaned out by the von Krehan family.

when he, for second time, had been informed by his deputy commander about what had taken place in the Slettebø camp. Consequently, **von Beeren** hadn't any misgivings prior to allowing his deputy commander to deal with the matter. Other than this conversation, there was no criticism directed towards **Probst** for the way he had handled the situation.

However, there was criticism directed towards the battalion in Eigersund, but not on the grounds of the executions. Those holding the highest positions of leadership were extremely unhappy. It was clear to them that their orders were not being satisfactorily obeyed. The glider in Eigersund had not been properly guarded during the night, and a large portion of the equipment and parts from the glider had been stolen by the Norwegians. **Von Beeren** sent a high ranking officer to the installation in Slettebø to investigate what had happened. When the officer returned to the headquarters in Stavanger, he brought with him a carton containing foreign money with a worth equivalent to 100,000 German marks. The bundle of paper currency had lain hidden in a package of medical equipment, and was turned in to the Germans by a Norwegian.

The top commander in Norway, **General von Falkenhorst,** also took no disciplinary action against **Probst**. This being the case, the responsibility for taking **Probst** to task rested on the shoulders of the division commander, **von Beeren**. To a certain extent, this had been accomplished by the reprimand he had given **Probst** in the course of their conversation about what had happened,. Given that **Probst** was a highly regarded officer and had acted in good faith, it was hardly likely that **Probst** would have been punished had **von Beeren** chosen to pursue the matter further.

Colonel Probst was formally questioned about his involvement on July 12, 1945 and gave a sworn account of what took place. But **Colonel Probst,** who appears to have played a central role in the execution of the 14 British soldiers, was never brought to trial after the war. He died of cancer before charges could be dawn against him.

Later, **von Beeren** came to admit that his deputy commander had grossly set aside standing regulations by not giving his immediate superior a complete account of the events that had taken place.

The day after the executions **von Beeren** sent a report to his immediate superior, **General Feuerstein.** A report on what had taken place was also sent to **von Falkenhorst,** but this report had not been written by **von Beeren,** personally. He did not, however, notify the German prisoner of war organization of British soldiers having been taken prisoner and then shot to death.

Simultaneous with the developments taking place at the division level, the incident involving the glider in Fylgjesdalen continued to move further ahead. Due to **Wilkens'** telephone call the previous night, **von Beeren** knew that the security police *(SP)* were already involved. Now, the *(SD)* would have responsibility for the British, a development **von Beeren** viewed as being in compliance with the Fuhrer Order. In this way, the soldiers from von Beeren's division weren't involved in what became of the survivors from the crashed glider in Fylgjesdalen.

At **von Beeren's** trial in Hamburg during the summer of 1946, the prosecutor called the fellow Norwegians **Trond Hovland,** from Helleland; farmer **Kristoffer Varden** from Sirevåg; worker **Hans Andreassen** and interpreter **Tellef G. Tellefsen** (who had been a member of the NS) as witnesses. The former division commander was freed of all charges, and thereby bears no responsibility for what had happened to the 14 executed British soldiers in the Slettebø military camp, or for the manner in which the fate of nine British soldiers from Fylgjesdaen had been decided.

Some weeks after **von Beeren** had been cleared, he testified in court against his former superior, **General Nicolaus von Falkenhorst.**[78]

Major General Karl Maria von Beeren, commander of the Wehrmacht in Rogaland, brought to trial for what had befallen the members of Operation Freshman. He was cleared by reason of the court's decision that he bore no responsibility for the executions in the Slettebø military camp. Photo loaned out by Trond Hovland..

78. *War Crimes Trials, Vol. VI, The Trial of von Falkenhorst, Formerly Generaloberst in the German Army, edited by E. H. Stevens,* Edinburgh, published 1949.
Asbjørn Barlaup: "Et system dømt till døden" (A system doomed to death) an article in Verdens Gang (Around the World), Aug. 7, 1946.

Chapter 18

The chief commander is brought to account

At the end of June 1946, the 61-year-old **Falkenhorst** was charged before a war crimes court in Braunschweig for actions he was guilty of committing in the course of his service in Norway during the war. Specifically, he was charged in connection with nine incidents of war-crime violations, among which the incident involving the nine *Freshman*-survivors was one of the most serious. **Falkenhorst** chose to witness in his own behalf under oath.

In April 1933, President Hindenburg had appointed him to the position of military attaché in Prague. At the breakout of war, he was a division commander in Pommern, and in April 1940 he was appointed to command the attack against Denmark and Norway.

That same summer he was selected to be the chief commander of the German occupying forces in Norway. He held this command through December 1944. After his service in Norway ended, he travelled to his home in Küstrin, and on May 10 he reported his present whereabouts to the allied victors. He had never been a member of the Nazi party or sympathized with its views.

As chief commander he received his orders from Supreme Command in Berlin *(OKW)*. He was the top commander in Norway, to whom all other high-ranking officers could turn. All territorial issues fell under his purview, but from a technical standpoint, it would only be under the circumstances of a probable invasion that he would have command of all three arm force branches. The air force and the navy were, in many respects and to a large degree, independent entities, with their own chain of command. And, like him, their high commanders had direct contact with the highest leadership in Berlin. The security service *(SD)* had not been delegated to serve under his command. It was a part of the German Security Police and, in common with all the police forces, it was headed by the **National Commissioner, Josef Terboven. Falkenhorst** cared neither for **Josef Terboven,** nor for the chief of the security police, and kept them both at arm's length. After the war, he came to learn that **Terboven's** organization had spied on him and sent reports to **Hitler**.

The Supreme Command in Berlin had drawn up special stipulations with regard to prisoners of war. In future cases, the army, air force and navy would take custody of enemy prisoners that came from the same branch of the military. If it was revealed that prisoners didn't belong to same force, they were to be transferred to the appropriate branch. The reason prompting this procedure was coupled to fact that every separate branch of the military had been trained in separate interrogation methods, and, in addition, each branch was particularly interested in gaining information about their counterpart branch in the enemy's forces.

General von Falkenhorst had received **Hitler's** order of October 18, 1942, and thereafter forwarded it to all his subordinate commanders. The top commanders of the air force and navy had likewise received and forwarded this order within their respective branches. As soldiers they were duty-bound to follow orders, and, since **Hitler** had been empowered by the German Parliament to make laws, they were compelled to follow them. Moreover, the order did not stand in opposition to internationally recognized law relating to how prisoners of war should be treated, because saboteurs took advantage of unusual methods in their manner of waging war, and such methods had not been taken into account in the stipulations worked out by the Geneva Convention. **Falkenhorst's** considered view was that this order must have been thoroughly discussed at a fundamental level by the Supreme Command in Berlin, from a comprehensive military, moral and international perspective. The only possibility of his not forwarding this order had been to shoot himself.

However, **von Falkenhorst** was opposed to this order because his conscience said, no. On grounds of this order he had contemplated resigning his command, but Hitler had forbidden proposals of this sort. Before **von Falkenhorst** forwarded **Hitler's** order, he attempted to tone-down the content. A sentence appearing in the order's second section, stipulating that prisoners be kept alive for purposes of interrogation – he moved to the first section. In addition, he had rewritten a formulation stating that prisoners should be shot at once, to read that they should be shot within 24 hours. The intent here was to win time. In official correspondence, instructions and directives concerning the Fuhrer Order, he was obligated to keep up a façade, but privately he was very open in the company of his generals about what he believed and thought about Hitler's order, and he impressed upon his subordinates that they were obligated to comply with the order in a noble and humanitarian manner. When **von Falkenhorst** had spoken with **Field Marshall Keitel** in Berlin about the problem, he was told that despite the Supreme Command's strong objection to this order, Hitler was not prepared to rescind it. This conversation between **von Falkenhorst** and **Keitel** occurred after the executions in Egersund, and **von Falkenhorst** tried to use this occasion to emphasize his earnest wish that what had happened at the Slettebø camp not be repeated. And, in fact, after these executions, no saboteurs were shot by the *Wehrmacht*. On the other hand, **von Falkenhorst** never personally sought to learn how it went for the prisoners of war that the *Wehrmacht* handed over to the security police. Had he done so, according to his own testimony, he would not have received an answer.

As chief commander, he could not become closely involved in every detail related to captured saboteurs. The majority of cases were handled by the various divisions. The commanders of these divisions were trained to be able to take care of this type of situation, an ability that also applied to **von Beeren.**

The commander of the Stavanger district had quite possibly already informed **von Falkenhorst** on the day after, about the British soldiers having been executed the previous evening, Since there wasn't an air force unit in Egersund, it was quite natural that the army had sent out a patrol.

Falkenhorst couldn't recall if the report he'd been sent had informed him about a certain number of saboteurs having been captured, or about them already having been executed. The events in Egersund had progressed very rapidly. In either event, he was shocked when he first heard of the executions. **Probst** had acted improperly. The 14 British soldiers should have been handed over to the security police and should not have been executed by the *Wehrmacht*. Just how the security police treated their prisoners, was not something he was aware of at that time.

As to the glider that had crashed in Fylgjesdalen, **von Falkenhorst** testified that he'd been informed about what had happened there in connection with the morning report the day after the crash. At that same time, he'd also been apprised of the wretched story in Egersund. But he had no documents or dairy that could corroborate what he said. He was forced to rely solely on his memory in his recapitulation of what had taken place almost four years earlier. He had made up his mind to prevent a repeat of what had happened to the Fylgjesdalen-survivors from occurring in Egersund. Consequently, he had instructed his chief-of-staff, **Lieutenant General Bamler,** to make arrangements to have these saboteurs brought before a military court. This, according to **von Falkenhorst,** would be an advantage to the saboteurs since they would thereby win time. Around lunchtime, **Bamler** telephoned Stavanger and learned the prisoners had already been handed over to the security police. The preceding midnight **von Beeren** had called the head of the security police in Stavanger, **Wilkens,** and told him that he was obligated to take custody of the saboteurs.

The soldiers had arrived in a glider, and therefore, it was the air force's responsibility to assist the security police in taking them prisoner. For this reason, **General Karl Koechy,** commander of the air force in Norway, was drawn into this task. Together with his soldiers and **Wilken's** men, they started off, but only to assist the security police in taking custody of the prisoners.

Another fact to consider is that with regard to the execution of the five British soldiers in Trandum at the beginning of 1943, **von Falkenhorst** had called for someone to take responsibility. The same applied to those who were murdered by *Sipo* in Stavanger in November 1942. Information derived from accessible documentation indicates that **von Falkenhorst** had, on other separate occasions, involved himself in the security police's business and succeeded in bringing about certain improvements for individuals who had been arrested. He could also have done this in the case of the British soldiers in Fylgjesdalen. Against this background, his denial of knowledge and influence over **Terboven's** men appears questionable.

After the *Freshman*-affair, **von Falkenhorst** sent out an instruction that serves to reveal his position vis-à-vis the Fuhrer Order. In this instruction, which was distributed to his subordinate commanders, he made it very explicit that when individuals who survived a sabotage action, and after having been interrogated, were to be executed, all civilians, Norwegian policemen, and all unwanted members of the *Wehrmacht* must be removed from the location.

Falkenhorst claimed that he couldn't remember having written that order, since saboteurs were not to be executed until they had first been interrogated by the security police. He reiterated that the Wehrmacht had only executed saboteurs on one occasion, namely, at the Slettebø military camp in 1942.

On several occasions after the *Freshman*-affair, many vital industries in Norway were subjected to sabotage by the allies, and during a meeting with his generals, **von Falkenhorst** had made it clear that effective safeguards must be taken in order to protect against such actions, but he had, at the same time, emphasized that the executions held in Egersund, under no circumstances, were something that was allowed to be repeated.

High-ranking officers from the air force and navy had also been invited to this meeting, as guests. Neither **National Commissioner Terboven,** nor other representatives from the security police, nor members of the Nazi party were invited. Had they asked to be present, **von Falkenhorst** would have replied, no.

On the fifth day of the trial, the court adjourned to make its decision. After four hours and ten minutes discussion, they commonly decided that **von Falkenhorst** was guilty of seven of the nine points he was charged with. All the points he was convicted of had their origin in the first point: He had forwarded Hitler's order down through the hierarchy of his command. For this, he bore the entire responsibility, and as for the rest, his involvement in the *Freshman*-affair was very serious, his revision of the text, directing that saboteurs taken prisoner were to be handed over to the *SD* for interrogation and be shot within 24 hours, closed the only creep-hole the *Wehrmacht* had been able to take advantage of to save its prisoners. As chief commander, he consequently bore entire responsibility for the events that took place in the Slettebø military camp. With respect to the murders of the remaining *Freshman*-prisoners carried out by the security police, he had failed to use his influence to try and prevent these executions.

After the court's verdict was made public, it met for a further 55 minutes before reaching a determination regarding the sentence to be carried out: **General von Falkenhorst** was sentenced to death by firing squad. When **von Falkenhorst** had the sentence read before him, he became, according to a Norwegian journalist who was in the courtroom, stone-still, only standing and staring straight ahead, as though he didn't understand what had been said. The guard was forced to pull on his suit jacket in order to make him aware it was time to go. With the same frozen stare but with his head held high and quick, short steps, he left the courtroom followed by two military policemen.

The sentence was later reduced to 20 years imprisonment. He was released in 1953 and died in 1968.

The court had placed the guilt on the *Wehrmacht's* highest commander. Given the background that **von Falkenberg's** guilt was based on his having forwarded Hitler's order to his subordinate commanders, these officers were thereby perceived as having been handcuffed by the Fuhrer Order. The same perception applied to the remaining lower levels in the power apparatus, all the way down to those who had obeyed the order "*Hoch – legt an Feuer frei*" (Ready! – Aim! – Fire!) and pulled the trigger.

The security police in Stavanger had refused to shoot the prisoners, and the same organization in Oslo held the five *Freshman*-prisoners imprisoned for over two months. From a formal standpoint, the *Gestapo* in Oslo had neither followed **Hitler's** order specifying that saboteurs were to be executed immediately after interrogation, nor had they complied with **von Falkenhorst's** revision specifying that saboteurs were to be shot within 24 hours after interrogation.

After **von Falkenberg** had been released in 1953 on the grounds of declining health, **Arne Bang-Andersen,** chief of the police station in Sola, tried to get in contact with the former German chief commander in Norway in order to talk about the *Freshman*-affair, but **Bang-Andersen** was given the cold-shoulder. **Falkenhorst** made it clear that the entire episode had brought about such severe consequences to his own person that he wasn't willing to talk about it.[79]

---

79. *War Crimes Trials, The Trial of von Falkenhorst, Formerly Generaloberst in the German Army,* Edited by E. H. Stevens, Edinburgh, published 1949
Interview with Arne Bang-Andersen, Stvanger, on Dec 23, !985. *Verdans Gang,* Aug. 8, 1946.

Operation Freshman ▲ ▼ ▲ The hunt for Hitlers heavy water

Chapter 19

The security police are brought to account

Heinrich Himmler was the supreme commander of all German police forces. The security police, with the undercover and investigation organ the *Gestapo*, and the security service were organized as separate sections within the *(SS) Schutstaffel* (Protective Squadron) organization. During the war the German police in all the occupied nations were organized in the same way as the police in Germany, and all these police forces, both within and outside Germany, were under the command of a head office in Berlin, *Reichssicherheitshauptamt* (the Reich Central Security Office – *RSHA*),

The *SS* also contained other sections, such as: Hitler's body guards, elitist military *SS*-units and its own "death-head" units which handled the administration and security of the concentration camps. *SS*-members were required to be racially pure Arians.

The *SS* was a power apparatus that Hitler and his men had built up parallel with building Germany's military strength and the NSDAP (the National Socialist German Workers' Party). The police within the *SS* were given broad powers. Their primary mission was to crush all opposition, and in that pursuit they could therefore arrest people without an arrest warrant and keep them incarcerated for however long they wished.

The organization within the security service and the security police that drew the most attention from people was the *Gestapo*, and it was also the *Gestapo* that came to represent Nazi Germany's ruthlessness and brutality in their minds. Entities from both the security police and security service were commonly referred to as *"gestapista"* by the Norwegians. As the national commissioner in Norway, Josef Terboven was the top commander of all the police forces in the country. Among the *SS*-officers serving in the hierarchy under his command we can point to **SS-Brigadeführer Wilhelm Rediess** and **SS-Standartenführer Heinrich Fehlis**.

The German police in the Stavanger district had, as already noted, an office on Eiganesveien (Eigane's Road). For a lengthy period of time, **SS-Obersturmbannführer Friedrich Wilkens** was head of that office.

Neither the highest police officials in Germany, nor those in Norway, were made to stand trial for what had happened in connection with the *Freshman*-affair. As it happened, all these men pre-empted he wheels of justice by committing suicide. Nor could **SS-Obersturmbannführer Wilkens** in Stavanger be brought to justice. He was killed in action by a Norwegian resistance force at Lutsivatnet (Lutsi Lake) in Sandes, in April 1945. One of people who had played a part in the executions in **Stavanger, Commissioner Petersen,** was arrested, but succeeded in hanging himself to death in his prison cell in Oslo before appearing before a court. **Arnold Hölscher** shot himself at a collection/processing center in Arendal where his real identity had been discovered. He had attempted to slip through among the regular army soldiers from the *Wehrmacht* who were waiting to be shipped out via Mandal to Germany.

Fritz Seeling, Erich Hoffman and **Fritz Feuerlein** were located, arrested and placed before a court in December 1945. The war-crimes court sentenced **Seeling** and **Hoffman** to death for their loathsome deeds against the four British soldiers. **Feuerlein** was sentenced to life-time imprisonment for his participation in the same crime. The two death-sentenced Germans sought pardons, but were rejected. **Seeling** was killed by a firing squad at Fort Akershus on the morning of January 10, 1946. **Hoffman** was transported to Germany where he was hung on the afternoon of May 15 of the same year. Precisely what became of **Feuerlein**, we can't say: After sentencing, he was handed over to the Russians where he was tried for the assault and murder of Russian prisoners of war.

After the war, the corpses of the five executed engineer soldiers from Fylgjesdalen were found in grave number 9 in Trandum. It was apparent that they had been blindfolded and bound, hand and foot. In the journals of the Medical-Legal Institute in Oslo is a detailed description of the clothes they wore at the time of their execution, along with the objects they had in their pockets.

Fehlis was the person most responsible for their murder. It was he who had signed the order to **SS-Hauptsturmführer Oskar Hans** directing their execution. **Fehlis,** as previously noted, succeeded in avoiding a court's determination of his misdeeds.

In the summer of 1946, charges were brought against **Oskar Hans** for the murder of prisoners. He stood accused of having executed people without due legal process. This turned out to be a difficult charge to prove, but he was nevertheless sentenced to death by the Eidsavating Lagmannsrett (Low court). This sentence was set aside by the Høyesrett (High court) on the grounds that the court's reasoning was unclear and contradictory.

Subsequently, **Oskar Hans** was handed to the British and was brought before the British war-crimes court in Germany. Here, the charges specified against him concerned the execution of the five engineer soldiers from *Operation Freshman* and one British agent in February 1943. In August 1948, he was sentenced to die by hanging, but this punishment was reduced to 15 years imprisonment. Nine of the 13 soldiers that had made up **Oskar Hans'** execution platoon in February 1943 were given 14 years imprisonment, while the rest were sentenced to death.

Hans Behnke, who acted as interpreter for **Oscar Hans'** *Sonderkommando,* was arrested but the charges were dropped. **SS-Hauptsturmführer Wilhelm Esser** was charged with use of excessive force in connection with his work for the security police and the security service (*BdS*) at Victoria Terrasse in Oslo, but it proved hard to establish that he was directly responsible for his subordinates having used excessive force. He was also head of the sections that handled issues relating to prisoners of war and sabotage. We have already seen an example of this responsibility in his interrogations of the five prisoners of war from the *Freshman*-affair who had survived the crash in Fylgjesdalen. **Esser** was sentenced to eight years imprisonment.[80]

---

80. Witness testimony of Fritz Seeling on Aug. 8, 1945, and of Fritz Feuerlein on July 6, 1945 and Aug. 16, 1945.
War Crimes Trials, The Trial of von Falkenhorst, Formerly Generaloberst in the German Army, edit. E. H. Stevens, Edinburgh, published 1949
Report PWIS/w, Consolidated Report on the Interrogation of two Prisoners (Oscar Hans, Wilhelm Esser), Akershus Prison, June 27, 1945. Execution of British Soldiers (A teletype message was sent to RSHA asking for instructions. A reply was received saying that the men were to be treated according to the Fuhrer Order)
Jostein Berglyd: The chapter, Hitler's SS, in Berglyd's book *Egerundere og dalbuer i kamp,* p. 333-338; Berit Nøkleby: Josef Terboven, *Hitlers mann I Norge,* (Hitler's man in Norway) Guldendal, 1992, and *Gestapo, Tysk politi I Norge* (German politics in Norway) 1940-1945, Aschehoug, 2003.
Tore Pryser: *Hitlers hemmelige agenter, Tysk etterreting I Norge 1939-1945,* (Hitler's secret agents, German executions in Norway) Universitets forlaget, 2001.

Operation Freshman — The hunt for Hitlers heavy water

Several Norwegian Nazis, who had been arrested after Norway's liberation, had the job of digging up the corpses of the English soldiers whom the Germans had attempted to remove all traces of. Due to the movement of sand, the dead bodies lay several meters deep by the time they were dug up in the early summer of 1945. Photo: Jørgen Tengesdal/Dalane Folkemuseum.

Chapter 20

Persuing Freshman

During the days when Norway's freedom was being restored, **Arne Bang-Andersen** worked as head of the police station in Sola, which once again fell under the Rogaland police district's jurisdiction. In May 1945, it therefore became his responsibility to meet the allied forces that landed at the airfield in Sola. Because of his position, he was invited on several occasions to dine at the British officers' mess, and in this way gained firsthand knowledge of the issues and questions that especially interested the British officers.

The first allied military units that came to Rolaland after the war belonged to the *1st Airborne Division*. The British immediately began to investigate what had happened with regard to *Freshman*. This suited **Bang-Andersen** perfectly since he was quite familiar with the crash in Fylgjesdalen. It had been his colleagues, **Legal-Police Officer Knut Leirvåg** and **Police Officer Tollef Ravn Tollefsen,** who had represented Rogaland's police district at the time these allied soldiers had been taken into custody. **Bang-Andersen** recounted these facts to a British investigator that he'd come to have a chat with.

The Brit represented the *Allied War Crimes Investigation*, the allied authority responsible for investigating possible war crime violations. The Brit thought that this information was interesting and, together with **Bang-Andersen** and an officer, they travelled out to Fylgjesdalen and visited the actual locations. There, they found people with relevant information, as well as the graves and parts and objects from the glider.

Over the summer, additional people from the War Crimes Commission arrived at Fylgjesdalen, and the tragedy was revealed. In time, the spore led to Fort Akerhus in Oslo, where several Germans were interrogated in connection with the *Freshman*-affair. **Bang-Andersen** was present at those sessions.

By that point in time, the Fuhrer Order was well-known, and **Bang-Andersen** asserted that if **von Falkenhorst** had acted as **General Erwin**

Rommel had done when he received Hitler's order, the *Freshman*-tragedy could have been avoided. It was said that Rommel, in the company of his staff, had torn apart the order saying: *So etwas macht man mit einer solchen Schweinerei* (This is what a man does with such filth).

The sorting-out of the *Freshman*-tragedy in Eigersund began during the first days following the war's end, but here progress appeared more accidental than planned – and this, despite the fact that as early as January 1943, both the British and Norwegian authorities had been informed, via the resistance cells in the area, about what had taken place. Alf Aakre had arrived from Great Britain to carry out his first illegal mission. During one of his many nightly journeys, he chanced to meet the chauffeur, **Lars Ramsland,** who told him about the two planes that had crashed. **Ramsland** had learned what had happened from **Trond Hovland,** the son of the government administrator in Helleland. Aakre believed both men to be loyal Norwegians, so he judged the information to be reliable.

The full story, however, came to be revealed by dint of an entirely separate and unofficial British initiative. The men onboard a British frigate, which happened to be tied up at a pier in Stavanger the day after the German capitulation in May, took part in the celebrations. The captain of the frigate was **Lieutenant Anthony Agutter,** nicknamed **Tony.** He was best friends with the father of one of the dead victims of the crash on Hæstad Mountain in Helleland, **Air Force Captain Arthur Edwin**

The unburied bodies lie ready to be transported to the Slettebø installation for autopsy. Photo: Jørgen Tengesdal/Dalane Folkemuseum.

Thomas. During the ship's stay in Stavanger, some of Tony's friends directed his attention to an article in a Norwegian newspaper: The article dealt with a British plane which had crash during the war in the Eigersund area. A colored man had been found among the deceased, a detail Tony found interesting. He recalled that a man from Sierra Leone had been the rear-gunner on the plane flown by Arthur Thomas. The plane's crew had nicknamed the colored man, *Snowball.* The article was published in the *Dalane Tidende,* Egersunds local paper.

Thereafter, Tony immediately travelled to Egersund, and from there to Helleland. Once there, he met several people who told him about the crashed plane. And one of them, **Martin Selmer Sandstøl,** even showed him photos that he'd removed from the dead pilot's pockets before the Germans showed up. In one of the photos **Tony** recognized Thomas's wife. **Tony** informed the **Thomas** family, and shortly thereafter, the widow and two close relatives travelled to Helleland. On arrival home, they informed the **de Gency Sewell** family who had also had a son among the deceased on Hæstad Mountain.

The family **de Gency Sewell** took it upon themselves to notify the remaining crew members' relatives. This was a time-consuming and complicated task since they had no address record of the remaining dead. Consequently, the family was forced to write to the *RAF* seeking help, and then wait for an answer. Letters addressed to Sierra Leone and Canada took a long time because they were shipped by boat, rather than by air. In due course, however, they finally received answering letters and photographs of the deceased.[81]

At the same time that this initiative had brought Helleland into the limelight, other pieces of the puzzle surrounding what had actually happened to the participants of *Operation Freshman* began to fall into place. During the latter half May, an officer from the *First Airborne Divisional Engineers* showed up in Kongsberg where, purely by chance, he met **Arne Kjelstrup,** the second-in-command with Grouse. **Kjelstrup** reported that on the night of November 20,1942, the four agents in the reconnaissance unit, who had been waiting for *Freshman* to arrive, heard the engine noise of a plane. In all probability, it was the plane with the leader of the flying operation aboard, Colonel Cooper. The plane was almost directly above their heads, when it suddenly disappeared towards the west. They were thoroughly convinced that a glider would be landing at any moment, but it never happened. A cloudbank put a stop to it. Other than this, Kjelstrup wasn't definitively certain as to what had happened to Freshman,

---

81. Interview, Arne Bang-Andersen, Stavanger, Dec. 23, 1985. Interview, Alf Aakre, July 23. 1986. Letter from Robin de Gency Sewell, Aston Upthorpe, England, Mar. 23, 2004, and mail from Robin Thomas, London, May 13, 2004.

except that he had heard that one of the gliders had crashed somewhere on Sørvestland.

The next, and most vital lead came from a British engineer soldier, who in the summer of 1945 travelled by train from Stavanger to Kristainsand. At the station in Sira he fell into a conversation with a railway worker who spoke about a glider that had crash-landed in Helleland in 1942 with 17 people onboard. Two men died from the crash, one became seriously injured. The engineer soldier later forwarded this information on to his superior in Stavanger, and soon the tragedy began to be revealed.[82]

A British investigative commission under the leadership of the British **Major Shrank Rawlings** arrived at Eigersund, Brusand and Ogna to carryout a crime-scene investigation. At the two last-named places, Kristoffer Varen, a land owner, joined the investigative team – not just because of his knowledge of the area, but also because he had witnessed the burial of the 17 dead soldiers from the glider in Helleland. Varden indicated the area of the gravesite, and several Norwegian Nazis who had been arrested began digging it up. It would take several days before the bodies, which lay pressed down in a sand grave, were finally found. The area had changed – more Nazis were added to the work crew. After days went by without a dead body having been found, one of the Nazis shouted: *The only thing buried here is a rumor!* After two weeks of digging, however, the grave where the 17 soldiers from the crash on Benkja Mountain lay buried was found. Due to the accumulated movement of sand, the dead bodies were now buried several meters below the surface.

"Have you found the rumor now?" questioned one of the guards. But the traitors, when it came down it, kept silent. The corpses were transported to the Slettebø camp to be autopsied.[83] The picture of what had happened to the *Freshman*-participants began to clear.

---

82. *Operation Freshman, An account of the raid by the 1st Airborne Div, Engineers on the Heavy water plant in Norway, By Q.M.S.D.F. Cooper, R.E.* In an interview with Jens-Anton Poulsson at his home in Kongsberg on Aug. 25, 2004, he informed me that it was Kjelstrup whom the British officers met in Kongsberg during the days after the war's end in 1945.
83. *Dalane Tidende,* June 27, 1945 and June 29, 1945.
Stavanger Aftenblad, July 16, 1945.
Interviews with Jørgen Tengesdal, Egersund, Kristoffer Varden, Sirevåg, summer of 1986.

Chapter 21

The Funerals

Early in the summer of 1945, the remains of the dead from the sand filled graves in Ogna were identified. They were re-interred in Eigane's burial park in Stavanger at the end of July 1945. Representatives from the British and Norwegian military authorities, the civil administration and the police were present.

Formal mourning began in the crematorium. The 17 caskets were draped with English flags and adorned with flowers, Church organist **Sagen** played Chopin's funeral march, and the English **Army-Chaplain, J. O. Jenkins,** held a short funeral service. The soldiers bore their dead comrades to their graves, and an honor guard was posted along the route. At the gravesite, **Army-Chaplain Jenkins** led the ceremony. A section of the honor guard fired-off a farewell salute before the soldiers were marched away. *Now, they are at last at rest in sanctified soil, those who the Germans had cast into a mass grave in Jæren.* Thus concluded the local paper in Egersund its report of the ceremony.[84]

In May 1945, a British military commission, under the leadership of **Captain Glynn Jones,** visited the government administrators' offices in Høle and Forsand. Accompanying them was a work force made up of German prisoners of war. The Germans were to dig up the corpses of the British soldiers buried in Fylgjesdalen, and then carry them down to Lysefjorden (the Lyse Fjord) on stretchers.

Lief Espedal represented the government administrator's office during this assignment, and, for all practical purposes, took charge of the stretcher-detail. When the Germans had carried the bodies down as far as Sagbackken, they balked at going down any further towards the fjord because the terrain was too steep. **Espedal** and **Trygve Fylgjesdalen** took it upon themselves to carry the dead bodies to Bakkånå. From there the remains were transported by boat to Stavanger, and the dead were laid to rest in Eigane's burial park at the same site as their comrades from Egersund.

---

84. *Dalane Tidende*, July , 1945.

Operation Freshman ⁓ ⁓ ⁓ The hunt for Hitlers heavy water

After the war, the remains of the executed British in Trandum were given a final resting place at the British Commonwealth's church cemetery in Vestre Gravlund in Oslo. There, they were buried alongside 97 other soldiers. On Hitler's express order, and counter to human rights, these men had been executed by the Germans. The dead bodies, as previously described, were found in a mass grave in Trandum.[85]

The seven dead bodies from the tow-plane at Hæstad Mountain, on the other hand, were buried in the churchyard in Helleland. All their closest relatives wished to see the deceased airmen buried there. They had been murdered in Helleland, and the memory of their loved ones had been mourned in the deepest, most genuine manner by the people from the area – something the surviving relatives were certain that the residents of Helleland would continue to do in the future. The *RAF* met with the decision of the relatives, and Helleland County and the *Commonwealth War Graves Commission* took on responsibility for the graves.[87]

The remains on the Hæstad moors were dug up, and once again, it was the local residents who undertook this task. It turned out the Germans had hammered together four boxes without lids in which to lay the dead bodies. **Tillert** and **Sigvart Helleren,** each man having volunteered himself, his horse and a sled, transported the corpses to the roadway. **Ola Kvinen** then drove the boxes down to the church by car, where **Erling Omdal** and **Sigurd Svalestad** laid the dead bodies in seven caskets.[88]

In Eigane's burial park in Stavanger lie the remains of the 14 executed engineer soldiers and the three victims of the crash at Benkja Mountain, together with the eight who died from the glider that crashed in Fylgjesdalen. Photo: Ingrid Worning Berglyd.

---

85. Interview with Leif Espedal at his home in Sola, Nov. 19, 2002. Visit in Vestre Gravlund, Oslo, Jan. 27, 2005.
86. Letter from the Forensic MedicalInstitute, Oslo, Director: Professor Dr. Jon Lundevall, March 3. 1982.
87. Letter from Robin de Gency Sewell, Aston Upthorpe, England, Mar. 23, 2004. Mail from Robin Thomas, London, May 13, 2004.
88. interview with Martin Selmer Sandstøl, Helleland, July 4, 1986.

At the burial on November 21, 1945, the church was fully seated. Norwegian soldiers stood honor-guard alongside the seven caskets. The priest, **Johan Uhl,** held the funeral eulogy, first in Norwegian, followed by a somewhat shorter version in English for the representatives from the British air force who were present. Uhl read from the Book of John, 14th chapter, verses 1 and 2, and among other points covered in his speech he said the following:

The bravery and self-sacrifice of these our friends will long shine as a glorious beacon in our history. Their graves, which will now join with all the other graves out here in this churchyard, will remind us of the debt we owe to our allies, and not least, to the British people who we Norwegians have always felt so closely related to.

The Norwegian soldiers also stood honor guard when the caskets were carried to the graves. Several wreaths were set beside them and the county board chairman, **Retsius Polden,** attested that the residents of Helleland considered it an honor to care for the graves of these men killed in the course of war. An English officer, air force **Lieutenant J. L. N. Canham,** thanked one and all for the fine ceremony. It would be a comfort to the relatives to know that their beloved had at last been buried in a respectful manner. He wished to give an especial thanks to those who had helped transport the dead soldiers down from the mountain to their last resting place.[89]

On the 1st of September of the following year, a memorial service was held in the church in Helleland. A number of relatives to the deceased British were present. After the church service, a formal ceremony in honor

The memorial stone by the British graves in Eigane's burial park in Stavanger, where 25 soldiers from the Freshman-tragedy lie buried. Photo: Ingrid Worning Berglyd..

IN MEMORY OF
THIRTY ROYAL ENGINEERS OF THE 1ST BRITISH AIRBORNE DIVISION
TWO GLIDER PILOTS OF THE ARMY AIR CORPS
AND
TWO PILOTS OF THE ROYAL AUSTRALIAN AIR FORCE
THE OCCUPANTS OF TWO GLIDERS WHICH CRASHED AT HELLELAND AND FYLGJESDALEN
ON 20 NOVEMBER 1942 WHILST ENGAGED ON A GALLANT MISSION AGAINST
THE GERMAN ATOMIC BOMB RESEARCH INSTALLATION AT RJUKAN

FOR DET ER DET STORE OG DET ER DET GLUPA AT MERKET DET STEND UM MANNEN HAN STUPA

---

89. *Dalane Tidende,* Nov. 23, 1945. Excerpt taken from Priest John Uhl's speech. A copy of the speech is with the Dalane Folkemuseum.

Norwegian soldiers carry the caskets of the deceased from the tow-plane to their graves. Photo: Jørgen Tengesdal.

of the seven British soldiers was held beside the graves. **Polden** spoke, emphasizing once again that Helleland considered it a great honor to care for the graves of their dead allied friends.

Two of the surviving relatives, **Joan Thomas** (widow) and **Robin Sewell** (brother), thanked the local people for looking after the grave sites. They would never forget the moments of remembrance shared in the church and out by the graves, [90] words that would come to have an especially poignant meaning in 1993. In that year, Joan Thomas died, and in accord with her express wishes, the urn containing her ashes was buried in the churchyard in Helleland. The grave lay right beside that of her first husband.[91]

The fate that befell the soldiers that made up operation *Freshman* has left a deep impression on the people of Norway, and most especially in Rogaland. The memory of this tragedy lives on among its residents, which has come to be expressed in various ways. These, we'll come to describe in the next chapter.

---

90. *Dalane Tidende*, Sept. 4, 1946.
91. Gravestone with an inscription in Helleland's churchyard.

The Funerals

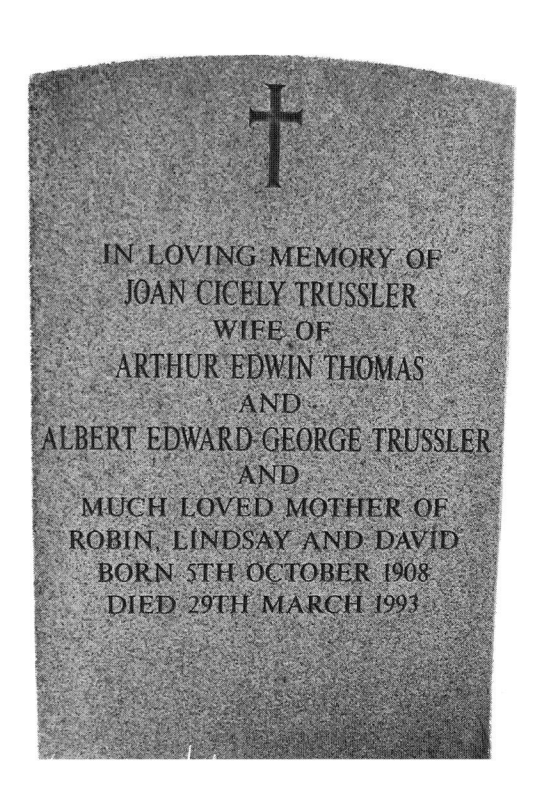

IN LOVING MEMORY OF
JOAN CICELY TRUSSLER
WIFE OF
ARTHUR EDWIN THOMAS
AND
ALBERT EDWARD GEORGE TRUSSLER
AND
MUCH LOVED MOTHER OF
ROBIN, LINDSAY AND DAVID
BORN 5TH OCTOBER 1908
DIED 29TH MARCH 1993

In 1993, the surviving widow of Flight-Lieutenant A, E. Thomas died. An urn containing her ashes was buried in Helleland's churchyard beside the grave of her first husband. Photo: Ingrid Worning Berglyd.

The British Commonwealth's burial plot at Vestre Gravlund in Oslo. Photo: Jostein Berglyd.

Operation Freshman ▲ ▼ ▲ The hunt for Hitlers heavy water

After the war, the seven airmen who crashed and died at Jønsokknuden in the Hæstad Mountain area were buried in the churchyard in Helleland.

Chapter 22

Memorial markers

The raising of several memorial markers over the post-war decades has ensured that the memory of the soldiers from the *Freshman*-tragedy who were executed in Egersund will last for many decades to come.

The first memorial plaque (outside of Slettebø)

The first memorial plaque was unveiled outside of Slettebø in 1957. The Egersund and Dalane Defence Association (*Egersund og Dalane orsvarsforening*) was the initiator. A large cross-section of people from both the lightly populated countryside, as well as the more populous urban areas, were present at the ceremony. The president of the Egersund and Dalane Defence Assn., **Reinhard Andersen,** explained how the idea of a memorial marker was born. Then the general secretary of the Norwegian Defence Association, **Major General Reichman,** said a few words and unveiled the memorial plaque. The British air attaché in

In 1957, the Egersund and Dalane Defence Association organized the first formal ceremony for the victims of the Freshman tragedy in Helleland and in Eigersund. At which time, the first memorial plaque was unveiled. Photo loaned out by the Dalane folkemuseum.

145

Norway, *Wing-Commander* **Morrisson,** expressed appreciation for the beautiful ceremony that had been held in honor of his dead countrymen, and placed a wreath by the plaque. Two additional wreaths were also placed by the memorial, one donated by the Norway Defence Association, and yet another from *kompani Linge* (Linge Company). The parish priest, **Guttorn Kallhovd,** closed with a short devotion. After the ceremony, many people laid a bouquet by the memorial plaque.[92]

Memorial stone (Helleland's churchyard)

Thirty years would go by before the unveiling of the next memorial marker. On November 20, 1987, a memorial stone was set to rest in Helleland's churchyard over the seven British soldiers whose lost their lives near Hæstad Mountain. The memorial stone came to be there at the initiative of **Hedly B. Duckworth,** the British aircraft mechanic who was scheduled to be onboard the first tow-plane – the one that had made it back to Great Britain. He also unveiled the memorial. **Duckworth** wanted to do something to ensure that the memory of the participants in the operation would not be forgotten. After the unveiling, the memorial stone was handed over to the Eigersund County Board Chairman, **Jostein Sirevåg,** who expressed his thanks on behalf of Eigersund County. The parish council's president, **Norden Øen,** promised to take good care of the memorial (the parish council is a church organization and its representatives are elected by the parish members). Both Norwegian and foreign authorities, as well

From the ceremony in 1987 – the memorial stone can be glimpsed behind the wreath of flowers. Photo loaned out by Rogaland's fylkeskommune.

---

92. *Dalane Tidende,* Nov. 18, 1957.

as representatives from the British and Canadian embassies attended the ceremonies. A large number of local residents were also present.[93]

The second memorial plaque (outside Slettebø)

On April 9, 1990, 50 years to the day after the German assault in 1940, a memorial plaque, set directly under first plaque from1957, was unveiled in Slettebø. On this plaque stood the name, rank, and military unit of all the soldiers who had been aboard the glider that had crashed on Benkja Mountain. By the addition of their names, the men who had so tragically met their fate in Eigersund became more visible. Approximately 100 people from the area were present for these moments of remembrance.

> *May we and our descendents look after and preserve the freedom that others have given their lives for. Let us in the future make certain that we shall not have need of more memorial plaques,*

So said the Eigersund County Council's vice-chairman, **Olaf Aurdal**, when he unveiled the memorial plaque.[94]

The second memorial plaque outside Slettebø was unveiled in 1990. Now the names of all the dead were engraved on the memorial. Photo: Ove Bowitz.

---

93. *Regarding my involvement in Operation Freshman*, an account by Hedly B. Duckworth, May 5, 1945
94. *Dalane Tidende*, Apr. 4, 1990, and Apr. 11, 1990.

Ceremonies

At the 1995 celebration of Norway's liberation, ceremonies were arranged both by the graves in Helleland's churchyard where lay the men who had died in the tow-plane crash during the *Freshman*-operation, and by the Burma Road outside Slettebø where the 14 British soldiers had been executed. The Brit, **Hedly B. Duckworth** from the Orkney Islands, was present at both ceremonies. Representatives from NATO's headquarters in Jåttåknuten were also present at both ceremonies.[95]

The photo shows British and Canadian soldiers with Lieutenant Colonel Pat Parson of the Royal Marines at the head. In 1998, they came from NATO's headquarters to Jåttåknuten in Stavanger, to the churchyard in Helleand, and to Slettebø in order to honor the soldiers from Operation Freshman who were executed in the vicinity of Eigersund. Photo: Olaf Aurdal.

95. *Dalane Tidende*, May 10, 1995.

Memorial markers (Benkja Mountain)

A memorial marker has also been erected at the site where the glider crashed at Benkja Mountain. The initiative for this memorial was furnished by two men from Australia who worked in Stavanger, **Neil Stagg** and **Philip Rubie.** They had both been in Eigane's burial park in Stavanger where two of their countrymen lie buried. **Stagg** and **Rubie** looked into the story behind *Operation Freshman* and decided that their countrymen should be honored with a memorial marker at the site of the plane crash. This memorial marker consists of a plaque attached to a large stone-mound. Eigersund County erected the mound, laid out a parking area, set up an information board in Hovland and marked out the route to the cash site. The memorial marker was unveiled on August 28, 1999. The ceremony included a fly-over by circa 1943 planes.

Approximately 100 people participated in the ceremony. Most of them were from the Australian colony in Stavanger, a few from NATO's installation at Jåttåknuten, along with people from the area. The Australian air attaché stationed in London, **Steven Drury,** the consul of the Australian Embassy in Sweden, **Ann-Grethe Noreide,** and the Eigersund County Board Chairman, **Marit Myklebust** were also notably present.

The two pilots of the glider that crashed in at Benkja Mountain, **Norman Davies** (28) and **Herbert Fraser** (29), who died on landing, were both Australians. In 1997, **Stagg** succeeded in finding out that both pilots came from Melbourne. Working through the war-veteran's club in Melbourne, he then succeeded in locating **Fraser's** window, **Elva Fraser.**

At the initiative of two Australians and Eigersund's County a memorial plaque was unveiled fastened to a stone mound up on Benkja Mountain in 1999

Operation Freshman ◆ ◡ ◆ The hunt for Hitlers heavy water

Ranking officers from NATO's headquarters on Jåttåknuten near Benkla Mountain, year 2000. Lieutenant General Torsten Skiaker is in the middle. Photo: Jostein Berglyd.

In 1942, she had received a telegram from the authorities, reading: *Missing and presumed dead.*

When she read the telegram, she didn't want to believe it was true, and over the years immediately following, she believed that her husband's whereabouts would be found. It wasn't until February 1946 that the young **Mrs, Fraser** finally received confirmation that her husband was dead, even if she had only gotten the briefest of summaries about what had happened. Several years later, she was able to derive some comfort on learning that the city of Stavanger was taking good care of her husband's grave. At the time he gave his life in the plane crash in Helleland, he had become the father of an infant dotter, **Jean,** only seven months earlier. After the war, the widow **Fraser** helped other families who had lost their nearest and dearest in action. This helped her contend with her own sorrow.

Stagg put an announcement in one of the Melbourne newspapers. Through this, he was able to locate the **Davies** family. It turned out that **Davies** had a brother, **John,** who was still alive. He was able to inform **Stagg** that their father, **Bert,** had visited Eigane's burial park in Stavanger in 1960. As a WW I veteran, it seemed as though the father had managed to get through what had happened, but his wife, **Sophie,** never got over her son's death. John had a letter his brother **Norman** had written to their father on October 26, 1942, just before *Operation Freshman* was launched. Among other things, Norman wrote;

> *This will be my last letter for a while, because next month I've got a lot to do on account of a special job. It's a shame that I can't tell you something about it. Don't let anyone else know. Don't say anything about this letter to anyone. I don't want Mama to worry herself over it. The sooner I'm given the mission, the better.*

Bert Davies was never to hear again from his eldest son. Exactly five years later, he received a letter from the Australian government confirming his son's death.

A month after the unveiling of the memorial plaque, **Rubie** was home in Australia on a visit, where he told the *Herald Sun* newspaper:

> *Last week's ceremony was fantastic – a dignified ceremony, honoring two brave Australian men.*[96]

Memorial marker (Eigersund's burial park)

A memorial marker was also erected outside of Eigersund.

In 1985, **Princess Astrid** unveiled a memorial marker in Eigane's burial park for the four British soldiers who were tortured to death by the *Gestapo* and then sunken into the depths of the sea. British war-veterans were present, together with Norwegian friends, to honor their fallen comrades. Among the war-veterans present was **Hedly B. Duckworth.** The men providing the initiative for the raising of the memorial stone were **Per Johnson** from Randaberg, and the Brits, **Peter B. N. Yeates** and **Eric Ward Mills.** At the very bottom of the memorial stone, it reads: FOR YOUR TOMORROW – WE GAVE OUR TODAY. These four British men also came to be remembered at Brookwool Memorial in England.[97]

Memorial marker (Lysebotn)

In connection with 1995's commemoration of liberation, Forsand's County raised a memorial to the crew of the glider that crashed in Fylgjesdalen, where eight men died on crashing – Four were tortured to death by the

---

96. *Dalane Tidende,* Aug. 25, 1999 and Aug. 8, 1999
Stavanger Aftenblad, Aug, 28, 1998
Aussie Post, Jan. 1, 1998
Sunday Herald Sun, Sept. 5, 1999.
97. Footnote 94, first section.
Telephone interview with Per Johnsen, Aug. 8, 2003. Information regarding *Brookwool Memorial* is located on a memorial plaque in the British Commonwealth churchyard, Vestre Gravlund, in Oslo.

Operation Freshman — The hunt for Hitlers heavy water

In 1985, Princess Astrid unveiled a memorial marker in Eigane's burial park in Stavanger for the four British soldiers who were tortured to death by the Gestapo and cast into the depths of the sea. Photo: Ingrid Worning Berglyd.

Gestapo in Stavanger, and five were shot to death in Trandum. The memorial plaque is located on the pier in Lysebotn.

> Eit engelsk glidefly på veg til Rjukan styrta i
> Fylgjesdalen natt til 20. november 1942.
>
> 8 av soldatane døydde her og dei 9 andre blei tatt
> til fange. Seinare blei dei avretta av tyskarane.
>
> James Frank Blackburn   Trevor Louis Masters
> Frank Bonner   David Alexander Methven
> James Dobson Cairncross Robert Norman
> Peter Doig   George Simkins
> Peter Paul Farrell   Eric John Smith
> Frederick Healey   Malcolm Frederick Strathdee
> John Glen Vernon Hunter John Wilfred Walsh
> Wallis Mahlon Jackson   Thomas William White
> William Jacques
>
> Minneplata blei reist av Forsand kommune ved
> 50 års markeringa for verdskrigens slutt i 1995.

The memorial plaque located on the pier in Lysebotn for the 17 soldiers in Freshman who were aboard the glider that crashed in Fylgjesdalen. The plaque was installed by Forsand's County in connection with the 1995 celebration of liberation.

Memorial marker (Skitten airfield)

In 1986, **Hedly B. Duckworth** gave out a book titled *Airfields in Scotland*. A passage in the book deals with the former airfield, Skitten. At the end of this narrative, the author expressed his wish to see a memorial marker put up on the location so that people would remember that it was from here that *Operation Freshman* had been launched. This inspired **Duckworth** to start getting things in motion. A memorial marker at the former airfield would now tie together the circle of memorial markers in Norway. He had a memorial marker designed, and sent it around to people in the area who would be involved with its being established. In doing so, he brought *The Royal British Legion*, Wick Branch, Scotland, county authorities, and the current owner of the land where the airfield once stood, **Ben Mackay,** into the picture. **Mackay** made a free grant of a portion of the former airfield's area where the memorial marker would be placed.

Duckworth's initiative sparked the enthusiasm of more and more people, and soon it became possible to begin plans for a larger memorial marker – not only for *Freshman*, but for all the soldiers who had lifted-off from the airfield at Skitten on their way towards the continent, never to come back. All costs reckoned in, it became very expensive and several years would go by before the necessary funding was taken in. The Norwegian ambassador was asked if any assistance could be given from their quarter, and on July 25, 1991, the ambassador had the following request sent to a large number of addresses:

> Enclosed, we are forwarding a request from George R. MacDonald, secretary of *The Royal British Legion* in Scotland, concerning plans to raise a memorial marker to the unsuccessful British sabotage effort against the heavy-water plant facility in November of 1942. The memorial will be unveiled on a day appropriate to commemorating the 50th anniversary of this operation, conditioned on the collection of sufficient funding. *I personally request that you earmark a sum to this project, for example, 1,000 – 2,000 crowns, and that you send the money directly to George R MacDonald.*
>
> H. Støvern (signature) Major/Asst. Defence Attaché

On September 5, 1992, the memorial marker to the fallen participants in *Operation Freshman* was unveiled at the site of the former Skitten airfield. On the memorial plaque, there stand these words, among others:

We Will Remember Them

The honor of unveiling the memorial went to the president of *The British Scottish Legion*, after having held a speech where he discussed the war's historical framework, followed by a detailed background account of the complications surrounding *Freshman*. The ceremony was lead by a parish priest who was assisted by another priest. The Salvation Army's local brass band played, and a number of wreaths were laid. A plane from the *RAF* ended the commemoration by flying an honor-circle over the memorial marker.

Near relatives to the honored dead, war-veterans, official representatives from the military authorities, and many others had assembled. Rogaland was represented at the unveiling, and at the subsequent memorial activities that followed, by people from the provincial council and Eigersund County. The provincial council's director, **Fredrik Wendt,** spoke and presented the provincial council's official account of *Operation Freshman* as a gift, an account that was written by the undersigned.

Remembrance Day

Every year, on the second Sunday of November, the British hold their Remembrance Day. On this day, the soldiers who died in *Operation Freshman* – in common with all the British citizens who died as a result of the war – are honored in a special ceremony.

Freshman and the memorial marker in Bellfield Park (Inverness)

When **Prince Philip,** in July of 2000, unveiled a memorial plaque on the memorial marker established by *The Aircrew Association* in Bellfield Park in Inverness, *Operation Freshman* was once again brought into focus. The airbase which was used by the members of *Operation Freshman* was found among the 32 bases that had been engraved on the plaque. The people who were in charge of organizing the ceremony in Bellfield Park on that July day lacked information about *Freshman*. They began to address this problem, and when they had digested sufficient material about it to know what had happened, they wanted to do something that would help to ensure that the story of this tragic event was not forgotten. This wish led to their organizing, together with the *British Legion* in Wick, a special ceremony, on November 20, 2002, at the *Freshman*-memorial marker standing on the former airfield at Skitten. In March 2004, T*he Aircrew Association* was able to notify the *British Legion* that a larger plaque, with the names of all the participants who had lost their lives in *Operation Freshman*, had now been affixed to the memorial marker.

Chauffeur Ray Burfitt has reached a noteworthy age. And though he didn't participate in the operation itself, he had functioned as chauffeur for the engineer soldiers when they were training in the mountain areas of Wales. **Mike Green and chauffeur Syd Brittain** were a part of *Freshman*, but due to their having incurred injuries during training, they never got to participate in the mission, something that in all probability saved their lives. *Green is still* alive, but **Brittain** passed away in the fall of 2004.

Another engineer soldier who took part in the training, **Bert Price,** was sent home after only ten days by reason of his father's death. This former engineer soldier is still alive. After learning the fate of the operation, his mother was to say, *It took a life to save a life.*[98]

---

98. *A Dunnett More Video (D.M.V.),* 1993. This is a three-hour-long recording of the unveiling ceremony at Skitten, outside Wick, Scotland. The film also contains several interviews, among them, Hedly B. Duckworth.
Letter from Don Owens, Apr. 30, 2004, secretary of *The Aircrew Association, Highland Branch*: Member's newsletter, *The Aircrew Association,* July 2000, Nov. 2002, May 2003, and Mar. 2004. Mail from Peter Yeates, Bristol, England, Jan. 25, 2005.

Operation Freshman ▲ ▼ ▲ The hunt for Hitlers heavy water

On September 5, 1992 a memorial marker was unveiled at the site of the former Skitten airfield in Scotland for the participants who died in connection with Operation Freshman. Priests A. Roy and R. S. Frizzel read from the Bible before and after the unveiling. Photo loaned out by Rogaland's provincial council.

Chapter 23

Hunting for the past

The Germans who came to the crash-sites of the planes involved in *Operation Freshman,* immediately began to collect weapons, equipment, and anything else strewn around the nearby terrain that might be of worth. This didn't stop the Norwegians who arrived at the site from successfully laying claim to a sizable amount of valuable objects and materials: Weapons, clothes, boots, money and gold disappeared in Norwegian pockets. As a result, significant *"Freshman*-collections" are, even today, still being held in private hands. During the post-wars years, both British and Norwegian museums have tried to gain possession of these stolen objects.

In the summer of 1981, a group of amateur British divers began searching for possible remnants and equipment from the glider that crashed at Benkja Mountain in Hellelnd in 1942. They searched in Gåsetjørn and in a small dam near the crash-site. There, they found remnants of light-wood boarding, which they surmised came from crates containing equipment from the glider. They concluded that perhaps this find concerned things that the survivors could have hidden in the water in order to prevent the Germans from taking them. They held off making a more detailed investigation in the expectation that experts would look into the whole situation, especially as they were afraid that explosive material might be found among the presumed objects.

The discovery of the scraps of boarding, plus information furnished by people in the area who had lived through the Freshman-tragedy, led to the launching of *Operation Gåsetjørn* in the summer of 1982. The decision to launch this operation should be viewed against the background of the fact that the *Royal Engineers* in England were already at work trying to put together an exhibition about heavy water in their museum in Chatham. A reconstruction of the *Freshman*-operation was said to be a vital part of this exhibition, which was envisioned as covering all aspects of the allied response to the heavy water alarm.

The British air attaché in Norway, who wanted to get a hold of the most interesting material possible, was drawn into the work involved in locating *Freshman* finds by following up tips and traces at both Benkja Mountain and at Fylgjesdalen.[99] He, along with other British authorities participating in this work, used an air force captain, **Per Johnsen** from Randaberg, as his contact man. The reason for engaging **Captain Per Johnsen** in this capacity was as follows:

In 1982, a British officer, **Lieutenant Colonel G. R. Owens,** applied for permission from the defence department to travel to Norway with a seven-man group of frogmen under the leadership of a lieutenant. The group would search in Gåsetjørn and in a nearby body of water for objects from the glider crash at Benkja Mountain in Helleland. The objects they recovered would then be transported to England to be presented in an exhibition about heavy water.

In response to an inquiry by the British, **Knut M. Haugland,** then the director of the Norwegian Home-front Museum, recommended that the British use **Captain Per Johnsen** as their contact man and helping hand for the duration of the work.[100] This advice was taken and, over the spring and summer of 1982, **Johnsen** was fully occupied with the job of locating and collecting relevant objects, especially in the Eigersund area.

By making use of the local paper, he received information which led to his coming upon equipment from the crash, such as: jackets, headwear, boots, leather jackets and radio receivers. But he was thoroughly convinced there were several other objects that could be of interest to the museum. He particularly mentioned a silk scarf with a panorama of the Rjukan area as a motif. He also believed that snowshoes and sundry parts of the glider itself were in private hands, specifically: The snowshoes that the engineer soldiers were to have used on their trek to the facility in Vemork, and parts of the glider's wooden construction, along with canvas. These were the sort of objects that he was quite certain private citizens would have taken before the Germans destroyed what remained of the plane.

The settlement of legal and regulatory matters, which were required before the diving for possible remnants of the plane and equipment in Gåsetjørn and in the nearby small dam could begin, were cleared up with the landowner, the police and the Defence Museum. The work commenced somewhat later than planned, but on Monday, the morning of September 13, 1982, the diving began. Necessary equipment was flown up to Benkja Mountain by helicopter. The heaviest item of equipment was a compressor to blow away the silt from the bottom of Gåsetjørn. The actual diving commenced on Monday afternoon and was completed on Thursday evening.

99. *Dalane Tidende,* Mar. 22, 1982 and Sept. 20, 1982.
100. Letter from Norway's Home-front Museum to Per Johnsen, dated Aug 19, 1982.

The seven frogmen did a thorough job. They laid out archeological, 4X4 meter squares on the bottom, and searched to a further depth of three meters, but without positive results. After four days diving, these professional frogmen were able to definitively state that neither remnants of the plane nor any relevant equipment were in Gåsetjørn or the small dam. All parties had to accept that the sought-after radio equipment, maps and weapons were gone for good.

The only remaining possibility was to make a new appeal to the local residents to turn in possible objects from the crash to the British. Several objects turned up as a result. Most of them came from a particular man in the Eigersund area, who during the course of years had collected so many parts and detailed items of equipment from the plane crashes at Helleland and Fylgjesdalen that he set up a little *Freshman*-museum.[101]

The museum in Chatham was also interested the objects and equipment from the glider that had crashed in Fygjesdalen, and an appeal was made both in the local newspapers and on radio. Johnsen could further add that the police chiefs of both Stavanger and Sandes had promised that anyone handing over firearms from the *Freshman*-operation to the museum's collection would avoid being penalized.

Johnsen's conviction that this issue was extremely important can be drawn from the special – though unfortunately fruitless – appeal he made to a person he knew had taken possession of a *Sten MKII sub-machinegun* from the glider that had crashed in Fylgjesdalen. He specifically pointed out how important it was and pleaded with the person in question to turn in the weapon to the museum run by the *Royal Engineers* in Chatham, England. By thus allowing this weapon to be included in the exhibit, he would be honoring the memory of the many soldiers who had died in connection with *Operation Freshman*.

At the same time, he reported that Hjørdis Espedal, who was one of the first to arrive at the crash site, had given the museum a Jew's harp. She had gotten this instrument from one the most seriously injured soldiers, who had wanted to show how grateful he was for the care and kindness she had given him. For as long as she lived, she would never forget how the British soldier, despite his pitiful condition, had tried to play some uplifting tones on his Jew's harp. Obviously, the affection she felt for this instrument was of great value to her, but she nonetheless considered that the right place for the Jew's harp was in the museum in Chatham, so that in this way it could be preserved for future generations,

The next British thrust to get a hold of equipment and objects connected to the Freshman-operation could be read in *Scotland on Sunday*. In an article appearing in its Aug, 8, 2004 edition, the magazine reports on

---

101. Authenticity certificate re objects, dated 1982.

a race that had gotten underway to save a crashed British glider. It had lain as wreckage in the mountains of Norway since the beginning of the Second World War – a forgotten memorial to the men who had died on one of the most vital and daring missions of the war: The objective of this mission was to put a stop to Hitler's atom bomb program.

The article's author thus described the essential facts of Operation Freshman, which the wreckage stemmed from, and at the same time posed that it had just been discovered only a month earlier after several years of searching. The exact location of the glider's crash had been kept a carefully guarded secret with the intent of hindering souvenir-hunters from showing up and plundering the wreck. But in point of fact, the whereabouts of the crash site had been known for 62 years! He went on to write that a certain **Peter Doig** had been aboard the glider, which would indicate that this wreckage must be the same glider as the one that had crashed in Fylgjesdalen, around midnight November 19, 1942. Because, as it happened, **Doig** was one of the pilots in that glider. In the Scottish magazine it was emphasized that a group of experts from the *RAF* were now struggling their way towards the crash site in order to gather in as many parts from the wreckage as possible before the souvenir-hunters arrived.

In the article, written by a **Yakub Qureshi**, one could also read that *Group-Captain* **(Colonel) David (Davie) Patton,** who was stationed at NATO's headquarters in Bodø, would be co-ordinating and leading the expedition which was on its way to the crash site to collect parts of the glider. A Norwegian, with good knowledge of the area, would guide the expedition to the exact location. The team would be making use of metal detectors to find material buried in the earth. They expected to discover metal parts and plates from the plane's landing gear section and cockpit. The parts recovered from the wreckage would then be flown from Stavanger to the *Assault-Glider Museum* at Shawbury in Shropshire, where they would be presented in a permanent exhibit. Wreckage parts of this sort, coming from a plane crash, were objects of cultural interest and value that were rightly at home in a museum in Great Britain. The work now waiting to be done was being undertaken, first and foremost, to honor those who had given their lives while attempting to carry out a desperate sabotage action.[102]

Rogaland's largest newspaper, *Stavanger Aftenblad*, became interested in the British effort to find possible aircraft parts. In the summer of 2004, the paper reported on the story in four large fold-out articles, contributed by three journalists. They had read the article in *Scotland on Sunday* and had also been in contact with **Patton**.

---

102. *Race to save lost glider of Telemark, Yakub Qureshi, article in Scotland on Sunday*, Aug. 8, 2004.

Thanks to the newspaper articles, the British got good publicity, and local residents who could contribute with information and objects from the crashed plane were brought into the picture. In a rather lengthy telephone conversation with **Patton** criticism was tendered with reference to the erroneous representations. The impression that remained after this conversation was that the result, despite all, was good. It was vital to draw the public's attention to this issue. The expedition had also been promised support from the Air force Museum and the Defence Museum. In addition, **Patton** had been in contact with the County Board's chairman in Forsand and the government administrators in Strand and Forsand to inform them about his plans.

The military experts were, moreover, followed by a film team consisting of two people from the *British Forces Broadcasting Service.* The film team was to do a news feature, and perhaps a documentary film, as well, about the expedition.

The expedition also had an added goal, namely, to bring attention in Great Britain to all the actions made against the plant facility in Vemork.

The highest ranking Brit to take part in **David (Davie) Patton's** expedition was **Colonel Martin Halsall.** Glider expert **Major Gary Wann** and Air Force **Captain Brian Hagan** also took part.

On Monday, the 6th of September, 2004, the expedition was assembled in Fylgjesdalen and began searching for parts from the wreckage. Combining the number of parts they had recovered themselves, and the fragments and objects they had gotten from the local-area residents, approximately 300 finds were registered, which they were very pleased with. Experts at the *Assault-Glider Museum* in England had already begun work on a full-scale model of a Second World War glider before the expedition had even started. To its great satisfaction and joy, they could now use some of the original parts from crashed plane in Fylgjesdalen.[103].

---

103. Articles in *Stavanger Aftenblad,* Aug. 26, 2004, Sept. 6, 2004, Sept. 10, 2004 and Oct. 23, 2004. Telephone conversation and interview with David (Davie) Patton, Aug. 24, 2004.

Operation Freshman – The hunt for Hitlers heavy water

Chapter 24

What the British knew

Around midnight, November 19, 1942, the British snapped up a transmission from the radio operator in the second tow-plane. He inquired about a course home. At that time, the plane was between 100-150 miles (160-240 km) east of Wick in Scotland. The plane didn't turn back, nor had the radio operator given any information about what had happened with the glider.

The first tow-plane had not been able to locate the site where the glider should be released, due to a fault in its special equipment (the *Rebecca*), and because of ice build-up that forced it down into a compact cover of clouds. In this situation, the tow-plane released the glider, which immediately became non-maneuverable and crashed. The tow-plane itself was able to return to the base in Scotland and the crew recounted the route they had flown.[104]

On November 20, the British received a message from *Grouse* reporting that the weather at the landing area had become worse at about 1900 hours (7:00 PM) the previous day. The wind had picked up and the sky became partially covered by low-lying clouds. The British, however, held fast to the timetable. On the ground at the landing site, the *Eureka* picked up the plane, and the men waiting there heard the rumble of a plane at 8:40 PM. An hour later, they again heard engine noise.[105]

On November 21, the British learned about a German communication asserting that two British bombers (the tow-planes), each one towing a glider, had come in over southwest Norway. According to this report a tow-plane and both gliders were forced to land. Those on board hadn't perished in the crash – all had fallen in battle.[106]

---
104. DEFE 224, p. 131, *piloting Error* (map sketch)
105. Ibid., p.14, p.131, point 3.
106. Ibid., p.134.

On December 5, the British received a report about *Operation Freshman* from its military attaché in Stockholm. The report wasn't completely thorough, but from what could be gleaned from it, two British tow-planes, each towing a glider, were forced to land on Norwegian soil because of bad weather. According to rumor, one of the tow-planes crashed against a mountain and was totally demolished. Everyone aboard died. Six men in the glider perished in the crash. The remainder were shot by the Germans. The second glider had landed up among the mountains above Flørli. Eight of the men onboard had died and nine were taken prisoner.[107]

The following day – December 6 – the British received a report from the Norwegian military attaché in Stockholm that two British gliders had landed in Rogaland on November 20, 1942. The soldiers in one of the gliders had come into contact with the government administrator, who, in turn, had informed the Germans.

All the British soldiers, with the exception of five men, had been shot to death. The still surviving five soldiers had been transported to a hospital in Egersund. The information source didn't know what had happened with the soldiers from the other glider, but according to rumor, they had also been shot to death. The information that the Norwegian attaché had passed on to the British had been furnished by, among other sources, **Major P. W: Lordahl** from the *7th Infantry Regiment*.[108]

On December 12, the British received a report via radio from one of its field agents in southwest Norway regarding a glider that had crashed near the church in Helleland. Five men had survived; two had died and several had been injured. The prisoners had been interrogated for two hours. All had stated that Rjukan was the sabotage mission's objective, and all had been executed by firing squad. The British regarded this agent as eminently reliable. He had contact with the local residents and could therefore access reliable information.[109]

On January 16, 1943, headquarters received intelligence concerning the *Freshman*-affair from an information source who had just recently arrived from Norway. The British referred to him as their *SOE*-agent with the *Sipo* in Stavanger, and further, as an interpreter. This information source recounted that he had occasion one day to follow along with a certain

---

107. ibid., p.15.
108. Ibid.
In the sections about Kristainstad and Setesdal in the series *Krigen i Norge* 1940 (The War in Norway), given out by The War's History section in the beginning of the 1950s, there is noted a battalion commander, Major P.W. Loerdahl who belonged to IR 7.
109. Ibid, p. 15-16.

Steer on car trip to an unfamiliar destination. This **Steer** was undoubtedly **Herbert Stehr, Criminal Secretary** with the *Gestapo,* section IV, Oslo. (see page 85.)

This "unfamiliar" destination proved to be the prison on Lagårdsveien (Lagårds Road) in Stavanger. Together with **Steer,** he was taken to the British prisoners who were incarcerated there. The source's task was to act as interpreter. This took place on the Tuesday or Wednesday immediately following the crash.

Four of the prisoners sat in a large cell, while the five others, who were severely injured, sat in a small cell. Among the injured was a Lance-Corporal who had broken both legs. In addition his jaw had been crushed and he was unable to eat. One of the prisoners was lame from the hip down. Aside from the care the prisoners received from the Norwegian doctor after the crash, they had been given no medical attention whatsoever.

The least injured prisoner had removed his uniform and was dressed in blue civilian clothes, while the rest wore uniforms without any insignia. The sanitary conditions were deplorable and it was quite apparent that the prisoners hadn't received any medical assistance. *Sipo* had confiscated all their personal effects and whatever other items they had with them. These items were shown to the information source and he was asked if he knew what they were used for, and how they worked, but he had no idea. *Sipo* told him that a map with a blue circle drawn around Rjukan had been found. The British were saboteurs and were to be shot. Namely, they had worn civilian clothes under their uniforms and had planned to flee to Sweden dressed as civilians.

The four men who were in the best shape were, one by one, subsequently interrogated by **Steer** and the information source. They gave their name, rank, serial number, birthplace, and their parents' nationality and address, but declined to answer any other questions. They were determined not to set their solidarity at risk.

Later, the information source learned that one, or several, of the soldiers had been tortured and then "volunteered" that they belonged to a unit in an airborne force that was to blow-up a facility in Vemork and then escape to Sweden in civilian clothes (*black undergarments*). This was told to him by **Siefried Fehmer,** who was later to head the *Gestapo* in Oslo. This can also indicate that the information source had some sort of connection to the *Gestapo* unit in Oslo

Based on all the details such methods had elicited, the information source had gotten the impression that the *Gestapo* knew the whole background of the *Freshman*-operation. They knew that the glider had been released at an altitude of 11,000 or 12,000 feet. The glider-pilot had immediately lost control over the plane which went into a spin and crashed. At an altitude of 2,000 feet, the pilot had shouted *Ditching Stations,* an expression used when a glider was about to land in water. It was very cold – cloudy with virtually no visibility. The glider didn't crash into the sea or into some other body of water, but in a mountain area. The men who had best survived the crash tried to help the injured but there wasn't much they could do, and so they decided to wait until it became light. Then some of them made their way down to a nearby farm and asked for help. One of the men they talked to walked to a house that had a telephone, and from there he rang for medical help. When the Norwegian doctor arrived, he warned them about *Sipo*. But the British soldiers who were in the best condition didn't want to leave their injured comrades. All the survivors were eventually transported to Stavanger. Among those who died instantly, or shortly after the crash, were the glider's two pilots, a lieutenant and a sergeant. In addition, there was another glider that had been shot down near Egersund. According to the information source, everyone in this glider had died, and the glider had come loose from the tow-plane.[110]

On February 23 1943, the head of *Combined Operations*, **Louis Mountbattan,** wrote to the *Chiefs of Staff Committee* that the British Intelligence Service had come to learn there existed a German order, drafted at the highest level, directing that all saboteurs within German-occupied areas were to be shot, no matter whether they were dressed in uniforms, or not. The intelligence service had gotten this information from the British military attaché in Stockholm. The military attaché had also reported that 17 survivors from the *Freshman*-tragedy had been executed by a firing squad in accordance with this order. The prime minister had requested that he be kept closely informed of this situation. But before **Mountbattan** complied with this, he wanted to know the committee's assessment. He held that it would be extremely difficult for him to plan raids in the future knowing that those taken captive or surrendering would be executed by the enemy.

---

110. Ibid., p. 162-165, p.172, point 3.

> Tuesday, 23rd February 1943
>
> Freshman
>
> To: The Secretary,
> Chiefs of Staff Committee,
>
> The Director of Military Intelligence has forwarded to me the attached letter from the Military Attaché, Stockholm, concerning the shooting of 17 British soldiers (which is understood to include some airmen) who forced landed in Norway during the abortive attempt to carry out Operation Freshman.
> It will be noted that there is a report graded B.2 that the German Military authorities have received orders from high authority that all persons landing from aircraft to carry out sabotage are to be shot out of hand irrespective of whether they are in uniform or not.
> This is a matter on which the Prime Minister asked me to keep him in touch, but before doing so I should like the Chiefs of Staffs' directions as to the action which they advise should be taken.
> I feel I shall be placed in a very difficult position if I continue to plan raids which may end in the execution of the men who take part, should they be captured or surrender.
>
> (signed) Louis Mountbatten
> Chief of Combined Operations

As early as February 11, **Mountbattan** had specified that all participants in the *Freshman*-operation were to wear uniforms (combat dress), and, in fact, had the sabotage succeeded, it would have been carried out by uniformed troops. The 160 kilometer (100 miles) escape to Sweden, however, was to have been accomplished in civilian clothes. It had been carefully pointed out in the operation order to the airborne troops that as soon as they shed their uniforms, they could no longer carry a weapon any sort. It was possible that the survivors had decided to attempt fleeing and had therefore taken off their uniforms after the glider had crashed.

On March 1, the committee addressed the communication from **Mountbattan.** Their decision was that this issue should be determined at government level. The *Foreign Office* and *Service Departments* should discuss the judicial aspects with respect to the Germans' alleged actions in the *Freshman*-affair. *The Chiefs of Staff should make this suggestion to their respective Ministers.*

A draft of the memorandum, which the committee formulated that same day, maintained that saboteurs should be clad in regular uniforms until the time their mission had been carried out. Under their uniforms the soldiers should wear civilian clothes (black underwear). Possibly, a personal weapon could be retained for self-defence. Otherwise, the committee was agreed that armed troops carrying out sabotage behind enemy lines, in accord with prevailing international law, should be handled a prisoners of war if taken captive by the enemy. Consequently, the Germans had no legally grounded justification for executing the soldiers from the *Freshman*-operation. In the case of soldiers who appeared in civilian clothes their position was not as self-evident. But even here, there still lacked legal justification for shooting them, not even after a judicial proceeding – not unless what they were engaged in could be proven. In the case of *Freshman*, there is no information that indicates the soldiers had changed to civilian clothes after the crash and in so-doing facilitate their proceeding to the target to carry out the sabotage. If such proof had been presented, then the situation for those who had worn civilian clothes would have appeared quite different. But the soldiers who had been taken prisoner had not been in civilian attire. They had surrendered and had been resigned to being taken prisoner.

In addition, the committee discussed other possible situations that participants in operations behind enemy lines could find themselves in. In summary, in the case of the *Freshman*-affair, there was nothing to justify the execution of the survivors. The Germans had violated the internationally recognized rules of war.[111]

On April 6, the British received a report from their agent **Alf Aakre** concerning the *Freshman*-tragedy in Egersund. The British regarded **Aakre** as very trustworthy, even though in this particular instance the information in question was not first hand. **Aakre** had gotten the information from **chauffeur Lars Ramsland**, who had talked with the government administrator in Helleland. The plane had crashed during a snowstorm, and the survivors had told the government administrator that they came from England and that their objective had been Rjukan. Their intention was to capitulate to the Germans.

The British soldiers had been badly knocked about and needed help. At their request, the government administrator rang up the Germans and reported that a plane had crashed, The *Arbeidstjenesten*, which was located in Helleland, was asked to act as a guard force until German soldiers could take custody of the British. The agent emphasized that the government administrator wasn't a Nazi.

---

111. Ibid., p. 166-169, 177-178.

The British soldiers were transported to Slettebø near Egersund. They were placed along the road between Slettebø and Tengsareid (the Burma road), and according to rumor, five of them were shot to death. The corpses were driven to Ogna and buried in the sand. The following day, the newspapers in Stavanger published articles reporting that British soldiers had landed in a glider, and subsequently been killed in action fighting against German soldiers. The government administrator's son had confided to **chauffeur Lars Ramsland** that just why the British had been executed was incomprehensible – all of them were wearing uniforms. There was also rumor about a glider having landed in the Stavanger area.[112]

In a commentary from headquarters, the *Air Marshall* pointed out that the flight-operation had been carried out under very difficult circumstances. Under such conditions, he should have set in his veto and halted the operation, but for the fact that the operation was vitally important. The effort couldn't be delayed, even though the planning had held forth for only short period of time. The *38th Wing* only had access to planes of the *Whitley* model, which couldn't handle the job of towing *Horsa*-gliders over the long trip from Scotland to Norway. Therefore, it was necessary to employ heavy bombers (*Halifax*). The three bombers they had at last succeeded in laying their hands on needed improvement on an extensive number of points. These the *38th Wing*, by exercising enormous strain, had succeeded in accomplishing with regard to two of the planes. But the plots were insufficiently educated and trained in carrying out this sort of operation. The British had now learned that, in the future, similar operations will require the best possible planes available and suitably well-trained crews. ***Group-Captain* Cooper** received high recognition for his having organized the expedition despite the difficult circumstances and for the fact of his having himself actually participated in the operation. Moreover, he had also succeeded in bringing the tow-plane back to the airbase unscathed.[113]

---

112. Ibid., p. 170.
113. *DEFE, 221, p. 5-6.*

Operation Freshman — The hunt for Hitlers heavy water

Chapter 25

Operation Freshman – an evaluation

How could the British win the war? This question became especially important for them in 1942. The British had long been aware that German scientists were working on atomic research, but in this year they received information that indicated the Germans would be able to produce an atom bomb. The British perception was that whoever was the first to succeed in producing an atom bomb would win the war. The British strove to contribute to a favourable outcome to this problem by sending its scientists and equipment to the USA, which had the best resources, and therefore, the greatest chance to win the race. On August 6, 1945 – the day the first bomb was released over Hiroshima – the British received ample confirmation they their assessment had been sound.

The British were also aware that the Germans had increased the production of heavy water in Vemork in 1942, and that the Germans were dependent on this substance, if they were going to produce an atom bomb. A decision was made to attempt destroying the plant facility in Vemork by means of a sabotage operation. After the British had been unsuccessful with their *Freshman*-operation, and likewise the Americans with their bombing, the mission was successfully executed by Norwegian saboteurs. Based on what we know today, it's doubtful that the operation had any significant impact on the outcome of the war. We now know that the Germans had shelved their plans to produce an atom bomb in 1942, since they had deemed that carrying out such a project would take too long. At the time, however, the British had no knowledge of this. For them, this was an extremely manifest and vital race that must be won at any price.

The training of the engineer soldiers selected to carry out *Operation Freshman* went off as planned without encountering any great obstacles along the way. The security/secrecy aspect of the operation also appears to have been satisfactorily seen to. When the planes lifted from the airfield at Skitten, the Germans had not been forewarned about the operation that had just been launched, and most of the men making up the sabotage force didn't know, for that matter, what the actual objective of their mission was.

The glider-pilots and other aircrew members had not undergone the same hard physical training as the engineer soldiers in preparation for the mission. And therefore, they weren't in the same top-shape as the soldiers. This was especially unfortunate for the glider-pilots who, contingent on a successful landing, for the most part would be facing the same demanding challenges as the saboteurs. The pilots of the tow-planes, on the other hand, had a very reasonable chance of making it home again after the gliders had been released over the landing areas.

Both the pilots of the gliders and the aircrews in the tow-planes understood better than the others the risky nature and possible consequences of undertaking the flight transport part of the operation. The *RAF* had no previous experience in using *Halifax*-bombers as tow-planes, and neither the tow-plane nor glider pilots had previously taken part in this sort of long range flight mission. Moreover, it was hard to foresee what the aircraft would encounter when flying over German occupied Norwegian territory. The Germans had already begun to build a comprehensive system of gun installations and defence fortifications in 1940 along the coastal southern area of Rogaland – and beginning in 1942, they had access to a large radar unit in Jæren. It was 16 meters high and a very prominent structure in the area. The radar's main purpose was to pick up oncoming enemy aircraft a long distance from the coast. A number of smaller radar installations were located over the area. The large radar installation was protected by nine anti-aircraft guns – and in an underground bunker east of the massive radar tower, the Germans had a liaison-station with direct communication to the air force. Would the British planes having been picked up on German radar or caught in the glare of German search lights, be subjected to anti-aircraft fire?. If the plane was forced to land, Norway's mountains and hilly landscape offered anything but ideal landing conditions.

Another complication was that the possibility of forecasting the weather, especially for a substantial period of time, was very limited. There was an overhanging risk that sudden icing, snow squalls, or heavy cloud cover would make the towing-phase impossible. In addition, the British hadn't acted on the warnings strongly recommended by the Norwegian meteorologist and, in hindsight, were forced to admit his prognosis was accurate.

With respect to the weather, the tow-flight over the North Sea went by without a problem for both flying units. The worst problem turned out be that the *Rebecca* in the first of the two tow-planes ceased to function as they neared the Norwegian coastline. Consequently, the chances of their locating the landing zone would be highly problematic. Nevertheless, this first tandem flying unit succeeded in reaching the immediate area of the landing zone, but a rapid weather change for the worst made it too dangerous to release the glider. According to *Grouse,* the communication between them functioned in one direction, but not in both. In any event, the glider was not released, even though the pilot kept the plane in the area and also flew in a large circle in the direction of Larvik, before setting course for returning home. Given the circumstances of the situation, this was understandable. The pilot couldn't continue to fly around blindly in the middle of clouds, hoping to catch a glimpse of the landing area, indefinitely. He had neither the time nor the fuel.

The problems encountered by this first flying unit developed into a tragedy as it reached the southwest coast of Norway on its way back. Just then, they were hit with sudden icing and snow squalls, weather phenomena that can possibly explain why the tow-line broke. But the message *Glider released at sea* would appear to indicate that it was the tow-plane itself that had uncoupled the glider. The tow-plane's fuel was beginning to run low, and the chances of making it back to Scotland were better if there was no glider in tow. In the stressful and excited situation that prevailed, the telegraph operator might well have formulated the message carelessly as it was being sent. In either event, the glider was separated and wound up flying towards the most hilly terrain imaginable rather than into the sea. Under these extreme circumstances, the pilot still attempted a successful landing. We know how it ended.

The second tandem-unit came in over Norway near Egersund. How far inland it succeeded n coming, is not known, but the plane must have circled around for a rather long time in heavy cloudbanks, accompanied by ice and snow. It was almost midnight when the tow-plane and glider crashed in what was then Helleland County. The glider crashed into Benkja Mountain, while the tow-plane touched ground and crashed in the Hæstad mountain area. In order to slip under the cloud cover the pilots flew low over the areas they landed in Helleland – too low an altitude, combined with poor visibility, led to catastrophe for both aircraft

With regard to the airborne landing of the saboteurs, the final choice came down to using parachutes or gliders. The glider was chosen and *Freshman* thereby became the first glider mission the British carried out during the war. Gliders could land without wheels and, if necessary, they could also negotiate frozen ground without incurring great damage. They could land both saboteurs and whatever equipment was called for at the same place, and relatively close to the targeted objective so that the attack force could reach Vemork and carryout the sabotage mission on the very same night they landed. In other words, it was thus realistic to pre-suppose that the glider would not be discovered by the Germans before the sabotage action had been completed. If the saboteurs came to be in need of skies or fold-up bicycles, there was room on the gliders to accommodate such equipment. An airborne landing using parachutes, on the other hand, would necessarily take place father away from Vemork in order to avoid the unmistakable sound of the plane's engine alerting the enemy. The risk of the parachutists being spread-out over an extensive area was also great. In addition, they would probably need to ski in order to cover the greater distance to the objective – a skill they were not trained in. It was hardly possible that they would be able to reach Vemork on snowshoes starting from some remotely situated place, and, even if they could, there was no question of them being able to carry any sizable amount of equipment.

Technical considerations resulted in the British choosing to go with two sabotage units, each one consisting of 15 men, to carry out the sabotage. The large number of men making up the total force can also point to a British awareness of the risk-filled nature of the operation, a concern we have earlier seen clearly expressed by **Cooper, Henniker** and **Wilson**. Just a few days before the operation went into action, **Henniker** suggested that, for sake of making double certain, the operation should be postponed to the summer.

If the gliders had been able to successfully land the engineers soldiers, and *Grouse* had then successfully led them to the plant facility in Vemork, then in all probability the British soldiers would have successfully blown it up. That was their job, and that was the mission they had been educated and trained to carry out. *Grouse* had the responsibility of determining how they would actually get into the facility. For *Freshman*, that problem never materialized. Possibly, the British would have forced their way into the area by attacking the suspension bridge over the ravine. That would likely have meant a high number of casualties, and may have been one the explanations for the large number of saboteurs.

After having carried out the sabotage, the survivors were to attempt escaping to Sweden. But who was going the help them along their long trek to the border? The plans say nothing about this, even though the escape in other respects was worked out in detail both as to security procedures and regulations and the various routes to be taken. The suggested routes point to the total ignorance of the British planers with respect to the geographical characteristics of the escape area. Perhaps "needless or naive risk-taking" is the right expression to describe the operation. The Norwegian saboteurs, on the other hand, knew they could manage in this type of environment, sufficient to carry out both the sabotage and the subsequent escape to safety, but they also had an entirely different background than the British engineer soldiers. The Norwegians were practiced skiers: They were hunters and had the ability to survive various Nordic weather conditions.

The British were soldiers, not hunters, and, all else aside, they couldn't ski. Therefore, they were equipped to proceed on snowshoes – which in itself is not an especially easy method of travel for beginners, even over relatively short distances, especially in deep snow.

The sabotage effort against Rjukan was conceived under the belief that the Germans had come farther in their development of an atom bomb than was actually the case. But the price was high. The first sabotage attempt cost the lives of 41 allied soldiers. In the efforts against the facility that followed, a large number of Norwegian civilians, and several American pilots, died. It was these human beings that died, and their surviving relatives, who paid the highest price. And of these people, it was the men who survived the respective crashes, who were subjected to the greatest suffering and the worst degradation. First they suffered through several hours wait by the wreckage, amidst their dead comrades in snow and ice. The injured were then carried on stretchers, under conditions of great pain, down steep mountain slopes, and thereafter, for better or worse, handed over to the German Security Police. The four men held in *Sipo's* cellar in Stavanger were subjected to torture and degradation. The remaining five men, having outlived their comrades, spent a further two months in prison and went to their deaths at the very moment they believed their situation would finally be bettered. The fourteen men who were placed along the Burma road in Egersund were shot in order, one after one – the youngest of them was barely 18 years old.

The British authorities became knowledgeable about what had happened to the participants in *Operation Freshman* relatively quickly, but at the time, they could not inform the families or relatives. The authorities had good cause for taking this stance, however, it's reprehensible that a portion of the nearest relatives were forced to wait entirely too long before they became informed. And even then, it was only after they had first tried over a period of several years to get the authorities to tell them what had happened. There is also ample reason to question why the British considered it necessary keep documentation concerning *Freshman* stamped "secret" until 1972.

Both the *Wehrmacht* and the secret police treated the dead British soldiers in a totally loathsome manner – both with regard to those who had died as a direct result of the crashes, as well as those who came to be murdered. The seven man crew of the tow-plane who died when their *Halixfax* crashed, the Germans buried in a crass manner under a thin layer of earth up on a mountain near the crash site, with no thought as to what would become of the corpses in the spring. The seventeen men from the glider that crashed on Benkja Mountain, they tossed down into a mass grave in a sandy heath near Ogna, where they remained buried for several years. The nine soldiers from the glider in Fylgjesdaen, they buried in Fylgjesdaen The five men who were shot to death in Østlandet, the Germans attempted to hide among the graves in Trandum. The four British soldiers who had been tortured to death in Stavanger were tossed into the sea, to sink in water several hundred meters deep, off Kvitsøy. In each and every one of these instances, the Germans were totally oblivious to any consideration of human dignity or ceremony. In this manner, the Germans had gone about annihilating the British saboteurs to the very last man.

There is nothing in the source material that indicates the British authorities were aware of Hitler's order at the time *Operation Freshman* was set into action. On the contrary, the saboteurs were told that if they were seized, they would wind up being prisoners of war. Those who managed to escape to Sweden would either be imprisoned there or shipped home. If the British authorities, despite all evidence to the contrary, actually knew about the Fuhrer Order, they may have had good reason not to pass this information along: Given that the point of the Fuhrer Order was that saboteurs were to be immediately executed, it would hardly have acted as a positive motivation for the men involved.

The facility in Vemork as it looks today (2001). Feed pipes in the background. The hydrogen plant was blown up on June 1, 1977. Photo: Ingrid Worning Berglyd.

The British had already charged several of the "November-executioners" from Stavanger before July 1945. It's said that one of the German attorneys, during a pause in the course of a war crimes trial, expressed the view that his countrymen didn't deserve to be put through this whole legal apparatus that was now being applied. He asserted that it was right and just to just ruthlessly shoot *diese Scweinehunde* (roughly: these filthy swine). This view was surely shared by others present during the trial, and the sentiment expressed is perhaps understandable, but it has nothing in common with the concept of justice we hold dear in a democracy.

The following year, charges based on the *Freshman*-tragedy were brought against the highest commander for the *Wehrmacht* in the Stavanger area. **Karl Maria von Beeren. Beeren** had direct responsibility for what had occurred in Stavanger and the surrounding area, and for having forwarded Hitler's order. But he maintained that he wasn't involved in the executions carried out at the Slettebø military camp. In this case, it was his subordinate who bore the responsibility. For his part, **von Beeren** had made it clear to his subordinates that, from a deep personal standpoint, he took exception to the order. Prisoners were to be treated in a proper manner that accorded with the deportment and spirit of a soldier. On the basis of this testimony, he was cleared. A similar argument was also advanced by **von Falkenhorst,** but a deaf ear was turned on his assertions. For despite the fact that Hitler's order clearly contravened fundamental human rights, **von Falkenhorst** had forwarded it down his chain of command. This had not only besmirched his honor as a German general, but also affirmed his responsibility for the violations of human rights inflicted by his soldiers when they executed the fourteen British soldiers alongside the Burma Road in Egersund. The early release of the person the court had held accountable as bearing the greatest guilt for what had happened in the Slettebø military camp in 1953, thus stands as something of a paradox.

During the trial, **von Falkenhorst** emphasized that the fourteen British soldiers should not have been shot but rather handed over to *Sipo*. That this had, in fact, actually been done never came out during the trial: Two men from *Sipo* in Stavanger had indeed been inside the Slettebø military camp and interrogated the prisoners. After this hearing procedure, one of these *Sipo* men had requested the soldiers in the Slettebø installation to voluntarily enlist in the execution platoon – which a number of soldiers from the *Wehrmacht* did. The only item in the source material that can possibly explain the action of these soldiers is that they may have become particularly embittered when they were told that the British mission had been to poison the Slettebø camp's water reservoir.

The government administrator in Helleland has been the subject of criticism from both individual local residents and in **Hoyle's** article in *The*

Times (2004) on the grounds that he didn't do enough to try and help the British, see page 185. The local residents, however, had been frightened by the reprisals the Germans had carried out after the British-Norwegian raids near Lofoten in March and December of 1941. The tragedy in Telaväg that took place on April 30, 1942 was also fresh in people's memory. Moreover, it was hard to keep anything secret in Helleland, and everyone knew the telephone network was tapped. Any attempt to help Germany's enemies could end in total catastrophe – for oneself, ones family and for ones friends and neighbors. This was the thinking of the government administrator in Forsand, and must also have been in the mind of Assistant Police Chief **Latham** with the Rogaland police, when he informed the German Security Police.

The execution of the fourteen soldiers alongside the Burma Road in Egersund made a strong impression on many of the German soldiers who bore witness to the entire affair. It was horrifying to see a line of young men - the youngest being 18 – lying on the ground, waiting to die. There were 50 meters between every man, each controlled by two German soldiers. The execution platoon was made up of eight men. With every execution, the remaining British soldiers were made to walk 50 meters closer to their death. It took over an hour before all the men were executed. Irregardless of whether the German soldiers had seen one or several of the executions, it was a horrifying experience that left a deep scar in their souls. For many of the German soldiers the memory of these executions became a psychological burden that remained with them for the rest of their lives – and the victors' charges with respect to collective guilt feel iniquitous. We have no sources that describe how the whole incident was viewed by the soldiers who carried out the actual executions. At that very moment in time, perhaps the assertion that the mission of the British soldiers had been to poison their water had served to sufficiently motivate them, but afterwards, surely many fell victim to psychological injury as a result of what they were guilty of having done.

Over the post-war decades, the participants in sabotage operations against the plant facility in Vemork have received much attention. This is perhaps especially true of those who took part in Freshman, the operation that failed and ended in tragedy. At the funerals, the trials, the raising of memorials, and during all the ceremonies that have been carried out over the course of years at the places where these tragedies took place, these men have been mourned so that what happened is not forgotten – which is as it should be. But the risk is that accessible sources, for a variety of reasons, will be misused. A shocking example of this is **Hoyles** article in *The Times*.

Chapter 26

Annotated sources and a literary overview

What occurred with Operation Freshman and the subsequent sabotage efforts against the plant facility in Vemork has been given a great amount of attention, both from military and legal authorities. Researchers, chroniclers and authors have all described their picture of what happened, and the surviving relatives have asked their questions. First and foremost, this attention has focused on what happened to the participants, followed second by where the planes had flown.

One of the first descriptions of what occurred with *Operation Freshman* is found in the war-diary of the *280th Infantry Division*, as recorded on the 19th and 20th of November 1942.

Later, the operation is noted in *Geschichte des Infanterieregiments 355, 1936-1945, eine Dokumentation.* This chronicle was printed in 1973 in a 250 copy edition which wasn't available to the general public. I got a hold of a copy in the beginning of the 1990s from **Hans Neeb** from Hanau who had served in the German occupation army in Norway.

In addition to the factual information contained in this white book from 1973, one could also read about how frustrated the surviving German soldiers from the *3rd Battalion* had become after the war due to their being held collectively responsible for the executions in the Slettebø military camp. This was also made very apparent when the author of this book interviewed four of these Germans during the 1980s.

The English military had already published its version of *Operation Freshman* in 1945. This was accomplished by making public a report in *The Royal Engineers Journal* immediately after the war ended. The article is especially interesting in that it contains a detailed account of the background to the operation. In addition, a portion of the work carried out by British and Norwegian authorities, during the hectic months immediately following the war's end in 1945, is also described, not only to bring clarity to what had happened, but also for purposes of bringing the responsible parties to account for the crimes they had committed.

In the British archives there are a number of dossiers concerning *Operation Freshman.* A portion of these files doesn't appear to have been well-arranged, and the same information can be found repeated in several of them. Gaining access to these files requires that an application to do so be submitted and approved. Thereafter, a *Reader Ticket* is issued, an archive pass that two representatives of Norway's Home-front Museum, **H. K. Sverdrup** and **G. Halle**, applied for and received in 1978 and 1979. They went through the dossiers and copied the most vital items on microfilm. A portion of the documentation is also recorded on Photostat copies. The microfilms and copies are now archived in Norway's Home-front Museum. Contained in this material are several documents and accounts about the operation, for example:

1. Report from *Ortskommandantur* (the District Commander) in Egersund regarding items commandeered from the British glider (Helleland), dated Nov. 11, 1942.
2. Report regarding hearings with *Hpt/Strmf.* **Oscar Hans** and *Hpt/Strmf.* **Wilhelm Esser,** dated June 6, 1945. (PWI no. 2).
3. Report from **Arne Lima,** dated Mar.13, 1944.
4. Information concerning tow- and glider-planes, along with information about the participants in the operation.
5. Several hearings with the German Security Police who tortured and murdered the four engineer soldiers in Stavanger. Hearings held by British and Norwegian authorities, and are written in German.

At Norway's Home-front Museum there is also a mass of documentation dealing with the subsequent Norwegian sabotage efforts against the plant facility in Vemork.

At the Dalane Folkemuseum, Egersund, there is a document that concerns the police investigation of the German's interpreter for the Eigersund area, dated May 24 1945. It contains a good deal of information about what happened to the participants of the *Freshman*-operation. Priest **Johan Uhl's** description of the words spoken over the Helleland churchyard's graves of the seven crew members of the tow-plane, dated November 21, 1945, are also stored at the museum, likewise stored are **G.Albrethsen's** war-diaries 1935-1947 which are on microfilm.

On pages 1496 b, 1497 b, 1506 and 2928 are accounts of the crash in Eigersund, written as the information about it unfolded at the time. The fate of the British soldiers is also recorded here. The original is located at the University Library in Oslo.

The book, *By Air to Battle*, is the official account of the *1ˢᵗ British Airborne Division* which was the military unit the British *Freshman*-soldiers belonged to. The book was published in 1945 at the behest of *His Majesty's Stationary Office*, which, among other things, sees to the publication of official publications and reports.

The history of the *38ᵗʰ Wing* was written and published by the pensioned air force **lieutenant colonel,** *Wing-Commaner* **D, H. Wood.** The book is titled *A history of Number 38. Group.*

!948 saw the release of the film *Kampen om tungtvannet* (roughly: The Battle for an Atom Bomb), the product of a French-Norwegian collaboration. Several of the actual Norwegian saboteurs got to play themselves in the film alongside trained actors. The film is factual and realistic, and it was well-received by the public.

In 1949, the trial of **Nicolaus von Falkenhorst,** top commander of the German forces in Norway at the time of *Operation Freshman,* was published in book form (see footnote 78). Here, the massacres that took place in the Eigersund and the Stavanger areas are dealt with as an integral part of the book.

Interest in this subject has also impacted the mass media, as for example in the local newspaper, *Dalane Tidende*, which has published articles about it on July. 28, 1974, July 28, 1982, and on Oct. 1, 1986. The newspaper, *Stavanger Aftenblad*, took up *Operation Freshman* in a big article on Nov. 18, 1967, and the *Rogaland-Avis* wrote about the affair that same year on the 18th and 25th of November. In addition, the national magazine *Verdens Gang* published interesting information about the complications surrounding *Operation Freshman* as early as 1945 and 1946.

In 1954, the publishing house William Kimber gave out a translation of **Knut Haukelid's** book *Kampen om Tungtvattnet* (Battle over Heavy Water) from 1947. The English edition was given the title *Skis against the Atom.* The book is exciting and an easy read, but lacks source references. It's quite likely that **Haukelid** used, among other references, his own four-page-long report on the sinking of the ferry "Hydro" on Tinnsjøen (Tinn Lake) on February 20, 1944, as part of his source material.

A memo from engineer **Kjell Nielsen,** dated May 9, 1983, shows, however, that **Nielsen,** along with **Haukelid** and **Rolf Sørlie,** wanted to make a number of corrections in the presentation of the preparation to the ferry-sabotage. And even as early as **Haukelid's** report of Mar. 3, 1945, **Nielsen** had, in fact, already pointed out that a mix-up, not covered in the report, had occurred between **Alf Larsen** and himself. Such errors are repeated in several books, and in the film produced by *BBC,* dealing with the sabotage action. According to **Nielsen, Haukelid** had, to a certain extent, accepted a portion of the criticisms made, and had promised to correct these mistakes in forthcoming editions of the book, but from a purely technical standpoint this proved to be difficult. Documentation about this dispute is on file at the Norway Home-front Museum.

In **Sverre Kjelstadli**s book *Hjemmestyrkene* (roughly: Home-front Forces) from 1959, there is a presentation on the *Freshman*-theme. In this account, the author by no means gives a complete picture of *Operation Freshman*. He neglects to mention the 14 British soldiers who were shot outside Slettebø in Egersund, and he blends together the two very separate crashes that took place in Fylgjesdalen and in Helleland. It's possible that **Kjelstadlis'** blunders were the result of his not having used carefully-organized source material.

Three years later, **Trygve Wyller** reconstructed the course of events in a large article titled *Da storkrigen suste inn over Rogaland* (roughly: When the World War blew in over Rogaland). The account is found in **Stahl's** book on the resistance effort in the Stavanger area. It's quite apparent that **Wyller's** article is built on comprehensive background material but the author provides no source references. Parallel with presenting the course of events, he makes an analysis of what occurred.

In 1962, the publishing house W.H, Allen, London, gave out a romanticised book about the operation with the title *But For These Men*, subtitled *How Eleven Commandos Saved Western Civilization*, written by **John D. Drummond.** The second edition was put out by Elmfield Press in 1974. The book's focus is directed mainly on the units that succeeded; *Grouse* and *Gunnerside*. **Drummond** maintains that when *Sipo* in Stavanger realized that the four British soldiers were too severely injured to be interrogated, they were executed by a doctor. The footnote attached to this contention indicates that the author has drawn this conclusion from information provided by someone who believed the four were poisoned. In the footnote, he further writes that another information provider had heard that the doctor had injected air into the victims' veins. The doctor had then sat and watched the victims' death throws. There are a number of pictures in the book, most of them borrowed from *Hero Films*. There are also a number of passport photos of the Norwegian saboteurs, but the texts attached to the pictures of **Joachim Rønneberg** and **Hans Storhaug** have been switched-around.

The major American film *The Heroes of Telemark* was shown in Rjukan in the winter of 1965, and featured the movie-star actor **Kirk Douglas** in the leading role. The film deviates a great deal from the factual course of the operation's events.

Assault In Norway/Sabotaging The Nazi Nuclear Bomb was published in 1975 by Harcourt Brace Jovanovich, New York and London. The book is written by **Thomas Gallagher.** On the book-jacket, the content is presented as the true story. The author is posed as a skilled writer and careful researcher. In the book's forward, **Gallagher** describes the *research* he did in Norway and Great Britain at the beginning of the 1970s enabling him to write about *the renowned raid that changed history.*

The book is exciting and easy to read, but contains serious errors. Gallagher writes that all *four* men aboard the *Halifax* plane that crashed in Helleland died, and that the fourteen British soldiers were stripped of their clothing before they were buried. He further writes that the four British who were transported to the *Gestapo's* headquarters in Stavanger were in such an injured state that they couldn't be interrogated. Therefore, they were poisoned by a German doctor. *There, when it became apparent that they were in no condition even to be tortured, they were poisoned by a German medical official.* The author also reports that the four British were commando soldiers, and that entire strength of the force totalled 34 men. Lastly, he writes that when the Norwegian saboteurs blew-up the plant in Vemork, there were German guards posted around the facility. It also appears that the author didn't grasp what the significance of a malfunctioning radio location apparatus, the *Rebecca,* meant to the operation.

In 1977, a book about *Freshman* was published in the USA titled *The Glider Gang* (author **Dank Milton**). The presentation is brief and accurate, and gives a reasonably reliable picture of what occurred.

Important information providers, who in the middle of the 1980s could give first-hand information about the *Freshman*-affair, were most prominently the Helleland natives, **Trond Hovland** and **Martin Selmer Sandstøl,** but there were also several more people in this small community who had been involved or affected by the whole scenario. In Egersund, both **Jørgen Tengesdal** and **Alf Aakre** were able leave interesting information, likewise the landowner near Ogna, **Kristoffer Varden.** The Germans: **Kurt Hagedorn, Fritz Bornschein, Friedrich Klippel** and **Hans Neeb** – all of whom had belonged to the 3rd *Battalion* – were also willing and able to contribute information. **Lief Espedal, Per Roth** and Johan Fredrik Thue had first-hand knowledge about what had happened in Fylgjesdalen. And there were still other people with information to impart, still living at that time.

The leader of the *Grouse/Swallow* unit, **Jens-Anton Poulsson**, gave out a book, *Aksjon Vemork,* in 1982 – subtitled *Vinterkrig på Hardangervidda* (The Winter War in the Hardanger Wilderness) through Gyldendal Norsk Forlag A/S. A large section of the book deals with the unit's mission to function as reconnaissance for both *Freshman* and the subsequent sabotage operation, *Gunnerside*, against the plant facility in Vemork. The book gives a factual presentation of the course of events, and **Poulsson** has taken care to refrain from hyperbole. In addition, the author has taken great pains to ensure that all the details in the presentation are correct. The last edition was given out as a facsimile by Tinn County in 1993.

As mentioned earlier, a number of close relatives to the deceased participants in *Operation Freshman* have been tracked down, both in Great Britain and Australia. Thus, a new dimension in the picture portraying *Freshman* has now been added.

The book, *Operation Freshman*, subtitled *The Rjukan Heavy Water Raid 1942*, is written by the British author **Richard Wiggan. Wiggan** has thoroughly studied the source material and has also had access to material that had, according to the author, not been available to the general public until that time-point. The book was released in 1986 and translated to Norwegian the following year. It's well-written and **Wiggan** has chosen a detailed approach to the subject. The author's source notations are reliable and lend themselves to being controlled without coming upon erroneous attributions. Insofar as I can discern, this is the best book about *Operation Freshman.* **Wiggan** has not visited the actual places in Norway, but a portion of this work was carried out by the author, **Gerd Schanche,** Sandnes, and her husband, at **Wiggan's** request.

On the other hand, the American author, **Dan Kurzman,** visited the actual sites, and insofar as possible, he also searched for people with relevant information he could question. As part of this research, **Kursman** and his wife came to Egersund where he got in contact with me, and I agreed to accompany him on his interviews with a number of information providers. **Kurzman,** in essence, said that he had decided to specialize in writing about especially dramatic events that had occurred during the Second World War – Do the research and publish the material in an exciting form. But based on the way he presented some of *Operation Freshman,* he proved to be more interested in fiction than fact. This is perhaps most apparent in the way he used the information he got from **Martin Selmer Sanstøl** and **Tor Nygård.**

This set of priorities also became apparent when we visited the crash-sites. Among other things, **Kurzman** wanted us to set out to the Hæstad Mountan area where the *Halifax*-bomber, i.e. the tow-plane, had crashed, but he absolutely insisted that our starting point should be from Highway 39, and from there climb straight up the steep mountainside to the location of the accident. I explained that this route wasn't practical, not even during favorable weather conditions, and that because of the snow and ice, such a climb was particularly dangerous, almost impossible. Despite this, **Kurzman** and his wife set off. They never succeeded in getting up to the cash-site, but **Kurzman** took a photo of his wife up on the side of the mountain. He then made use of this picture in the book and in the accompanying text he describes, among other things, that his wife is pointing to the place at Benkja Mountain where a glider crashed and the seven men onboard died.

The point here is not only the fact of a fictional setting being brought to the readers attention, but that he somehow managed to use the wrong geographical area. In addition, as it happened, it wasn't a glider that had crashed in the Hæstad Mountain area but a tow-plane.

The author maintains that **Groves** made contact with **General Strong** and suggested that he should establish a line of communication with **General Dwight D, Eisenhower,** Commander of the allied forces in Europe (p.17 in Kurzman's book) *Groves ... contacted General Strong ... to suggest he get in touch with Genera Dwight D, Eisenhower, the Allied Supreme Commander in Europe.* This took place in 1942, but Eisenhower was not appointed to joint commander until 1944. Kurzman further writes that Welsh appointed Tronstad to head the Norwegian exile government's intelligence service, *Chief of Intelligence for the Norwegian Government-in-exile* (p. 46 in Kurzman's book). The British **Welsh** had no authority to do this.

Kurzman had let it known that his books come out in large editions, and indeed, this was the case when *Blood and Water – Sabotaging Hitler's Bomb* was published in 1997. Several of the book's chapters deal with *Freshman*. He also sets aside a considerable number of pages to the situation and complexities surrounding the production of an atom bomb and the Norwegian saboteurs' contribution.

On a Norwegian television program, *Gutta på tur* (roughly: Gutta on a journey) on TV 2, that was broadcast in 2001, a group of men was shown wandering over the Hardanger wilderness and down towards the installation in Vemork where a band of Norwegian saboteurs had journeyed to one night in the past. All the men from *Grouse*, aside from **Arne Kjelstrop,** took part.

Naturally enough, during the program *Freshman* came up for discussion. At this point, confusion arose among the participants in the operation about what had happened at the various places in Sørvestlandet. This awakened reaction around the countryside, especially with the members of the Dalane Folkemuseum, and in the Egersund and Dalane Defence Association. The author of this book was then asked to take up the program's misinformation with the responsible parties. On December 14, 2001, I wrote a letter about this matter to TV 2, with enclosed copies for the attention of the program leader, **Arne Hjeltnes**, and the information-provider whose assertions were sufficiently misleading that ample cause existed to correct them. An answer to this criticism was never forthcoming, and a half-year later the program was rebroadcast without any of its material errors having been corrected.

On October 20, 2004, an article titled *The murdered heroes of Telemark* was published in *The Times*. The article was written by Ben Hoyle. Hoyle asserted that documents, duly classified and stamped as secret – which purportedly made it apparent that the British engineer soldiers who had crashed in Norway in the early winter of 1942 had been betrayed by local residents in the area, whom the soldiers had come in contact with and whose help they had sought – had recently been taken away. The British soldiers had still hoped they would escape – or so the article maintained. The engineer soldiers all belonged to *Operation Freshman* and their mission had been to blow up the plant facility in Rjukan. Hoyle further maintained that most of soldiers died when the plane crashed, but five had survived: Three were injured, but the other two had walked to the nearest "village." There, they had asked the government administrator for help, instead he rang the German authorities who arrived and took the British prisoner. After which they were forced to show the Germans the way to their three injured comrades and the glider. The five were thereafter transported to Oslo, interrogated and later shot in Trandum. The presentation goes on to show that the executions in Slettebø took place after the events in Trandum. And finally, the German witness, *Corporal* **Kurt Hagedorn,** is described as a Norwegian soldier.

On December 9, 2004, a recapitulation of Hoyle's article was printed in *Verdens Gang* under the heading: *Telemarks hjältar förrädda och sjutna* (Telemark's heroes betrayed and shot).In the article nothing is said about the erroneous facts of the presentation, nor did the magazine later print some form of apology or notice of correction.

According to a mail from Peter Yeates on April 4, 2005, the assertion that Norwegians had betrayed the Freshman-soldiers was repeated in *Glider Pilots Magazine* and in *The Royal Engineers Airborne Magazine* in the spring of 2005. Yeates was intent on refuting this assertion, but wondered how he should go about it: *I want to refute the allegations. How do I do this?*

Much of what has been written about *Operation Freshman* has suffered from inaccuracies and misunderstanding. Such articles, and especially the one in *The Times,* but also those that appeared in the two above-mentioned magazines, represent the absolute lowest watermark and are properly at home in the trash basket.

Syd Brittain, the engineer soldier who watched his comrades take off on their mission without him, has always reacted strongly against people who claim knowledge about the *Freshman*-operation, without having conducted an objective and thorough study of the source material. This distain is made apparent in a long poem he wrote honoring his dead comrades. One of the verses reads:

> *A lot of strangers will not understand, but then, they were not here, to learn first hand.*

He also states that his dead comrades live on in his thoughts and in his heart, and he describes the loyalty he feels for them, thusly:

To have known such men as you, was more than just a pleasure, it's something that no one can take away, My greatest treasure. And when my number's called, I'll do my very best, to see my ashes join, the other part of me, in Norway, Where you rest.

As far as I'm aware, the latest literature to be published about *Freshman*, and the subsequent sabotage actions against the plant facility in Vemork, is the book *The Real Heroes of Telemark* by Ray Mears, Hodder & Stoughton, London, in 2003. The presentation is mainly derived from the films Mears has produced for the *BBC* on that theme. Over recent years, these films have also been shown on Norwegian television several times, as original showings and as repeats. Mears has done an impressive job, but he has lent entirely too much emphasis on the saboteurs who succeeded. The *Freshman*-force's failed attempt need not have been regulated to the background, as has clearly been the case in this instance.

1. The *Gestapo* tortured and murdered four British soldiers and heaved them into the sea at approximately this location. The British had been a part of the crew aboard glider *DP349* that crashed in Fylgjesdalen. There is a small memorial stone with their names listed, in Eigane's Burial Park in Stavanger.
2. Eigane's Burial Park in Stavanger, where most of the participants in *Operation Freshman* lie buried.
3. The 14 survivors from glider *HS114*, which crashed at Benkja Mountain in Helleland, were shot by the *Wehrmacht* in the Slettlebø military camp near Egersund. The Germans tried to hide the corpses in a sandy heath near Ogna. After the war, the corpses were dug up and buried in Eigane's Burial Park in Stavanger.
4. Slettebø just outside Egersund, where the Germans had a large installation.
5. Helleland: The seven aircrew members of the tow-plane, *Halifax W7801*, were buried in Helleland's churchyard at the end of the war.
6. The mountainous area where the *Halifax W7801* crashed in the Hæstad Mountan area in Helleland.
7. The place where the glider *HS114* crashed at Benkja Mountan in Helleland.
8. The glider *DP349* crashed in Fylgjesdalen. The tow-plane pulling *DP349* was the only aircraft to successfully make it back to Scotland
9. The targeted objective that *Freshman* attempted to reach, the plant facility for producing heavy water in Vemork, near Rjukan.
10. The Grini concentration camp, several kilometre west of Oslo: The Gestapo held five soldiers from the plane that crashed in Fylgjesdalen isolated here, until Jan. 18, 1943.
11. The five soldiers from *Operation Freshman* who were shot by the execution platoon from the *Gestapo* in Oslo, lie buried in Vestre Gravlund.
12. Trandum, where many Norwegian resistance fighters and allied agents were shot by the Germans during the war: It's also the place where the five *Freshman*-soldiers from glider *DP349* met their fate in January 1943.

Annotated sources and a literary overview

The circled numbers mark vital places in southern Norway in connection with Operation Freshman. The map was drawn by Robin Sewell de Gency.

189

Operation Freshman — The hunt for Hitlers heavy water

Footnotes

1. *Operation Freshman (An account of the raid by the 1st Airborne Div. Engineers on the Heavy water plant in Norway)*, By Q.M.S.D.F.Cooper, R.E., 1945, p.31
2. Brun, Jomar: *Brennpunkt Vemork 1940-1945*, Universityforlaget (University Press), 1985, p.5-7.
3. Wiggan, Richard: *Operation Freshman, The Rjukan Heavy Water Raid 1942*, William Kimber, London, 1986, p.23-24.
4. *Public Record Office (PRO). Richmond, Surrey, England, Group Letter DEFE 2, Piece Number 2245, Freshman paragraphs 1 and 3.* the documents contain 70 text examples concerning the period September 8, 1942 to November 18 1942, and describe the pre-planning of operation *Freshman*. Norway's Home Front Museum has copies of the documentation, both on microfilm and as Photostat-copies
5. *Norsk Krigsleksikon* (Norwegian Combat Dictionary) 1940-1945, p.390, 249.
6. Footnote 4, paragraphs: 4,6,7,8,9,57,62,63,65,66.
7. Footnote 3, p.22.
8. Encyclopedia Britannica, Vol. 7, p.576-577
9. Speer Albert,; *Erindringer*, Gyldendal, Oslo, 1971, p.203-205
10. *Führerbefehl* or the Fuhrer Order. "The Order" is presented in both German and English in *War Crimes Trials, Vol, VI, The Trial of von Falkenhorst*, edit. E. H. Stevens, p.9 and 250.
11. Interview with Jens-Anton Poulsson in his home in Kongsberg, on Aug. 25, 2004. Letters from Poulsson to the author with information/comments on the subject, as follows: Sept. 2, 2004, Sept. 21, 2004, Nov. 21 2004 and Dec 28, 2004. Poulsson has also lent the following written documents to the author: the operation order that *Grouse* received on Oct. 17, 1942 – written in English. A report about the work of *Grouse* during the winter of 1942/43, written by Warrant Officer Jens-Anton Poulsson, London, Apr. 1943, Jens-Anton Poulsson: *Aksjon Vemork, Vinterkrig på Hardangervidda* (Ak Lake, Vemork, Winter combat on the Hardanger Wilderness), Facsimil, 1993, Tinn County.
12. *Operation Freshman (An account of the raid by the 1st Airborne Div. Engineers on the Heavy water plant in Norway)*, By Q.M.S.D.F.Cooper, R.E., 1945, p.31

13. Just who Tronstad was, is discussed in Chapter 1, Heavy Water.
14. Brun, Jomar: *Brennpunkt Vemork 1940-1945*, Universityforlaget (University Press), 1985, p.66-67.
15. See footnote 12
16. See chapter 2, A risk-filled mission
17. Footnote 12, much of the detailed information is taken from the *Public Record Office (PRO). Richmond, Surrey, England, Group Letter DEFE 2, Piece Number224*, See *Outline plan*, dated Oct. 13, 1942 and notations about *Freshman*, dated Nov. 17, 1942, p.117, Freshman, passages 59, 60 and 61, p.12.
18. Dank, Milton: *Glideflygergjengen* (Glider flying), Tiden Norsk Forlag (Publishing Co.), 1979, p 43-44
19. *Public Record Office (PRO). Richmond, Surrey, England, Group Letter DEFE 2, Piece Number 224, p.46-52. (Briefing notes on Escaping from Vemork to Sweden).*
20. Radio program about Operation *Freshman*, NRK Stavanger, 1983
21. Footnote 14.
22. Footnote 12, Footnote 19, p 5, passage 7.
23. *Operation "Freshman" (An account of the raid by the 1st Airborne Div. Engineers on the Heavy water plant in Norway),* By Q.M.S.D.F.Cooper, R.E., p.33; NRK Savanger, program about Operation Freshman, 1983. Over the period July 20-27, I travelled around a part of the area where *Freshman* was trained.
24. Mail from PeterYeates, Nov. 5, 2004. He was a close friend of Syd Brittain's and his confidant. See also: Wiggan, Richard: *Operation Freshman, The Rjukan Heavy Water Raid 1942,* William Kimber, London, 1986, p.52, 163164.
25. Footnote 23, a written account from Hedley B. Duckworth, dated May 12, 1995: *Regarding my investment in Operation Freshman.* An undated report by Duckworth; *Freshman: Aftermath of Operation Freshman, end of September 1942 to 20th November 1942. The sequel to Operation Freshman. Up to present time.*
A Dunnett More Video (D.M.V.) This is a three-hour-long recording of the ceremony that took place when a memorial to the participants in Freshman was unveiled at the air field at Skitten, Wick, in Scotland in 1992. This recording contains several interviews, among them, one with Duckworth. It's been difficult to confirm Duckworth's information. I haven't been able to find his

name in the British military documents. However, the remarkable job performed by the ground personnel under the leadership of Sergeant Gale is noted: *The admirable work cheerfully carried out by the ground-maintenance party under Sgt. Gale (DEFE 2, 221, p.13).* In the register listing those who were onboard the tow-plane, Sgt. Gale's name does not appear, but this doesn't necessarily mean very much. Falconer, for example, is on the list, but obviously wasn't on the tow-plane since he lay buried in a churchyard in Helleland. Personnel comprising the plane's crew could have been changed at the last moment. See also: chapter 5, footnote 30.

26. Petterssen, Sverre: *Kuling fra nord,* Aschehoug & Co. (W. Nygaard) Oslo, 1974, p.158-162

27. *Public Record Office (PRO).* Richmond, *Surrey, England, Group Letter DEFE 2, Piece Number 224, Freshman, p.14, 71 passages,* dated Nov. 19, 1942. According to another British document, dated the same day, *Group Letter DEFE 2, Piece Number 221, p.5,* the first plane's take-off occurred at 17:55(5:55 PM). The next take-off was a half-hour later.

28. *Operation "Freshman" (An account of the raid by the 1st Airborne Div. Engineers on the Heavy water plant in Norway),* By Q.M.S.D.F. Cooper, p.32-37.

29. Ibid.

30. Report about the operation, dated Dec. 8, 1942, *Group Letter DEFE 2, Piece Number 221, p.8,* see Chapter 4, footnote 25.

31. Footnote 28, Map, *Plotting Eries,* covering the route the tow-plane used on the return flight to Scotland: Located at the Dalane Folkemuseum (public museum), Egersund. In his letter dated Apr. 4, 2006, Jens-Anton Poulsson indicates that his present understanding is as follows: It was the 2nd tandem-flight that came into close proximity of the landing area, and the one they made contact with. His reasoning is that, in as much as flight number 1 reached the target area, there really isn't any reason to think that that the navigator for flight number 2 should not have accomplished the same. Moreover, there isn't any reason to assume that the *Rebecca* in flight number 2 should also have ceased functioning. Therefore, it must have been the 2nd flight that *Grouse* was in contact with.

32. Interview with Trond Hovland, Helleland, Aug. 14, 1986. Wandering and observing with Hovland in the Benkja Mountain area, Helleland, on Aug. 8, 1986. Rapport from Government

Administrator Theodore Hovland to the police chief in Rogalund concerning the plane crash in Helleland, dated Nov. 21, 1942.
Interrogation, police investigation of Tellef G. Tellefsen (interpreter), May 24, 1945.
Report from Arne Lima concerning the crash in Helleland, dated Jan. 20, 1944, Report no. 775.
Written communication from Arne Lima to Per Johnson, Randaberg, concerning the British airborne landing attempt on Hardangervidda in Nov. 1942, dated Nov. 16, 1981
Undated memorandum by Gunvor Benestad, wife to Per Johnson, Randaberg, concerning the plane crash on Benkja Mountain, Helleland. *Public Record Office (PRO)*. Richmond, *Surrey, England, Group Letter DEFE 2, Piece Number 219, p.59,* dated May 19, 1943. *Gescheite des Infanteriregiments* 355, 1936-1945. *Eine Dokumentation, mit Auszügen aus den authetischen Verlustlisten.* Dr, Fritz Amberger, Frankfurt/M, 1973, Eigenverlag. Zum Verkauf an Buchhandlungen nicht zugelassen.
Kriegstagesbuch der 280, Infanteridivision (280th Infantry Division war diary), Nov. 11, 1942, Nov. 21, 1942.

33. Interrogation report, document in connection to the police investigation of the Norwegian Nazi interpreter in Eigersund, dated May 24, 1945. *Kriegstagesbuch der 280, Infanteridivision, Nov. 20, 1942. Public Record Office (PRO)*. Richmond, *Surrey, England, Group Letter DEFE 2, Piece Number 21, p.58,* dated May 19, 1943, report from G.T. Rapport to the police board in Vest-Agder, Flekkefjord, on Apr. 5, 1946.
Witness testimony from Kurt Herbert Scheulen on Oct. 23, 1945, Heinz Schneider on Oct. 23, 1945 and Werner Fritz Seeling on Aug. 20 1945. Scheulen and Schneider were both employed by the security police (*Sipo*) in Stavanger. All three confirmed that Petersen worked at the *Gestapo's* headquarters in Stavanger.

34. *War trials of von Falkenhorst, Vol. 6, p.50-52.*
Kurt Hagedorn, Erfurt, East Germany, interview on Dec. 17, 1985 and Jan. 1, 1986.
Observations made wandering through Slettebø on Dec 18, 1985. Fritz Bornschein, Emden, West Germany, interview on June 22, 1987. Observations made wandering through Slettebø on Sep.3, 1987. Friedrich Klippel, Mainz, West Germany, interview.

35. Kurt Hagedorn (1920-1986) East Germany, interview on Dec. 12, 1985, Dec. 18, 1985 and Jan. 30, 1986. Observations made wandering through Slettebø on Dec. 18, 1985.

Fritz Bornschein, Emden, West Germany, interview on June 22, 1987. Observations made wandering through Slettebø on Sep.3, 1987.
Friedrich Klippel, Mainz, West Germany, interview on June 22, 1987. Hans Neeb, Hanau, West Germany, interview on June 10, 1992. Observations made wandering through Slettebø on June 10, 1992.

36. *War trials of von Falkenhorst, Vol. 6, p.53-54*

37. Kristoffer Varen, Sievåg, interview on Aug 11, 1986. Observations made wandering through Ogna that same day.
Jörgen Tengesdahl, Egersund, interview on July 7, 1987.

38. Egersund's resident, Hans Andreassen's witness testimony according to the *Dalane Tidende,* in an article published on June 7, 1946 about the investigation of the German commander in the Stavanger area, Karl Maria von Beeren (Behren).
Interview with Per Rasmussen, Egersund, on July 10, 1999.
Kriegstagesbuch der 280, Infanteridivision, Nov. 20, 1942, p.8-9.

39. In Geirulf Albrethsen's *War diaries 1935-1947,* p.1496 b, 1497 b, 1506 and 2928 are observations of the plane crash. The fate of the British soldiers is also mentioned. These diaries are in the University Library, Oslo, and on microfilm in the Dalane Folkemuseum, Egersund.

40. *Gescheite des Infanteriregiments 355, 1936-1945. Eine Dokumentation, mit Auszügen aus den authetischen Verlustlisten.* Dr, Fritz Amberger, Frankfurt/M, 1973, Eigenverlag. Zum Verkauf an Buchhandlungen nicht zugelassen, p.49-50.

41. Martin Selmer Sandstøl, Helleland, interview on July 7, 1986. Observations made while wandering on Hæstadfjellet that same day. I was also present when the American author, Dan Kurzman, interviewed Sandstøl at his home in the fall of 1943. See the last chapter. Also see the magazine, *Hellelands buen,* November 1992 and *Kriegstagesbuch der 280, Infanteridivision, Nov. 20, 1942.*

42. Per Johnsen, Randaberg: The Fylgjesdal Glider, 1982, unpublished work.
Interview with Leif Espedal, Sola, on Nov. 19, 2002.
Reports from Knut Leirvåg, Stavanger, on Mar. 23, 1982 and Sep. 16, 1982, lent out by Per Johnsen, Randaberg.
Kriegstagesbuch der 280, Infanteridivision, Nov. 21, 1942, p.10-12.
Witness testimony, Martine Fylgjesdal on Aug. #, 1945.
Report, Tollef Ravn Tollefsen on Nov. 23, 1942

Witness testimony, Finn Bjønnes on Aug. 7, 1945 and Oct. 27, 1943

43. Per Johnsen, Randaberg: *The Fylgjesdal Glider,* 1982, unpublished work.
Interview with Leif Espedal, Sola, on Nov. 19, 2002.
Reports from Knut Leirvåg, Stavanger, on Mar. 23, 1982 and Sep. 16, 1982, borrowed by Per Johnsen, Randaberg.
Wandering around the crash site on June 24, 2001 and Aug. 8, 2002. On the last-cited date, the author, along with people from the area, continued to walk in a southerly direction , down along lake Fylgjesdal towards the ravine at Sagbakken, and then turned west at the side of the mountain along the Lyse Fjord towards Håheller.
Witness testimony, Finn Bjønnes on Aug. 7, 1945 and Oct. 27, 1943.

44. Interviews with Per Roth, Hafsfjord, on Nov. 19, 2002, and with John Fredrik Thue, Sandnes, on Nov, 19, 2002.
In addition, further confirmation is found in the accounts of several information contributors; written in 1982, and lent to the author by Per Johnsen, Randaberg.
Also see Trygve Wyller and Knut Stahl: *Av Stavangers historie under okkupajonen, 1940-1945. De lange arena* (The long years 1940-1945, Stavanger's history during the occupation), Stavanger, 1964, p 13 ff.
Witness testimony, Johan Fredrich Thue on Oct 7, 1945.
Witness testimony, Sigurd Stangeland (interpreter) on July 7, 1945.

45. Beginning in 1939, the German Security Police, *Sicherheitspolizei (Sipo),* all the German police forces, the *Gestapo* (secret police), and the security police – *Sicherheitsdienst (SD,)* were all part of the same organization. This organization was Hitler's most vital tool for crushing all opposition to the regime.
Norsk Krigsleksikon (Norwegian War-Dictionary) *1940-1945,* J.W. Cappelens Publishing, 1995, p 398.
Witness testimony; Fritx Seeling, Aug. 20, 1945 and Nov. 6, 1945
Witness testimony: Fritz Feuerlein, July 6, 1945 and Aug. 16, 1945
Witness testimony: Arthur Wolfgang Heinz Schneider, Oct. 23, 1945
Witness testimony: Georg Schomaker, Oct. 23, 1945.
Witness testimony: Kurt Herbert Scheulen, Oct. 23, 1945
Witness testimony: Karl Dawe, Aug. 17, 1945.
Witness testimony: Erich Hoffmann, Sep. 9, 1945, Oct 23, 1945, and Oct. 22, 1945
Witness testimony Ohan Esser, July 17, 1945.

Also see: *War Crimes Trials, Volume VI, -The Trial of von Falkenhorst*, 1949, and Richard Wiggan: *Operation Freshman*, William Kimber, London, 1986.

46. Major General Colin Gubbins forward in Knut Haukelid's book *Kampen om tungtvannet* (roughly: The battle over heavy water) Ernst G. Mortensen's publishing A/S, Oslo 1983.

47. Letters from Joachim Rønneberg to the author, Nov. 9, 2004, Nov. 24, 2004 and Dec. 9, 2004. *Operation Gunnerside,* Warrant-Officer Rønneberg's report. It's written in English and is in Norway's Home-front Museum.

48. Knut Haukelid: *Kampen om tungtvannet,* Ernst G. Mortensen's publishing A/S, 1983, p.12.

49. Footnote 47.

50. Footnote 48, p.51 and p.55.

51. Ibid., p.54-56

52. Footnote 47.

53. Interview with Jens-Anton Poulsson at his home in Kongsberg, on Aug. 25, 2004.
Letters from Poulsson to the author with information and comments concerning complications, Sep. 9, 2004, Sep. 21, 2004 and Dec. 28, 2004. Poulsson has also lent the author the following written source material: the operation-order that *Grouse* received on October 17, 1942; Report concerning *Grouse's* work in the Norwegian winter of 1942/43 written by Jens.Anton Poulsson, London, April 1943. Also see Jens-Anton Poulsson: *Aksjon Vemork, Vinterkrig på Hardangervidda,* Faksimil, 1993, Tinn kommune.

54. Letters from Joachim Rønneberg to the author, Nov. 9, 2004 and Dec. 12, 2004. Operation *Gunnerside,* Warrant-Officer Rønnegberg's report. It's written in English and is in Norway's Home-front Museum.

55. Ibid. Interview with Jens-Anton Poulsson at his home in Kongsberg, on Aug. 25, 2004.
Letters from Poulsson to the author with information and comments concerning complications, Sep. 2, 2004, Sep. 21, 2004 and Sep. 29, 2004. The operation-order that *Grouse* received on October 17, 1942; Report concerning *Grouse's* work in the Norwegian winter of 1942/43 written by Jens.Anton Poulsson, London, April 1943. Also see Jens-Anton Poulsson: *Aksjon Vemork, Vinterkrig på Hardangervidda,* Faksimil, 1993, Tinn kommune.

56. Footnote 54.
57. Footnote 55.
58. Jomar Brun: *Brennpunkt Vemork* (Burning Point, Vemork), 1940-1945, Universityforlaget (University Publishing) 1983, p.73.
59. Operaton *Gunnerside*, Warrant Officer Rønneberg's report.
60. Letters from Joachim Rønneberg to the author, Nov. 9, 2004 and Dec. 12, 2004.
    Knut Haukelid: *Kampen om tungtvannet*, Ernst G. Mortensens Forlag A/S, 1983, p.96-105..
61. Interview with Jens-Anton Poulsson at his home in Kongsberg, on Aug. 25, 2004.
    Letters from Poulsson to the author with information and comments concerning complications, Sep. 2, 2004, Sep. 21, 2004 and Sep, 29 2004. The operation-order that *Grouse* received on October 17, 1942; Report concerning *Grouse's* work in the Norwegian winter of 1942/43 written by Jens-Anton Poulsson, London, April 1943. Also see Jens-Anton Poulsson: *Aksjon Vemork, Vinterkrig på Hardangervidda*, Faksimil, 1993, Tinn kommune.
62. Archive Box NHM10B – This box contains a number of documents concerning the bombing of Vemork, and is in Norway's Home-front Museum.
63. Letter to the author from Jens-Anton Poulsson, Nov. 29, 2004. Also see: The report written by Warrant Officer Knut Haukelid concerning the sinking of the ferry "Hydro" on Tinnsjøen (Tinn Lake) at 10:15 AM on Feb. 20, 1944, and engineer Kjell Nielsen's account about the sabotage mounted against the ferry in Rjukan in February 1944, dated Nov. 9, 1983.
64. Footnote 62.
65. Ibid., p.13. Report written by Warrant Officer Knut Haukelid concerning the sinking of the ferry "Hydro" on Tinnsjøen (Tinn Lake) at 10:15 AM on Feb. 20, 1944. This report is letter-dated "Stockholm, Mar. 3, 1944" and is undersigned by Knut Haukelid.
66. The British soldiers' fate should be seen against the background of the Fuhrer Order, dated Oct. 18, 1942. Hitler formulated this order, personally. Subsequently, it was then distributed to the chief commanders of a list of occupied nations by *Field Marshall, General* Wilhelm Keitel. Nicolaus von Falkenhorst, the chief commander of the German forces in Norway, was among those who received this order, and he further forwarded it to his sub-commanders at

the various military installations. The order's content is given at the beginning of chapter 2. The Fuhrer Order is presented in German, p.8ff and in an English-version translation on p.250-255 in the *War Crimes Trials, Vol. VI, The Trial of von Falkenhorst. Edit. E.H. Stevens,* Edinburgh, 1949.

67. Radio program on the topic of Operation Freshman broadcast in 1983 by NRK Stavanger. Knut Haukelid: *Kampen om tungtvannet,* Ernst G. Mortensens Forlag A/S, 1983, p.48.

68. *An Feldkommandosteele, BDS in Oslo berichtet, 21.11.1942* (roughly: A Field-command Installation (BDS) in Oslo, Feb. 21, 1942) Also see Richard Wiggan: *Operation Freshman, The Rjukan Heavy Water Raid 1942,* William Kimber, London, 1986, p.81.

69. Interview with Hans Neeb on June 10, 1992.

70. Ibid. Report from the *Ortskommandantur* (District Commander) in Egersund concerning seizure of objects from the British glider, dated Nov. 23, 1942, this document is at Norway's Home-front Museum.

71. See footnote 68.

72. Interrogation hearing with the Nazi's interpreter on May 24, 1945. This document is in the Dalane Folkemuseum, Egersund.

73. Interview, Fritz Bornschein, Emden, West Germany on Sep.9, 1986.

74. Berit Nøkleby: *Gestapo, German politics in Norway 1945-50.* p.120.

75. Footnote 8, interviews with Kurt Hagedorn, Egersund, earlier resided in Erfurt, East Germany, Dec. 17, 1985, Dec. 18, 1985.

76. *War Crimes Trials, Vol. VI, The Trial of von Falkenhorst. Edit. E.H. Stevens,* Edinburgh, 1949.

77. Information via letters from Hans Neeb, Hanau am Main, West Germany, on Feb. 3, 1986 and May 6, 1986.
Gescheite des Infanteriregiments 355, 1936-1945. *Eine Dokumentation, mit Auszügen aus den authetischen Verlustlisten.* Dr, Fritz Amberger, Frankfurt/M, 1973, Eigenverlag. Zum Verkauf an Buchhandlungen nicht zugelassen.

78. *War Crimes Trials, Vol. VI, The Trial of von Falkenhorst, Formerly Generaloberst in the German Army, edited by E. H. Stevens,* Edinburgh, published 1949.
Asbjørn Barlaup: "Et system dømt till døden" (A system doomed to death) an article in *Verdens Gang* (Around the World), Aug. 7, 1946.

79. *War Crimes Trials, The Trial of von Falkenhorst, Formerly Generaloberst in the German Army,* Edited by E. H. Stevens,

Edinburgh, published 1949
Interview with Arne Bang-Andersen, Stvanger, on Dec 23, !985.
Verdans Gang, Aug. 8, 1946.

80. Witness testimony of Fritz Seeling on Aug. 8, 1945, and of Fritz Feuerlein on July 6, 1945 and Aug. 16, 1945.
    War Crimes Trials, The Trial of von Falkenhorst, Formerly Generaloberst in the German Army, edit. E. H. Stevens, Edinburgh, published 1949
    Report PWIS/w, Consolidated Report on the Interrogation of two Prisoners (Oscar Hans, Wilhelm Esser), Akershus Prison, June 27, 1945. Execution of British Soldiers (A teletype message was sent to RSHA asking for instructions. A reply was received saying that the men were to be treated according to the Fuhrer Order)
    Jostein Berglyd: The chapter, Hitler's SS, in Berglyd's book *Egerundere og dalbuer i kamp,* p.333-338; Berit Nøkleby: *Josef Terboven, Hitlers mann I Norge,* (Hitler's man in Norway) Guldendal, 1992, and *Gestapo, Tysk politi I Norge* (German politics in Norway) *1940-1945,* Ascheoug, 2003.
    Tore Pryser: *Hitlers hemmelige agenter, Tysk etterreting I Norge 1939-1945,* (Hitler's secret agents, German executions in Norway) Universitets forlaget, 2001.

81. Interview, Arne Bang-Andersen, Stavanger, Dec. 23, 1985. Interview, Alf Aakre, July 23. 1986. Letter from Robin de Gency Sewell, Aston Upthorpe, England, Mar. 23, 2004, and mail from Robin Thomas, London, May 13, 2004.

82. *Operation Freshman, An account of the raid by the 1st Airborne Div, Engineers on the Heavy water plant in Norway, By Q.M.S.D.F. Cooper, R.E.* In an interview with Jens-Anton Poulsson at his home in Kongsberg on Aug. 25, 2004, he informed me that it was Kjelstrup whom the British officers met in Kongsberg during the days after the war's end in 1945.

83. *Dalane Tidende,* June 27, 1945 and June 29, 1945.
    Stavanger Aftenblad, July 16, 1945.
    Interviews with Jørgen Tengesdal, Egersund, Kristoffer Varden, Sirevåg, summer of 1986.

84. *Dalane Tidende, July, 1945.*

85. Interview with Leif Espedal at his home in Sola, Nov. 19, 2002. Visit in Vestre Gravlund, Oslo, Jan. 27, 2005.

86. Letter from the Forensic MedicalInstitute, Oslo, Director: Professor Dr. Jon Lundevall, March 3. 1982.

87. Letter from Robin de Gency Sewell, Aston Upthorpe, England, Mar. 23, 2004. Mail from Robin Thomas, London, May 13, 2004.
88. interview with Martin Selmer Sandstøl, Helleland, July 4, 1986.
89. *Dalane Tidende,* Nov. 23, 1945. Excerpt taken from Priest John Uhl's speech. A copy of the speech is with the Dalane Folkemuseum.
90. *Dalane Tidende,* Sept. 4, 1946.
91. Gravestone with an inscription in Helleland's churchyard.
92. *Dalane Tidende,* Nov. 18, 1957.
93. *Regarding my involvement in Operation Freshman,* an account by Hedly B. Duckworth, May 5, 1945
94. *Dalane Tidende,* Apr. 4, 1990, and Apr. 11, 1990.
95. *Dalane Tidende,* May 10, 1995.
96. *Dalane Tidende,* Aug. 25, 1999 and Aug. 8, 1999
    Stavanger Aftenblad, Aug, 28, 1998
    Aussie Post, Jan. 1, 1998
    Sunday Herald Sun, Sept. 5, 1999.
97. Footnote 94, first section.
    Telephone interview with Per Johnsen, Aug. 8, 2003. Information regarding *Brookwool Memorial* is located on a memorial plaque in the British Commonwealth churchyard, Vestre Gravlund, in Oslo.
98. *A Dunnett More Video (D.M.V.), 1993.* This is a three-hour-long recording of the unveiling ceremony at Skitten, outside Wick, Scotland. The film also contains several interviews, among them, Hedly B. Duckworth.
    Letter from Don Owens, Apr. 30, 2004, secretary of *The Aircrew Association, Highland Branch:* Member's newsletter, *The Aircrew Association,* July 2000, Nov. 2002, May 2003, and Mar. 2004. Mail from Peter Yeates, Bristol, England, Jan. 25, 2005.
99. *Dalane Tidende,* Mar. 22, 1982 and Sept. 20, 1982.
100. Letter from Norway's Home-front Museum to Per Johnsen, dated Aug 19, 1982.
101. Authenticity certificate re objects, dated 1982.
102. *Race to save lost glider of Telemark,* Yakub Qureshi, article in *Scotland on Sunday,* Aug. 8, 2004.

103. Articles in *Stavanger Aftenblad*, Aug. 26, 2004, Sept. 6, 2004, Sept. 10, 2004 and Oct. 23, 2004. Telephone conversation and interview with David (Davie) Patton, Aug. 24, 2004.
104. *DEFE 224, p.131, piloting Error* (map sketch)
105. Ibid., p.14, p.131, point 3.
106. Ibid., p.134.
107. ibid., p.15.
108. Ibid.
In the sections about Kristainstad and Setesdal in the series *Krigen i Norge1940* (The War in Norway), given out by The War's History section in the beginning of the 1950s, there is noted a battalion commander, Major P.W. Loerdahl who belonged to IR 7.
109. Ibid, p.15-16.
110. Ibid., p.162-165, p.172, point 3.
111. Ibid., p.166-169, 177-178.
112. Ibid., p.170.
113. *DEFE, 221, p.5-6.*